DARK CLOUDS AND SILVER LININGS

To "Doctor Jim" who
tries so hard to keep
my Honey healthy.

Gratefully

Dot

The Author

DARK CLOUDS
AND
SILVER LININGS

A True Story Of Love, Families, and WWII

Dorothy Shepherd Fibush

"Keep the home fires burning,
While our hearts are yearning.
Though our boys are far away
They dream of home.
There's a silver lining,
Through the dark clouds shining.
Turn the dark clouds inside out
Till the boys come home."

Popular song of World War I.
("The war to end all wars.")
Music • I. Novello / Lyrics • L.G. Ford

Creative Arts Book Company
Berkeley • 1995

First Edition August 1995

Dark Clouds and Silver Linings is published by Donald S. Ellis
and distributed by Creative Arts Book Company.

For Informatioin contact:
Creative Arts Book Company
833 Bancroft way
Berkeley, California 94710

ISBN 0-88739-108-7
Library of Congress Catalog Number 95-69094

Printed in the United States of America

Dedicated to my "Honey"
without whom there never would have been a story,
and without whose help there never could have been a book.

The logo above represents the word 'HONEY' which has been
used as Don's and my signature to each other since 1929.

ACKNOWLEDGEMENTS

The children of Leta and Charlie Ide
who saved letters and shared them,
Shirley Thompson and Sandy Little, who
encouraged me from the very start, Irwin Cohn
for preparing the manuscript for submission,
Suzanne Guyette, Dave McElhatton, Bob and
Fran Schroder, Michael Woo, Barbara Storment,
numerous Contra Costa County librarians,
and last but far from least, my publisher,
Don Ellis, for his boundless enthusiasm
and innovative suggestions.

TABLE OF CONTENTS

*Of course this should read, "This Is the Navy." However according to the terms of Irving Berlin's will, not one word of this can be changed.

FOREWORD

When I was a small child, my British father told me lurid tales about the Boer War, and read to me from the newspaper about the Balkan Wars and the savagery of the Turks and the Bulgarians. To me that was exciting and was made even more so by the dramatic way in which it was presented by my adored father.

When World War I began in 1914, it had no reality for me until April of 1917, when the United States joined the allies in "The War to End All Wars." Then I began to worry about my beloved Papa. One of the popular songs of the day brought tears to my eyes whenever I heard it:

> "My Papa's all dressed up today. He never looked so fine
> And every time I look at him, I'm glad my Papa's mine.
> He's got a beautiful new suit. The old one was so old.
> It's blue with buttons oh so bright, I guess they must be
>   gold.
> Oh, my Papa just belongs to me and Mama,
> And I guess the folks are blind who cannot see
> That his buttons are marked U.S.
> And that spells 'us,' I guess,
> So he just belongs to dear Mama and me.
>
> My Papa's kind of glad, and kind of sad, I wonder why.
> And every time she looks at him, It makes my Mama cry.
> Who's Uncle Sam?, My Papa says that he belongs to him.
> But Papa's joking 'cause he knows my uncle's name is Jim.
> So my Papa just belongs to me and Mama,
> And I guess the folks are blind who cannot see
> That his buttons are marked U.S.
> And that spells 'us,' I guess,
> So he just belongs to dear Mama and me."

With the simplistic faith of an eight-year-old, I told my father that I would not let him go to war, and if he tried to go, I would tie him up with ropes. Then, since I had taken care of that situation, I put all my childish efforts into earning and saving money for War Stamps. In my patriotic fervor, I even knocked down a rather large boy who scoffed that War Stamps were no good, and I would never get my money back. To my patriotic little heart such a statement was high treason requiring prompt action on my part. Unfortunately, just as I knocked him flat, a very good friend of my parents happened to walk by and promptly reported to them my excessively unladylike behavior!

Little did I dream in those days that some day I would have a husband who would leave us all for nearly three years to fight the Japanese in the Pacific. Could I possibly have imagined that our oldest son would join the U.S. Navy during the Korean War? Could I have foreseen that some day our youngest son would be enduring "Tet" in Saigon, a time when all the South Vietnamese troops left the scene to go home for the big holiday season and five hundred American boys were left to defend the city against over five thousand North Vietnamese?

What happens next? Will our five grandsons and five great-grandsons, or even our three granddaughters and six great-granddaughters, be required to continue the killing? How much longer will our world as we know it continue to exist?

D.S.F., January 1995

AUTHOR'S NOTES

This is a story of World War II. It is a story of families, not battles. Most of it is told by letters—his to her and the children, and their's to him. There are letters from best friends stationed at Pearl Harbor on December 7, 1941, as well as other letters and items of interest.

In Part I, from January to June of 1943, most of her letters to him have been lost, and her diary is used. Also, during the summer together at the beach, diary entries are necessary.

His letters to her are a constant source of frustration, because of censorship. Very little can be told of what is happening and where it is happening.

Because of the innumerable people mentioned, a cast of characters is in order.

THE IMMEDIATE FAMILY

Don and Dot Fibush

Children: Donny (1934) Beverly (1937) Judy (1938) Chuck (1942) Brett (1946)

THE EXTENDED FAMILY

Don's brother Ken, his wife Esther and son David (1937)

Don's sister Rae, her husband Harry, son Stevie (1942) and daughter Frances (1943). Rae is Don's "baby sister," nine years younger, often referred to as "Baby." Harry was drafted into the Army very shortly after Frances was born.

Harry's sister "Babe", and her husband "Mitch."

Don's aunt Nettie, her daughter Edie and granddaughter Ann (1934); daughter Phil and sons Dicky (1937) and Michael (1941); and daughter Elaine, "seeking her fortune in Hollywood."

Don's uncle George and his wife Gertie.

Don's cousin Art and his wife Mary; their daughters Amy (1935) and Mary (1938).

Dot's Daddy, Mama, brother John, and sister Midge, eleven & fourteen years younger, respectively.

NEIGHBORS ON SPRINGHILL ROAD

Springhill Road was, in 1943, a narrow dirt road, winding for a mile and a half through pear and walnut orchards in a blind valley located three miles from the village of Lafayette. It was populated by a handful of families, most of whom had just built "in the country" or were in the process of building.

Jack and Marky Schneider and daughter Susan (1941) on one side of Dot and Don,

Dan and Bernice Condit and son Philip (1941) on the other side

Jack and Betty Imrie, daughter Betty Jean, (1938) son Johnny, (Dec. 7, 1941)

Bob and Leslie Underhill and daughter Phyllis (1943)

Tom Slaven, retired attorney, his wife Verna and teenagers, Tommy and Mardi

Gary and Helen Brown and their daughters, Nancy and Lois (1934) and (1937)

The Martinos, a farming family who had originally owned most of the property on the west side of the road.

The Hinks, a wealthy older couple who owned much of the land in the valley.

Professor Hoskins and family at the far end of the valley.

LAFAYETTE GRAMMAR SCHOOL

Mr. Ellis, Principal and District Superintendent

Mrs. Christian, elderly fifth-grade teacher, beloved by all.

Mrs. Burkhead, delightful third-grade teacher.

FRIENDS FROM OAKLAND AND BERKELEY

Leta and Charlie Ide and their five children

Catharine and Bob Bruce

Ruth and Arleigh Williams

Marjorie and John Kemmeries

The Matthews, the Alkires, and the Woods

THE HOUSE MATES

(All stationed at St. Mary's Navy Pre-Flight School)

The Kellehers

Catherine and Melvin Pickens, son Gary (1942)

Mabel and Rusty Meyers

Myrtle and Holly Hollingsworth, son Lee (1942)

Betty and Bert Lembeck, sons Michael and Lance (1942) and (1943) and Gretchen, their German Shepherd. Bert was a Marine captain and gunnery instructor at St. Mary's Pre-Flight School.

A NOTE ON THE DESIGN

To help the reader follow the flow of the correspondence back and forth, Don's letters are set in italics and my diary entries are noted and indented.

PROLOGUE

Redmond, Washington
May 5, 1941

Dear Dot and Don,

When Charlie joined the very first Naval R.O.T.C. Unit at Cal in 1926, we never dreamed we would some day be "paying" for that aura of glamour and romance! Now that he has received orders to report as Commanding Officer of a net tender[1], it's time to pay the piper.

We left Oakland on April 27th. Driving north on the main highway, the dogwood was just coming out and the redbuds were in all their glory. As we headed for Crater Lake and started up Mount Mazuma the snow deepened until it covered the buildings, which were accessible only through tunnels.

We drove through Oregon, around Mt. Hood and down the Columbia River. Washington is so beautiful I can't believe it! I keep looking for the ugly barren spot that must be just around the corner but never is.

When we arrived at Kirkland, on the east shore of Lake Washington, we called on every realtor and found just one furnished place. It was in an auto camp near the shipyards. For $40 a month we could have a cabin: two rooms, kitchenette with a wood cook stove, the lids so broken they could only be removed in segments by hand. No closets, just three coat hangers on a nail in the corner. There was no inside bathroom! I don't mind living in squalor if necessary, but I'm darned if I'll pay FORTY DOLLARS A MONTH for the privilege!

After spending the night in an exceedingly crummy auto court, the seven of us dressed to go out for breakfast in the pouring rain. Charlie had to report to his ship, immaculately accoutered. That's when we discovered the kids had been standing on his uniform coat and cap for three days!

As soon as he left, I went to a realtor, asked for an unfurnished house, and miraculously, they had one! I came, I saw, I grabbed it. It's a four room cottage, brown shingle exterior, plywood interior. It actually has a bathroom and a large semi-finished loft, a wood range in the kitchen and a wood stove for heating the living room. There is linoleum on all the floors except in the living room where the floor is finished in yellow shellac all around the edges of a rug that isn't there. The rent is $20 a month and we furnished it for $30.

Charlie made a deal with the second hand store man so that when we leave, he will buy it all back, at half what we paid. That includes an

---

[1] A ship which installs and maintains submerged metal barriers at the entrance to harbors, to prevent submarines from entering.

oak table, six reed bottom chairs, three mattresses, a large iron pot and a huge copper kettle which leaks only a little.

We also have a combination barn, garage, and woodshed, two wells, one with an old hand pump, one with an automatic electric pump which supplies the house with running water. The water is slightly rusty and it carries a certain amount of floating debris, but so far we haven't found any snakes, frogs or lizards in it. The whole place simply crawls with water snakes and slugs—big black slugs. Have you ever seen big black slugs? Ugh!

Good heavens! I just read over what I've written, and I've made the place sound like a nightmare. It isn't at all. It's all grown two feet high with weeds and clover, and has the most luxurious soil it has ever been my pleasure to dig, so loose that the weeds almost jump out of it, if you give them a tiny tug. We have two cherry trees, one peach, one pear, and several apple trees, loaded with young fruit, and caterpillars! Whenever it stops raining, I go out and gather them! It seems to me there should be better way to get rid of them.

The second evening here, Charlie and I took our striped canvas chairs out into the balmy spring twilight to sit and admire our farm. We have a lovely big raspberry patch, and it occurred to me that in all those four acres of weeds there MUST be a strawberry patch somewhere. Soon I found a cabbage patch, last year's, with all the cabbages gone, four feet high with yellow blooms. Then I found a corn patch, also last year's. Also nice big patches of carrots and potatoes. At last, I found the strawberry patch—big beautiful strong plants loaded with blossoms, and berries ready to ripen.

I yearn for a cow and chickens, but Charlie says, "I let you furnish a house for just one month but don't think I'll let you stock a barnyard!" He expects to be sent to Honolulu in a month. I'd like to stay right here till school starts. Moving this mob to Hawaii in the middle of a war is a big undertaking. Charlie says he's going to reserve six cells on the brig ship for us. That should make it a peaceful crossing for me!

I love this place. I have the feeling of having come home. It surprises me that I don't find it difficult to cook on a wood stove after so many years. Right now I have a pot of beans simmering on the front of the stove, four loaves of bread and an apple strudel on the back and some bean seed sprouting on the warming shelf. Our water is heated by passing through copper coils in the firebox of the stove. The supper fire heats about a quarter of a tankful, so with the tea kettle full of very hot water, we have enough for one good hot bath. Consequently we all stagger our baths.

It's so restful here! No radio or phonograph. What could be more relaxing than an evening spent side by side in deck chairs, watching our carrots grow?

But don't get the idea that nothing ever happens around here. Only last week a driver ran his truck into the City Hall and moved the building nearly five inches off it's foundations. That was over in the city of Kirkland. We don't have a City Hall. But we do have a drug store, a doctor, a veterinarian, and a general trading post that sells Charlie's Fuller Paints, so we feel right at home. If I only had some chickens! Love to you all, we miss you.

Lovingly, Leta

December 17, 1941

Dear Leta and Charlie,

Of course we were frantic when we heard the news. However we soon learned from Charlie's folks that you were all ok, except for the fact that Charlie's hair had turned white before he got to the ship, due to the Jap planes that were strafing the road. I always thought "His hair turned white overnight" was an old wive's tale. Anyhow, Charlie, I expect you look very distinguished, although it must feel strange to you at age thirty one!

There's a Japanese family up the road who live in a shack on the Hink place and take care of the pear crops for all of us. The girl, who walks home from school with our kids, complained bitterly about having had their radio taken away, and that they are to be shipped away to a concentration camp. I know it's not their fault, but I found myself not feeling a bit sorry for them. "What is she complaining about?" I thought, "She isn't going through what Leta and her family are going through." Then I was ashamed of myself for even thinking that, but just the same, it's the way I felt. Of course, at that time we didn't know what might have happened to all of you and were frantic.

On the 7th we had a date with Rae and Harry. We stopped off in San Francisco at the Prudential office because Don needed something from his desk. As we came out the door, a man getting out of the elevator called to us, " The Japs have bombed Pearl Harbor." We looked at him askance thinking, "Boy! How crazy can you get? Some people will do anything for attention!" When we got to the parking lot, the attendant ran up to us excitedly with the same statement. We were still skeptical. It was impossible! We turned on the car radio to listen on the way to Burlingame, and spent the rest of the day huddled around Rae and Harry's radio worrying about all of you.

Will you and the kids be sent home? It would be great to have you back here, but I know how you would hate leaving Charlie. We read the news so carefully, looking for anything that might tell us if you are OK. . . .

Honolulu, December 17, 1941

Dear Dot and Don:

We are all ok, and I am <u>SO</u> glad that we are here with Charlie and not safely at home. It's a good feeling when the smoke of battle clears to be able to see him and know that at least for one more day we are together, the kids still have a Dad, and all is right in our own very small world.

We were still in bed the morning of the 7th, which already seems months ago. We were rocked by the first explosion, but they are so common here, with all the blasting and big gun practice, that I thought nothing of it. However, Charlie leaped out of bed, ran to the window and shouted to me. When I joined him I saw a battleship in flames. Planes going toward Scofield, the military air field, had geysers of muddy water flying up beneath them. Charlie recognized them by the red dots on their wings, but it was the geysers that told me what was happening. Charlie was in uniform, out the door, through Hickam Field and on the last stretch before they started strafing him.

I threw together a bomb shelter of the dining room table, sofa cushions, and bedding. <u>Then</u> (Where was my head?) I went outside to get the kids in! They were fascinated by the falling bombs and had to be forcibly hauled indoors. All morning I was pulling them away from the windows and shoving them back under the table. Not that I blamed them. The only reason I stayed under the table myself was to keep them there. It's much worse when you can't see what's happening. The noise was so shattering that, after each attack ended, I went out fully expecting to find every house except our own destroyed. It's always a shock to see the sun shining, the grass still green, the neighbors all alive.

One fifty caliber Jap machine gun bullet came through our roof. A bomb destroyed the children's tree house, and a piece of casing fell in our garage.

You have undoubtedly read the details of everything that happened, but can you imagine the horror of watching all those sailors trying to swim away through burning oil, their bodies in flames? For days as I stood at my sink washing dishes, I saw truck loads of pine boxes coming out of the gate, on their way to Red Hill, the military cemetery, and I found myself wondering if any of them held boys that I have known and might have been a little nicer to.

I haven't seen Charlie in a week. We're on another alert. I only wish they'd get it settled before the kids and I have to leave. Once we've licked them, there won't be any need to send us home . . .
Lovingly, Leta

Honolulu, December 24, 1941

Dear Dot and Don:

I woke up to a terrible fracas of whistles and realized an air raid is on. By the time I got Charlie off and the bathroom full of steam to protect us from gas in case of an attack, I was too wide awake to go back to sleep. I think I had better stop and move the dining room table back to its December 7th spot in the safest corner, and start making it bullet proof. Once an enemy plane gets overhead we are in great danger from the fire from our own guns.

It's 3 a.m. Somebody's cat has taken shelter with me and insists on being in my lap while I write. I wish I knew whether it's "all clear" yet. Nothing is happening right now except an occasional plane overhead and distant explosions. Oh! I think the raid is over. I hear cars coming home. Ah! The man next door just came in. He says we're still on alert but things have quieted down.

The kids are happy here. The only reason they'd like to go home is because they think they'd be big shots at school with tales of December 7th. There are thirty-eight children in our group of fifteen duplexes, eighteen of them in the four houses at our end. What with Christmas, the war hysteria, no gas, and no playgrounds, it's a wonder we hang onto our sanity. To make matters worse all of us are packed, subject to evacuation on a few hours' notice.

Our rationing system allows enough food for an average family of four, but it's difficult to feed seven on that amount. I hear rationing is tight at home. How is it with you?

Lovingly, Leta.

Part One

"THIS IS THE ARMY, MR. JONES" *

"This is the Army Mr. Jones.
No private rooms or telephones.
You had your breakfast in bed before
But you won't have it there any more.
This is the Army Mr. Green.
We like our barracks nice and clean.
You had a housemaid to do your floor
But she won't help you out anymore.
Do as the bugler commands
You're in the Army and not in the band.
You're in the Army Mr. Brown.
You and your baby went to town.
She had you worried but this is war
And she won't worry you any more, more, more.
No she won't worry you any more."

Irving Berlin
From the musical production,
    "This is the Army", 1943

---

* Of course this should read, "This Is the Navy." However according to the terms of Irving Berlin's will, not one word of this can be changed.

December 27, 1942

Dear Leta and Charlie,

I am in a daze. Don has joined the Navy and will be leaving on January 13th for indoctrination at the University of Arizona. It has happened so fast, but actually it had been simmering inside of us for a long time.

One evening as we sat reading, Don tossed the Cal Alumni Monthly over to me and said, "Read this." The article was a plea for more officer material. It said the Navy was in dire need of more well-educated men. As I read it, vague feelings I had been having for some time took shape. "Let's go for a walk," I said, and we called upstairs to tell Donny we'd be walking up the road for a little while.

As we strolled along the path, we both expressed feelings of guilt that we were not contributing to the defense of our country, the feelings that we were so fortunate to have each other, our lovely spot in the country, and most of all, to have been able to adopt our four wonderful children. We felt that we should be taking part more actively in defending what we had. The article demonstrated that it might be financially feasible, and we felt that somehow we could manage. So just like that, the decision was made, and the next morning Don set the wheels in motion.

Now that the time is approaching, I am scared to death. Christmas has been a very bittersweet occasion. Every moment is so precious. We took movies of each one of the kids gazing in wonderment as their Daddy came out of the bedroom door in each one of his uniforms. Quite an impressive fashion show: first his khakis, then his blues, and then his whites.

Donny is excited over the whole thing. Bev doesn't like having her Daddy go away. You know how special their relationship is. Judy is bewildered. Poor little kid. She has had so many changes in her young life. I hope this won't discombobulate her further. She has only been with us eight months, and having had eleven homes in her three-and-a-half years, she is so very insecure. Of course the whole thing is way over Chuck's head. At six months he is interested only in the next meal and an endless supply of holding and hugging!

Lots of love to all of you from all of us,

Dot

DIARY

January 1st, 1943. I approach this year with dread. Took down all the Christmas decorations and filled the house with flowers. It looks and smells beautiful. Lovely evening, just the two of us after so much company.

January 12th. Our butane froze again. What a nuisance, going out in our robes to pour kettles of hot water over the tank so the furnace would go on. Had a last "fun" trip to San Francisco. Took Chuckie to feed the ducks at Golden Gate Park. He was a lamb all day.

January 13th. Don told the kids goodbye before they left for school. I don't think it's real to them. Well, it's not real to me either. He's gone! Read myself to sleep. I suppose that's better than crying.

Midnight, January 13, 1943

Oh Honey,

When the train left I was in despair. I went to Martinez to see Mrs. Edgar. She tried to be comforting. She said, when her husband died, she was numb. Then she was frantic, desperate, and hopeless. But she said, "Believe it or not, the day <u>WILL</u> come when you'll wake up in the morning glad to face the day and want to pitch in and enjoy life." I find that very hard to believe.

As you know, the reason I went was to find out how Judy's and Chuck's adoptions are proceeding. She gave me more information about Judy, but she feels we should not try to go ahead with finalizing, because with you away there's the possibility of our applications being turned down. Of course I was extremely disappointed, but I guess we have no choice. If only we could have finalized them before you left, but of course that was impossible since they had been with us such a short time.

Goodnight, Honey

January 14, 1943

My Own Sweet Family,

The trip on the train to L.A. last night was very interesting. I met several fellows who were at Cal with us and whom I haven't seen since then. You can imagine the conversations we had, far into the night.

Charlie Cook met me at the station. We picked up Roscoe Holmes at the Prudential office, and they took me to a fabulous lunch at the Brown Derby.

After that we went to CBS to see Elaine, and she showed us the whole place. I was really impressed with "my bratty little cousin," her poise and her responsibilities. I had no idea how much there is to producing radio programs.

Then Charlie took me out to his home—it is GRAND! He has a C card entitling him to all the gas he needs because he is in the Auxiliary Police. Lucky guy!

John was at the station when we arrived in Tucson. It was swell seeing your "Baby Brother" after so long. We plan to meet again at church next Sunday.

We are billeted (bunked) in the University Gym in double-deckers. There are 500 in my class and 500 in the bunch ahead of us. They are called Senior Student Officers. We are Juniors.

I am SO lonesome for all of you and especially you my lovely one.

Your loving Honey and Daddy

January 16, 1943

Oh Honey, my Honey:

It is freezing around here, and I mean that literally. Last night it was 22 degrees. Yesterday a couple of the boys from the little Army radar camp up on the hill came down to help me dig, but the ground was too hard. Naturally we asked them to have lunch with us, which I am sure they were hoping we would do. They are nice kids and so far from home. They love being around our kids.

I think I'll ask a half dozen or so of them to come down next Saturday evening to have dinner with us and play ping pong and badminton. I'll see if I can round up some of the neighbors too, and we could have dancing in the rumpus room. Our children love having them around. To the children they are men. To me they're kids.

Honey, I hate to quit, but I am SOOOOOO tired and think I had better get to bed. Sorry this is such a short letter. Oh Honey, I am so lonesome. Sometimes I think I can't stand it, but then I get to working hard and concentrating on what I am doing and that helps.

Love, love, love from your Honey.

January 17, 1943

Dearest Wonderful You:

It was such a thrill to talk to you and the children last night. I feel so much better. Don't forget to keep the tires inflated to 32 lbs. all around, and have the spare checked from time to time. I am certain you will have to have Dad advance you some money on our war bonds as he offered to do. On top of the other things I mentioned, and the normal expenses, the life insurance is due before the 15th of next month.

Saturday we had three shots; tetanus, typhoid, and small pox. Right after that we had movies on drilling and then classes till noon. After lunch we had Captain's Inspection and, despite the fact that the weather was cold and windy,

*several fellows passed out from the shots. My reaction started about that time,
so I went to bed and slept until muster for Watch Squad at 5:30.*

I was fortunate in the first quiz. I got a 3.8, (95%).

All my love to my wonderful family,

January 18, 1943

Honey:

It makes me so mad that you aren't receiving my letters yet. I'm glad
you are meeting so many interesting people and enjoying that part of it
even though it seems as though they are working you at least twenty-five
hours a day.

Today I planted carrots, strawberries and sweet peas. Some more of the
boys from the camp on the hill came down and helped. They did all the
digging. What a break that was for me.

NEXT MORNING. That is as far as I got yesterday. Too much going on
after the kids got home from school. Chuckie is playing in his pen beside
me and is making the loveliest noises, "talking" to me. I just hate for you to
miss this part of his life as he changes and develops so rapidly. We are all
trying our best to get movie film but it looks pretty hopeless.

Bernice and Markie take turns taking me out each day for a driving
lesson. We pile our collective kids into the car during school hours so we
won't have more than three to take with us. Good night, my darling.

Your Honey

January 19, 1943

Dearest One:

I can't stand it! Still no mail from you, and I know you have written.

*Last night we heard an excellent talk from a member of our class who
escaped from a Japanese internment camp there.*

*I'm eating like a horse at every meal. If I don't put on weight now, I never
will. Incidentally a BIG box of cookies would be much appreciated.*

*We are to have a stiff exam tomorrow and no time to study for it. The
courses we are taking are Seamanship, Navigation, and Administration. This
exam will cover the names of EVERY part of a battleship, the memorizing of
signal pennants and flags, sixty five of them, and half of a text book on
Seamanship.*

*The average age of our bunch is about 34–35. All college grads, of course,
and many with a Ph.D., so the competition is keen.*

No time for more today. All my love to my precious ones,

Your Honey

January 21, 1943

Dearest,

We had our first BIG exam today, and it was a dilly. I am tired and stiff from all the gymnastics, also from lack of sleep. Usually I get six hours or less per night—like the old days in law school.

I hope you are able to get meat and the other necessities. Our meals here are really wonderful although it is supposed to be proper to complain.

We just returned from drill. Two letters from you were had arrived. What a thrill! I don't see how you can find time to write me such terrific letters. I am afraid you are overdoing. PLEASE don't work so hard. PLEASE have some fun.

I thought I would get used to sleeping here pretty soon, but I don't. Every time I turn I reach out for you in my sleep, I wake up with a start because I can't reach you. Last night it was at least ten times.

The drill field is over a mile away. We march both ways as well as one-and-a-half hours while we are there. We do everything by platoons of forty men. We have weekly examinations, and the results go on our fitness reports to Washington. Despite all this I am determined that letters to you will come first, whenever I have a few minutes.

I enjoy the studying but we are so cramped for time. I got a 3.3 on my second quiz. Last night we had another lecture on navigation. I certainly enjoy that course. Today we also had instruction in pistols and guns.

So Bev has chicken pox. What a shame. Be sure that you are well for your birthday, my little Poochy. I hope it doesn't bother you too much.

In the Navy books I sent to Donny you will find a lot of answers to your questions. "Blue-Able" refers to the flag A-able and the other to the flag B-Baker. Irish pennants are bits of sheets or blankets or anything that hangs out from under the bed springs. The "head" is the washroom and toilet.

The weather here is amazing. We have a temperature range of about 40–50 degrees. From 30 in the morning at 5:30, it goes up to 75 or 80 by noon.

I get a lump in my throat at least 100 times a day when I think of you.

February 1, 1943

My Precious One:

Your letter of Friday came today and also the box of delicious cookies. I just finished passing them around and have over half the box left.

It seems I am the medical wonder of the age. My smallpox vaccination is taking even though I had smallpox twenty four years ago. After evening lecture I reported to sick bay and since my temperature was 102, they made me stay. Two-thirds of the fellows have had serious shot reactions since we arrived.

This is a beautiful campus. All the buildings are red brick, and most of them are Southern Colonial with tall white pillars. We see many of the students as we march to and from our classes. Most of the coeds wear jeans to class.

Isn't that amazing? Also a lot of the students ride bikes. There are bike racks on the campus. Can you imagine?

We spend a great deal of time standing in line. After marching to class and meals, we stand in line to get in when we get there, stand in line to get a clean towel, to get our laundry, to buy anything at the ship's store, to get a haircut, to wash, shave or take a shower, even to sit on the throne!

It was such a thrill to talk with you and the children last night. I hope the phone call didn't make you cry this time. It made a new man out of me.

We were all invited to a Fiesta Ball last night, but it cost $2.75 a person, and if I am to save enough money to come home on leave, I can't squander it that way. Instead, five of us went to the Pioneer Hotel, which is the nicest one in town. It was a treat to see someone besides Navy officers. They have a good orchestra, and the cover charge is only fifty-five cents. I didn't dance because my legs and arms are still much too painful.

So Chuck patty-cakes now. I wish I could see him. Maybe you can get that on the next roll of movie film. I am trying hard to get some for you.

I will be going to a formal dance on Tuesday evening. The city of Tucson has one for each senior class, and our class is invited too. We get special leave for the occasion and they fix us up with dates.

I learned a little more today about communications school in L.A. In our battalion there are thirty one others who have orders there. The course is for two months, six days a week. They provide meals, but no quarters, so I'll have to rent a room somewhere. The training is extremely confidential. Nothing in writing. No pencils or pens allowed in lectures. On completion one becomes an expert communications officer, ready for assignment.

I must get back to the books now. All my love to all my loves,

DIARY

February 3rd. Had the jitters all day. Tried to get rid of them by riding my bike up and down the road. No sleep till 1:30 a.m.

Feb 5th. Mabel and I to the commissary. What a madhouse. Out of most of the things we needed. Everyone trying to spend their new ration points.[1] Took Donny to eye doctor in S.F. Package from Don with gifts for the kids when we got home. Such excitement!

Feb 7th. Drove the car all over the neighborhood by myself. Can't believe I am actually driving a car. But I'm a long way from being able to take it out on the highway. Lucky I can practice in our secluded valley.

Feb 8th. Donny broke out and is SO SICK, much sicker than Beverly. Poor kid. Poor me, too. He is so badly broken out, and the

---

[1]Periodically, Ration Boards issued stamp books, one for each member of the family. These stamps were required in order to buy meat, canned goods, various other food items, gasoline, and tires. If the needed items were not available within the time period, the stamps (points) went to waste.

itch drives him wild. Sometimes he can't help crying and that makes me feel terrible.

Feb 11th. I'm dying for a letter. Beautiful weather but what good does it do? Bev is feeling much better, but her face is still a mess.

Feb 13th. Big day! Donny feels much better, but Chucky is SO SICK. Fortunately he isn't well enough coordinated yet to be able to scratch. He tries, poor little thing, but luckily he can't get his hands focused on the right spot. We managed to have Bev's birthday party by inviting anyone on the road who had already had chicken pox—Nancy and Lois, and all three Condits. So with streamers, hats, and cake it turned out to be quite a splendid affair.

Feb 17th. No letter, and this was the 14th anniversary of our first date. Woe is me! Worked on curtains.

Feb 22nd. Washington's birthday! Nice weather, and everyone feeling better. To the rationing board with Bernice in the afternoon. Need more shoe coupons, desperately.[2] Judy wears shoes out in less than two months.

Feb 26th. I am on my own now. I have a license, and I can drive the highway without my kind and patient neighbors to ride herd on me. I didn't think I would live through the driving test, but I did!

February 11, 1943

Dearest Mine:

The 3rd Battalion is leaving this afternoon and I am green with envy. Each month during the week of "graduation," the student officers put on a skit. There were about fifty in it, and what talent! Script writing, directing, and acting were all so professional, and the jokes were marvelous, especially so with an all male audience and most of the jokes directed at staff members.

Our classes were shortened today, but not the quiz. First there was a regimental review. After that we changed to our blues for the graduation exercises. At least a hundred of the officers' wives attended.

Ernie Steiner just walked by and said "Say hello to Mama for me and tell her the cookies were good."

I am assigned to be Student Officer in charge of the watch all night tonight and all day Saturday. It's quite a responsibility as the watch squad consists of two full platoons of about eighty men. I'm crossing my fingers and hope I don't make any mistakes.

You might be interested in knowing a little more about the members of my platoon. We have four attorneys, besides me, one of whom was the D.A. in San Antonio. Another one was a Superior Court Judge in Topeka, Kansas. There are seven teachers, five high school and two college, two civil engineers, four mechanical and four electrical engineers.

---

[2]Each person was allowed two shoe coupons a year. Sometimes a special request, accompanied by signed forms and an urgent plea, would be granted.

I can't impress on you strongly enough that my orders are NEVER to be discussed with ANYONE. We knew all along that I would be going to L.A. when I leave here but didn't know the significance of it.

Your Honey and Daddy.

February 14, 1943

Dearest Mine:

It certainly was a relief to talk with you last night. I was so worried all week about the chicken pox. I'm glad Bev liked the doll suitcase I sent her and that she had such a nice party in spite of everything.

You asked me what the student officer in charge of the watch has to do. Well, it would take too much time to tell you in a letter. However, this might clarify it a bit. At every station and on every ship every day, there is what is known as the " Officer of the Day" or "Officer of the Watch." He is responsible for the complete running of the entire station or ship, in ALL respects, for a twenty four hour period. During that time he is in complete command, subject only to the Captain and the Executive Officer. At this station we have the entire watch handled by the student officers with a staff officer as Officer of the Watch. However, he is there merely to see that nothing goes wrong, and the Student Officer in charge has the full responsibility. There are whole books written on the duties of the O.O.D. So you can see why it would be difficult to describe in a letter.

As soon as I learned my specific duties as officer in charge, my apprehension disappeared. At the end of the watch we were complimented highly. After that a bunch of us went downtown. Everywhere we went we bumped into members of our platoon. Finally we went to the Old Pueblo Club. It's a private club, but they have guest cards for officers. One of the officers introduced me to his date, and I had a dance with her. She is a graduate of the University of Iowa and is now a social worker. I met another officer from our battalion who will also be going to L.A. He is from Washington and his name is Jim Phelan. He is bringing his wife and two little girls to be with him in L.A.

I am glad Donny is feeling better. Please take care of yourself, Honey. I worry about you so much. You have your hands so full.

Yesterday after lunch Ernie and I got a ride downtown. All a Naval officer has to do in this town is to stand on the corner, and practically the first car that comes along stops to pick him up. We went to meet the fellows who were coming in on the train. I felt that Arleigh might be one of them, and he was. It was swell to see Arleigh and hear the latest about all of you.

Gee, I feel so terrible about poor little Chuckie. I get so much pleasure out of looking at all your pictures every day.

All my love to my cherished five.

February 17, 1943

Dearest Mine:

As soon as we finished athletics and calisthenics yesterday, we made a dash for the showers. Can you imagine what it's like when 500 men shower at the same time with only 50 showers? The dance was a very nice affair. Everyone was so friendly, and I danced every dance. Each of the girls, or should I say women, as they ranged from seventeen to seventy, had her name on a card pinned to her formal. Also the last half was entirely tag dances[1].

Several of the fellows in our platoon were quite shy, so I would dance with a girl and then introduce her to a shy one in order to get him started.

I forgot to tell you about the talk we had Monday evening. The speaker, a colonel in the Marines, was in command of the invasion force on Guadalcanal. His talk was very confidential and restricted, but it was by far the best we have had. His medals covered the entire upper left side of his coat.

I should knock on wood. I haven't had any reactions to the two shots I had last night. They did all five hundred of us in an hour and fifteen minutes with one man giving the tetanus in the left arm and the other giving the yellow fever in the right. My right arm feels o.k., but oh that left!

I had better study now. Please give each one of the children a kiss for me and a big hug too. Oh if only I could do it in person . . .

February 23, 1943

Dearest Mine,

Soon, I'll be able to help you in the vegetable garden. You'll need those vegetables more than ever with the new stricter rationing.

Last night, instead of one of our rare and precious study periods, we had an abandon ship drill, then an emergency drill, and then joined in a station-wide black out drill. After that about fifteen or twenty fellows gathered on and around my bunk and had crackers and peanut butter, crackers and jelly, cookies and candy, all from a box the girls from the office sent.

I received a 3.9 in my quiz this morning. It was on comprehensive "restricted" material for which we have had only four days to study. So far we have taken or are taking Naval Administration, Seamanship, Navigation, Ordnance, Naval Fundamentals, and Naval Communications. Each one covers quite a variety of subjects. In Fundamentals alone we have covered four books in two weeks and have another to cover in the next five days.

Tonight we had an hour's study period, and I surprised myself by learning the entire semaphore system. By bedtime I was able to receive whole sentences as fast as any of the fellows could send them. It just goes to show what a fellow could do if he had a little time to study. . . .

---

[1]In a tag dance it is acceptable for someone not dancing to tap a person of the same sex on the shoulder. The person tagged must then yield his partner for the balance of that dance. Those not dancing are encouraged to tag someone.

February 27, 1943

Dearest, Darling:

Poor Arleigh! He is having his first watch today—a sixteen hour one, outside patrol, which means that he has to walk all day, on top of having his second typhoid shot (double dose) this a.m.

Ernie and I had inquired about swimming at the Arizona Inn, and they said we could, so we started to walk over, not realizing how far it was. With the assistance of a ride part way we were there in an hour. It is certainly a swell hotel, by far the most exclusive around here—$30 a day for a couple. Wow! It is quite similar to the Del Monte, with each of the rooms a separate cottage. The swimming pool is beautiful and is protected by shrubbery and lattice work on all four sides and with lawns and deck chairs all around it.

There was so much going on that we never did get around to swimming. It was enjoyable just being there and watching everyone. Before we knew it the fellows started arriving for our platoon party, and then the fun began.

The banquet was terrific. But the fellow who was to be toastmaster couldn't come at the last minute, so five minutes before dinner started, I was drafted to act in his place. Luckily everything went off ok, and I had a lot of compliments afterwards, much to my surprise. I called on everyone to say a few words, and they were all swell, some in a serious tone and some in a humorous one. There were a lot of surprises. Some of the quietest fellows made the best talks of all. We had fun ribbing the staff.

When it was over, seven of us managed to get a taxi to take us into town. We asked the driver about a good place to go, and he suggested the La Jolla, which is a night club with a floor show. There was no cover charge or minimum charge, and the show was excellent. The place was jammed, but we spoke to the head waitress, and she managed to fix us up with a ringside table. Weren't we lucky? By the time we got back we were really ready to hit the sack.

All that "fun" last night seems senseless when you aren't with me. But we have to keep going and make the most of this experience, or we would go nuts.

Your loving, lonesome, anxious-to-be-home Honey and Daddy

February 27, 1943

Honey,

I forgot to tell you about the day I got my license. I was absolutely petrified for fear I would do something terrible. We always practiced with a car full of children, and I had gotten in the habit of putting my arm out in a protective way whenever I put on the brakes suddenly. So at one point in the examination, when we stopped suddenly, I did this instinctively and felt so foolish. I hoped that the examiner would laugh it off, but he made no attempt to make me feel less uncomfortable.

I had been practicing parallel parking for weeks and was still very unsure of myself. After we had driven all over Martinez and he indicated that we were to finish up, I asked him if he wanted me to park. His answer was, "Heavens no! I can tell by the way you drive you could never park. Why do you want a license, anyway?" I told him, "I live three miles from schools, stores, and buses. I have four children, and my husband is overseas." "Well," he said, "I'll give you a license, but for HEAVEN'S SAKE stay out of traffic!" What a morale booster!

Today I went to the nursery and got oleanders, roses, and grapes. It was too big a job to start planting by the time I got back, so I just did a lot of weeding. Right now the soil is perfect for pulling weeds and you know how seldom that happens. The Schneiders call it "fifteen minute adobe" because there is just fifteen minutes in the whole year when it is workable!

Tom Slaven dropped by last night to see if there was anything he could do for us. He is such a dear. I don't know what we would do without him around. He pushed our car all the way into Lafayette the other day because our battery was dead. Last week he took Donny's bike to Berkeley to try to get a tire for it. I think it is killing him to be too old to get involved in the war effort in a more exciting way. Oh, also yesterday the Burkes came by AGAIN—at meal time AGAIN! It is getting to be a joke, and one of these days I am NOT going to invite them to stay and eat with us!

Oh Honey, I am so terribly lonesome for you. It seems as though you have been gone forever. I find that every tiny decision I have to make assumes enormous proportions; for example, whether or not I should send Bev to school when she didn't seem to be acting normal. I tried so hard to decide, as though the fate of a nation hung on my decision. Then I thought if you were here you probably would say, "Oh go ahead and send her. She looks fine to me." When Mr. Ellis drove up a few hours later I wondered why on earth the principal would be coming here in the middle of a school day. There was poor little Bev all broken out and miserable. He explained that since he knew I was home with two little ones, he thought the best thing to do was bring her home himself rather than bother me. What a nice man! But I was SO terribly embarrassed at her having exposed the whole class to chicken pox.

Honey, please get the war over with and come home TOMORROW!

DIARY

February 28. Rae and Harry came for the weekend. The kids were delighted to see them, especially Harry. They do love to have a man around. They took me to see "The Major and the Minor" in Martinez, and it was so good to be going somewhere with adults for a change— the first time I had been out in the evening for so many weeks. We had trouble with our car coming home, but Harry managed to fix it, whatever IT was. He is so good at things like that. . . .

March 2, 1943

Dearest Mine:

They need another fellow for Saturday night, so Arleigh is going. Our dates are to pick us up, and we are to go to a cocktail party at 6:30 and then the formal dinner dance at 8:00 at the Santa Rita Hotel. The name of the girl I am supposed to take is Ruth Fuller. I'm so glad we were able to get Arleigh in on it. He's pretty low and lonesome with the baby due so soon.

You asked about what I want to do when I come home on leave. MOST OF ALL I WANT TO BE WITH YOU PRACTICALLY ALL THE TIME. ALONE. Of course I will want to see Rae and Harry, and I'll want to drop in at the office, but mainly I just want all of my family that I can get. I'm sure everyone will understand. If they don't, it's too bad. Only a few more days. Kiss the children for me.

March 7, 1943

Dearest:

Yesterday after Captain's Inspection, Arleigh and I and three other fellows went downtown. At 6:30 we met our dates for the party at the gateway to the campus. The party consisted of twenty-five couples: fifteen Navy and nine Army, plus the host and hostess of the cocktail party. Their home is a beautiful one, with an intriguing garden, lots of lawn, shade trees, a barbecue, and ping pong tables. It was nice having the get-together there, so we could meet and get acquainted ahead of time.

When we left there, Arleigh and I and our "dates" rode together. The girl who was supposed to be my date was the exotic type. She is Dean of Girls at the local high school. However, as things turned out, I had a different date before the evening was over. That one was the identical twin of the girl who invited us to the party. They are identical in every way, even their names both begin with a V—Velma and Vera. No one could tell them apart. They dressed alike except for different color ribbons in their hair. They kept changing ribbons, so we were never sure which one was which.

One of the fellows didn't show up, and the way the seats were arranged, I was left with two girls. Finally I found a fellow in my platoon in the hotel lobby, dragged him in, and gave him the exotic one.

The party was fun, and when I discovered that Velma has an eleven-year-old daughter and a seven-year-old son, we talked about our children for the rest of the evening. I figured out from the little she could tell me that her husband is on a destroyer in the Pacific. We all have to work hard at remembering the poster which says, "LOOSE LIPS SINK SHIPS."

Today Arleigh and I went for a postman's holiday. We walked at least eleven miles and really saw the town, including all of the Mexican quarter. I am going to try to get a really good sleep tonight.

This is my last letter before I leave, because anything written later wouldn't get to you until I am there. Can I possibly live until then Honey?

DIARY

March 6th. Leta and her gang came over, and we had a wonderful day. The nine kids had a great time together. Charlie is at sea now. Leta assumes he is in the Pacific.

March 7th. Another horrible lonely Sunday almost over. Chuck, Judy, and I all have runny colds. Tried to stay in bed and keep them down too.

March 8th. Oh Joy! Oh bliss! Five letters from Don. Life looks worth living again.

March 11th. Ruth and Arleigh Williams' baby girl, Linda, arrived today at 3:11 a.m. Two letters from my Honey, lovely long ones.

March 12th. Rushed to get ready, cleaned house, got food, cooked, had my hair done. Dashed to meet his plane. HE MISSED IT! The Underhill baby arrived at six, a little girl, Phyllis.

March 13th. He's here! It's wonderful!

March 14th. Rae and Harry, my folks, and the Stocktons all arrived at once. Shortly thereafter a mass invasion by Don's aunts and cousins. So much for Don's plans for us just to be alone and enjoy being together.

March 17th. Up at 5. Took Don to the bus at 6. Rainy and dark. Our time was so short, but we did have fun taking the kids to Fleishacker Zoo, Treasure Island, and Golden Gate park. But Oh! I can't bear it. Well, in two months maybe—

Part Two

"DON'T SIT UNDER THE APPLE TREE."

Don't sit under the apple tree
With anyone else but me,
Anyone else but me,
Anyone else but me, No! No! No!
Don't sit under the apple tree
With anyone else but me
Till I come marching home.

Don't go walking down lovers' lane
With anyone else but me,
Anyone else but me,
Anyone else but me, No! No! No!
Don't go walking down lover's lane
With anyone else but me
Till I come marching home.

Lew Brown, Charlie Tobias, & Sam H. Stept
Made famous by the Andrews sisters
during WW II.

March 18, 1943

Dearest Mine:

I am terribly homesick and lonesome already. The parting this time was much worse, wasn't it? Oh how I enjoyed our few precious days.

I arrived about 6:45. The rain was coming down in sheets. After much difficulty I located a bus which took me within three blocks of Wil's hotel. He was waiting for me in the lobby and had reserved the only room left. It was $5! It was lucky that we could share the cost.

This morning, as soon as we presented our orders to the O.O.D., we were taken to the wardroom (officers' lounge) where we all sat and talked for a while. After that we had a talk from one of the staff members and were issued our books. We were then secured for the day in order to find living quarters. There are thirty four Naval officers and thirteen Marine officers in our class. Most of the Marines have been in Communications for some time and have just come from three months of schooling at Ft. Benning, Georgia.

I won't be able to write much about school here. They keep stressing the necessity of secrecy all day long. We worked hard from 7:40 a.m. to 5:30 p.m. with twenty minutes for lunch and have an entire book to learn before Friday.

Oh Honey, our time together was so short but so wonderful. I thought I would die that first day though, when everybody descended upon us.

It was so much fun at Fleishacker Zoo and Golden Gate Park. Young as Chuckie is he seemed to enjoy it a lot. And the kids were all so well behaved. I can just hear you saying, "For a change!" Seeing "Me and My Gal" and "Random Harvest" with you was such a delight.

I left my heart with you and my thoughts are there continually.
Your Honey

DIARY

March 18th. Susan and Philip pushed Chuckie's buggy off the porch, and he landed upside down in the flower bed. I was petrified, but after I brushed him off and found he was unhurt, I really felt good. AT LAST some one else in the neighborhood has children old enough to do naughty things.

March 22nd. Planted carrots, chard, and artichokes, also did a lot of weeding. Chuckie watched and loved it. Three letters! Oh Joy!

March 29th. Pouring rain and then bright sun. Took all the kids to the doctor. What a workout! Donny has to have a basal metabolism test because his second teeth aren't coming in. Tried to shop for food but couldn't find much. Washed windows, planted petunias, typed till 11:30, then read till 2 a.m.

March 21, 1943

My Very Dearest Dear:

Yesterday we secured at 4:30 and Wil and I went to look for a place to live. One of the fellows knew someone whose place would be available, so we were lucky. After depositing our belongings, we went to the Officer's Club at the Beverly Hills Hotel. It took us over an hour by foot and by bus. We had an excellent dinner, one of the best meals I have EVER had. Excellent service and a thick tender T-bone steak. Not bad for a buck.

We walked a couple of miles through the beautiful Beverly Hills section before going to the Open House. Hostesses greeted us, and we had a few dances to a five-piece orchestra. One of the girls is a Theta and a Junior at U.C.L.A. The other one is from Vienna and has been in this country about a year. The one from UCLA told our fortunes from the lines in our palms. She told me I would be married twice, the first marriage wouldn't last long, and that I would have one child. You should have seen her face when I told her I've been married eleven years and have four children.

This morning I had to walk nearly a mile for breakfast, but it was worth it. I had eggs, fried potatoes, two hot cakes, and coffee, all for thirty cents. I have lots of studying to do so am glad I have the rest of the day for it.

I am coming along pretty well in taking code. However in typing I am quite handicapped. There are only six of us who don't already know how to type by the touch method. We only have forty minutes a day, and I have to be able to type 45 words per minute by the end of two months in order to get 4.0.

So poor little Chuckie can't sit down because of his shot. What next? Have all his pock marks disappeared yet? Oh how I wish you were all here with me. Most of the men here are married, and about half of those have children. Most of them have their families here with them, but there's not a chance in the world of finding a place for a family the size of ours.

Your ever lovin' Honey and Daddy.

March 28,1943

My Dearest Sweetheart:

I am so excited about next Friday that I can hardly wait. I finally found a room in a small, respectable hotel five blocks from here and about six blocks from the ship. It's right on Sunset, so the streetcar is very handy. Be sure to bring your bathing suit. We could go either to the Beverly Hills Hotel or to the beach. I can hardly wait. My heart is jumping for joy.

As soon as I finished writing you yesterday, Wil and I left for Elaine's. She has a little three room cottage about ten minutes' walk from Hollywood and Vine. It's secluded and quite old. She has been fixing it up and has planted both a Victory garden and a flower garden. We had a meatless dinner but it was excellent. Wil couldn't get over how good it was. I am amazed at how Elaine's personality has blossomed since she came down here. Wil thought she was tops.

This morning I had a good breakfast at the corner drug store. However it was much too expensive—sixty cents. I can't do that very often.

I keep forgetting to tell you. They have Li'l Abner and Harold Teen in the L.A. Times but no Little Orphan Annie or Tarzan. Somehow I will manage to get along without them! Oh the trials and tribulations of war!

DIARY

April 1st. Getting really jittery. Will my clothes be ok? Will the kids be ok without me? Rae and Harry are coming to take charge.

April 2nd. Up at 5. Markie took me to the train. Horrible trip. Train jam packed with soldiers. So many stops and delays. What bliss to see his face. Dingy, dirty room in old crummy hotel in down town L.A. next to the fire station, with engines going in and out all night long. Poor Don was so very disappointed not to have a nicer place for us. Walked and talked, found a lovely place for dinner. It's HEAVEN to be together!

April 3rd. To Hollywood, met Elaine at CBS for a tour. Then an hour and a half on three street cars to Don's special place. The only thing left on the menu was calves' brains and eggs! For dessert, only carrot ice cream! Oh well, "C'est la guerre." At least we are together. Then by streetcar to the Beverly Wilshire to go dancing at the officers' club. They wouldn't let me in because I didn't have on a long formal. Don's uniform was acceptable but not me! So, again by streetcar, to the Ambassador Hotel to dance.

April 4th. Late breakfast. "Blackouts Of 1943." Terrific show! Walked and walked, nice dinner, then dancing at "The Palladium." Tommy Dorsey was playing. Marvelous! The jitterbuggers were WILD!

April 6th. Sooooo low. Cried off and on most of the day. Everything went wrong while I was gone.

April 5, 1943

Lovely Lady Mine:

I just finished dinner and am waiting for the downpour to subside so I can make a dash for it. Right now you must be getting pretty tired of the train. Wasn't our weekend marvelous? You were so wonderful and you looked terrific. I thought you looked as though you had just stepped out of Vogue Magazine.

I'm enclosing a letter from Rae. She is willing to come over again. So be sure to make your train reservations right away, and tell her which weekend.

I am up to eight-and-a-half words per minute in my code now. As soon as I get to nine I will have a 4.0 for the course and be excused to study during that period. I had my first test in typing today and got 4.0, which pleased me, inasmuch as I was starting from scratch. In semaphore I can send and take twelve words per minute now and will have 4.0 as soon as I can do fifteen.

DIARY

April 8th. Low and lonesome. Cleaned house. Sewed at Red cross. Planted carrots, lettuce, radishes. MARVELOUS letter from my Honey.

April 11th. After Sunday School I spent most of the day in the kitchen. Among other things we made ice cream in an old fashioned crank freezer. The kids loved it and all wanted their turn at turning the crank and licking the paddles. My disposition is terrible. I know I'm lucky with four darling children and a wonderful Honey, but I am so tired of being without him.

April 12, 1943

Dearest Beautiful:

I had a marvelous time yesterday and forgot my lonesomeness for a while. When I finished writing to you, I barely had time to get to the Ambassador in time to be taken to the Open House. The hostesses were there to drive us. A couple of Marines from our bunch were the only others I knew before going, but they made us feel so at home that I got acquainted with almost everyone. There were about thirty officers and about twenty girls plus five mothers.

The affair is at a different home every week. This home is like one you might see in the movies. We danced in the den, which is the size of our living room, and played the piano and sang songs in the living room. We had the library, patio, sun porch and a walled garden for sitting and conversation. In the garden they have ping pong, a huge swimming pool, and a tennis court. The party lasted from two to six, and I enjoyed every minute of it.

I was invited by one of the mothers to go to a dinner dance at 7 p.m. at the Town House, which is about four blocks from the Ambassador. That dance was given by the Flower Guild of the Junior League. All of the older women wore so many diamonds that it almost put my eyes out! Just five of us had been invited to join them, and we ate our dinner with five ladies, the youngest of whom was at least forty, but we enjoyed their company and conversation very much.

After dinner we danced, and later one of the girls drove me to Hollywood Blvd. in her Cadillac Coupe so I could take the streetcar home. I had most of the dances with her, and she was a lot of fun. She is involved in volunteer work and also goes to San Pedro twice a week as a hostess at the USO. She was floored when I told her we have four children. Wish I didn't have to stop . . .

April 15, 1943

My Precious One:

For the past two days we've been having two hour talks by the Marines in our class about the action they have seen, with particular reference to communications, as well as personal experiences at the battle of Midway, in the Solomons, in the New Hebrides, at Guadalcanal, etc. You can imagine how very interesting it has been.

I'm glad you write your letters the way you do because I want to know the bad as well as the good news. If we keep things from each other, we can't stay as close. Of course, it makes me feel bad to know when you are down, but I can imagine how it would be if I had to keep my feelings to myself.

Last night I received a telegram from Trix and Marty asking me to call them. Marty has to go to Las Vegas on a case, and his club is having a dinner dance at the Hollywood Roosevelt tonight. Trix wanted to know if I could take her. Of course I will. I am certainly getting in on a lot of entertainment.

NEXT DAY. We had a swell time at the dinner dance. Their club had taken over the entire ballroom plus the Hollywood Roosevelt orchestra. We had fun telling different stories as to why I was there and Marty wasn't. There were about three hundred there. Practically all were married couples about our age with several children. I enjoyed driving their car, a 1941 Buick sedan.

Today Wil and I took the electric train to Long Beach and arrived at the Navy Landing Pier just in time to catch the launch to the battleship we wanted to visit. I can't tell you anything about the ship except that it was quite overwhelming. One of the Junior communications officers showed us around. Going back on the officer's launch I learned a lot from a gunnery officer who took Naval ROTC at the University of Washington. He is now a full Lieutenant. He suggested that we have dinner at the Officers Club. The price of the dinner was based on the entree. The most expensive was turkey for $1. We both had thick juicy tender steaks (.95), and the whole dinner was excellent.

By the time we took the bus to Long Beach, the train from there to L.A., and the streetcar home, we were bushed, but I wanted to be sure to get this finished and off to you right away. Goodnight, My Beloved.

Your Honey.

DAIRY

April 13th. Visited school a.m. Rode the bike into town. Three miles on the highway is scary for a novice like me. I think learning to ride the bike was harder than learning to drive the car. Sewed on dresses for the girls p.m. Cried all over the sewing machine. I'm lower than low.

April 16th. Got a lot done outside, also sewing. Almost finished the girls' dresses. Gave the house a good cleaning. Twelve-thirty by the time I got to bed. Writing to Don cheered me up a little.

April 21st. The kids are having a great time. The weather is gorgeous. They play hide-and-seek in the mustard, but the Martinos came this afternoon to plow the orchards, so that's the end of that. The mustard is high this year again. The little ones can walk unseen and the taller ones crawl unseen through it. Everyone in the neighborhood gravitates here most of the time. I counted sixteen this morning and practically no squabbles.

April 22, 1943

Dearest Sweetheart:

What a perfect day! Two letters from you, and on top of that I had two exams and received 3.7 in one and 4.0 in the other. I have five more tomorrow.

Taking the children to open house at school must have been fun. It is such a relief to me to know that you can drive now and get out when you want to. That reminds me, would you please contact the gas rationing board? Tell them I'll be home on leave, and we will need some extra gas so I can take care of all necessary business details before I am sent overseas? Send the forms for me to sign right away so we will have it by the time I get there.

I can't wait for the next five days to pass. I just reserved a very nice room for us. It's in a convenient location where the Sunset Blvd. street car runs. I went to seven hotels before I found this one. It is attractive and comfortable. I hope you are as excited about our coming weekend as I am.

Friday was a killer! I had five exams and did all right in all of them but was worn out when I finished. Yesterday I had two more. When I finally finished I had a very nice dinner at Elaine's, and then we walked to the dance at the Hollywood Athletic club. There were no street cars or buses after midnight, so we also walked back. By the time I got home I had walked over eleven miles!

DIARY

April 25th. After Sunday School, we drove to Oakland and Berkeley. Dinner at the folks. Home dead. Got in a traffic jam at Broadway and MacArthur and was petrified. Thought I would never get across the intersection but finally made it and was proud of myself.

April 27th. Started getting ready for the trip. So much to do. I am so excited. It won't be long now, if I can live through the preparations.

April 29th. What a day! Got groceries, hair done, put Donny on a bus to Burlingame. Took Bev to Imries at 6:30. Worked till 11:30 getting ready.

April 30th. Up at 5:30. Took Judy and Chuckie to the folks at 6:30 and dashed for the train. Arrived L.A. 6:05 P.M. GOOD dinner, lovely movie, "Journey For Margaret," with Margaret O'Brian. Our hotel is delightful.

May 1st. Don had to be at the base, so I spent the day with Trix. Farmer's Market, what a great place! Then Little Olivera Street— Fascinating. Took a short cut, got lost, and stranded on a cliff. Then dinner with Art and Mary and dancing at the Ambassador Hotel. Wonderful!

May 3rd. Yesterday was a nice leisurely day, got up late, read the papers, movie in the afternoon, "The Amazing Mrs. Halliday." Swell! Dinner at the Cooks.(What a mansion!) Then the sad parting. Oh how I hated to leave my Honey. Trip went quickly, but collecting everyone and getting home took ages. Everyone finally in bed by 9:30. Oh! Am I bushed!

May 5, 1943

Oh Lovely Lady!

My heart dropped to the ground as I watched you get on the street car taking you to the train. Wasn't our weekend wonderful? You were perfection!

NEXT DAY. Your letter just came! I'm so glad the children all had a good time and that everything went well this time.

MAY 7th! I'm hoping you will receive this on the most important day in the year for us—May 10th. I wish I could give you a wonderful present. Anyway I gave you one eleven years ago that you will have forever,—my heart. These have been eleven wonderful years, haven't they?

Last night Wil and I went to the fights. Uncle Otto gave us the tickets and the seats were perfect. It was a kick to watch the people as they came in. There were celebrities galore. We recognized Alice Fay, Bert Wheeler, and Joe DiMaggio, also a lot of faces whose names we didn't remember. It was obvious that many of them came just to be seen.

May 10th. OUR SPECIAL DAY. I can't go to bed until I write a few lines to tell you how wonderful it was to hear your voice. How could three minutes go by so quickly? The operator said they had so many calls waiting that it would be after midnight before I could get through to you. I asked for the supervisor and told her why it was so urgent that I get you. Wasn't I lucky that she got it through for me?

About Donny's room—please ask Jack to figure how much sheetrock and insulation we will need. If it doesn't come to over $25, order it so I can work on it as soon as I get home. Perhaps Donny and I can work on it together, *even though I would probably accomplish more without his "help". Speaking of help—I am so glad to hear how much the children are helping you. Be sure to tell them how happy it makes me.*

I did forty-eight words a minute without a mistake in my typing final. We had four hours of finals today. I have between 3.7 and 4.0 in all of them.

Sunday at Elaine's, I talked with Aunt Nettie for several hours. She showed me some poetry she had just written to Uncle Nate, and it was beautiful. She always writes poetry to him when she can't stand the separation any longer. Later Elaine and I took a bus to Santa Monica, walked along the beach and out on the pier. If only you had been walking with me. What a lovely evening it could have been. It was swell not having time to get too lonesome on OUR DAY.

DIARY

May 7th. Planted tomatoes and finally got them all in. What a relief. I'm so late getting them in this year because of the late frosts.

May 8th. Worked in the garden most of the day. The Leckners came and the Kemmeries, multiple naps with kids in every bed! Everyone helped to plant corn until it got dark. Got in seven long rows.

May 15th. Don phoned. He's coming! He's coming! Oh Joy!

May 16th. Started to clean house after Sunday School, but the Stocktons came for a picnic. Then the folks arrived with the Stiegles and Mac. Then Bob, Sharlene, and her cousin. "Oh Day Of Rest and Gladness!"

May 17th. Cleaned house like mad. Made an angel food cake for him. Got all of us dressed to meet the plane. He didn't come. The suspense is killing me! I can't STAND this!

May 17, 1943

My Love:

I just finished making the phone call to you. I expect you are in tears right now. I don't blame you. I feel that way myself. The letdown is terrible after the joy, excitement, and anticipation yesterday. I'll just have to resign myself to waiting and won't count on anything until I have my orders and my plane ticket in my hand.

If we don't get our orders soon, I am going to be in a real spot since most of my clothes are in my trunk, which is on it's way! If Mrs. Kaufman rents our apartment, Wil and I will have to go to a hotel.

Saturday I slept as late as I could to make the day disappear faster and then went over to the armory. That is when I got the false news. I arranged about my trunk and my plane ticket, phoned you, then got the bad news. Everyone is sunk, and many of the fellows are really on the spot, especially those whose families are here. Their apartments are rented, and they must move out today.

DIARY

May 19th. No sense in hanging on to Don's angel food cake, so I served it at Red Cross. Waited and waited for the phone to ring. He finally called. Can't believe my Honey is really coming.

May 21st. He actually arrived. Got here about midnight. The children woke up and were so excited. Chuckie was bewildered and distant at first but was soon clinging to him.

May 22nd. Spent yesterday in S.F. Had a great time. Today is blazing hot. Don got loads done. New sandbox, swing, clothesline poles.

May 23rd. Took the kids swimming after Sunday School and a picnic lunch. Met Catharine and Bob at the Leamington Hotel for dinner and dancing.

May 24th. He's gone. I wallowed in work all day without getting anywhere. What happens next? This see-saw existence is wearing.

May 24, 1943

Dearest Honey Mine:

Our weekend was so wonderful. The plane ride was SWELL!. I don't believe we had any air pockets on the whole trip and I didn't even know when we took off or landed. Some difference from my first and last flight fifteen years ago in a biplane! Air travel is TOPS! The day was beautiful until we reached this side of the ridge when we hit thick fog.

It took three hours for the Greyhound bus to go the sixty miles to Oxnard. I spent the last two hours talking to a lady who has been renting her three bedroom home in Ventura for $65 a month. She expects it to be vacant June 15th. We can have it if we want. By the time I got to the base it was 6 p.m.

There is every indication that I will be here two or three months, possibly longer, but you never know. We'll just have to take our chances. Ventura is a nice town with a beach and is only thirteen miles from here. We are through at 4:30 daily, and Saturday till Monday. Also no studying to do.

The officers' quarters are like an advance base in the Pacific, little tin huts with nine Army cots each and a separate hut for the head. Our meals cost us eighty cents per day. Jim Phelan is in the same hut with me until he can find a place for his family. This morning I started to get all the details attended to that should have been handled yesterday, such as seeing the personnel officer, the disbursing office, the dispensary, and being interviewed by the Skipper.

Jim Phelan and I spent the rest of the afternoon walking around part of this place and seeing what we could see. We walked at least six miles. We also went aboard two different ships and enjoyed that very much. I wish I could tell you about everything, but there is even more secrecy here than in Los Angeles.

I had my first ride in a jeep today. I also rode in a station wagon, a private car, and four different buses—quite a collection! It looks as though a person can learn as much or as little as he wants to here. I think Jim and I will be a good influence on each other in that respect.

In the evening we studied aircraft identification together. It is very interesting, and I think I'll do it every day until I'm familiar with all of the planes at all angles. A person is supposed to be able to identify them in one-tenth of a second; not very long, is it?

I took my old shoes to be soled and heeled today for seventy five cents. They will be ready tomorrow. Haircuts are fifteen cents so I guess I'll take my chances!

This place is very informal in dress and punctuality. I was the first one up at 6:45 yesterday and today. I bought a wind-breaker and wear it most of the time, as do all the other officers.

I wish we would get a little sunshine. First, because it feels so good, and second, to stop the ribbing we Californians take from the rest of the fellows. But most of all I wish you were all here with me. Soon, I hope.

DIARY

May 27th. Bitterly cold and windy. Chopped out weeds and watered, washed the car. No letter today. I am really down. Oh oh oh! Just got a phone call. He has found us a house, but not in Ventura!

May 27, 1943

Dearest Honey:

I've been in bed since 6:30. I finally got the bug. I began to feel awful about the middle of the morning while taking Donny to Dr. Hartman. To make matters worse, the gas tank was registering empty as we left Berkeley. I was apprehensive because we had to take a bunch of detours where they were fixing the road. I stopped at the gas station in Lafayette, and it was closed (out of gas)! I got in such a tangle of school buses, trucks and a Navy bus, I thought I'd never get out with enough gas to get home, but I made it, put twelve gallons in when I got home, dished out dinner, and tumbled achingly into bed. My temp is 101.6.

I picked up an elderly lady walking to the Happy Valley bus stop, a very interesting person. She pioneered public school kindergartens in California when she came from Switzerland many years ago. She was amazed that I could talk and drive at the same time, which pleased me no end. . . . Love you to pieces.

May 29, 1943

My Precious Beloved:

When the Ventura house didn't work out, I hitched a ride to Santa Barbara and went to a real estate office but found nothing. Santa Barbara is a nice town, very much like Carmel—very quiet. There is one nice place to go dinner dancing. The beach is superb, but the weather is still foggy.

I hope I have some good news soon. In the meantime, perhaps you had better start finding out what you would have to do in regard to the O.P.A. (Office of Price Administration) if we rent our house.

NEXT DAY. You can't possibly imagine what it has meant to me mentally ever since I talked with you last night. Now that I have rented a house, I'm a new man. As I told you over the phone, the house needs cleaning. The back yard is a mass of weeds which we'll have to cut through to make a path to the beach. It has two bedrooms and a separate guest house with two bedrooms and a bath. The nearest town is Carpinteria, two and a half miles away. It's thirteen miles to Santa Barbara and forty-five miles to the base. Several of the fellows drive from Santa Barbara, so we can arrange a car pool. Bring blankets and linens.

At last we are really going to be together. Honey, is it really true?

May 30, 1943

Honey:

I have been so busy since you phoned. Jack was here fixing the john. He went right home and woke Marky up to tell her the good news, and she came over, took home the material and started making the girls' sunsuits because now I won't have time.

This morning I was still feeling lousy, but I had to get food. Everyone, just like me, was trying to use up their ration points at the last minute. Two hours later, I came home without meat and with sixty-six meat points wasted.

After struggling through the rest of the day in and out of bed, I managed to fix the kids dinner and get them to bed. Then I gave myself the works—hot lemonade, mustard plaster, aspirin, etc.

This morning I still felt awfully bum. To help matters along, Beverly vomited twice, and Judy had a nosebleed all over the place. So I spent most of the morning mopping up. I simply have to quit, my Darling.

May 31, 1943

Dearest Honey:

I could write reams about the difficulties that are involved in this trip, but what's the use. It seems to me you are always giving me things to do which are beyond my capabilities, and this is certainly one of them, but I guess I'll live through it—and a week from now everything will be terrific.

When I phoned the chaplain at St. Mary's he just about hit the ceiling, he was so thrilled to hear about a house for rent. I told him it would be $125, and if they would do some work around the place, we would make it less. Donny is so thrilled, he even worked without coercion. He finished cleaning the attic, then worked in the yard and cleaned the garage. I'm trying to get hold of a trunk so I can send some things down by express. It has to be in Oakland tomorrow in order to get to Santa Barbara by Saturday.

I had my heart set on leaving at about 10 o'clock Saturday night, then we could be almost there before we had to stop for meals or bathroom, but my folks are having a fit about my traveling at night. I am going to phone the A.A.A. and find out just how much dim-out there is to travel through with just the parking lights. If there is much, it would be too trying at night.

Tomorrow I must go to the ration board and try to get extra gas coupons. Tonight I must get some sleep. Oh Honey, it won't be long now!

NEXT DAY. This will be my last letter. I just finished packing the trunk I borrowed from the Ingrams. Tom Slaven will take it in tomorrow morning. They practically promised to have it in Santa Barbara by Saturday. It will cost $4.

When I filled out my application for twenty-four gallons of gas they acted as though I was trying to rob a bank. There was one nice girl there. She tried really hard to get it through for me on time. I'm to phone Friday a.m.

Oh Honey, isn't it marvelous? Soon I'll be able to keep house for you? I hate to leave our lettuce. It is a dream now, so tender and soft and lovely.

With the trunk packed, I feel as though we're really on our way to you. Your anxious, eager, can't hardly wait, Honey

Dear, dear, Daddy:

Are you really going to be at the beach with us? I wish I could type this, and I wish I could write. When we are at the beach, I am going to hug you and kiss you and hug you and kiss you, and we will go in the waves. What are waves? Tonight we have had skunks, and the dogs barked and I didn't see them, but I could smell them. And I love you.

Judy

Part Three

"BY THE SEA, BY THE SEA, BY THE BEAUTIFUL SEA."

Sandyland, June 8, 1943

Dear Midge,

Although leaving home was absolutely H---, this is definitely HEAVEN! You just HAVE TO COME DOWN FOR YOUR VACATION. We have loads of room. Chuck and Judy share the second bedroom, and Donny and Beverly each have a room in the guest house, each with two bunks. Beverly would be in seventh heaven if you would share her room with her.

Our back yard is the beach, and our front yard is a mass of New Zealand spinach, two feet high! It'll save me tons of ration points. The kids are on the beach all day, and only Chuck needs supervision. Since he still naps both morning and afternoon, that makes it simple. So far the weather has been foggy, so we have had no need to worry about sunstroke or burning.

Don was able to get leave and come get us. We met him at the bus at nine, the morning of the 5th. By noon our house was rented to a Navy officer stationed at St. Mary's. They are from Oxnard. If only we had known, we could have traded houses, but it's much more fun to be here on the beach. Besides they are paying us $125 a month and we are only paying $50.

We got away by 11 p.m. carrying all the kids out to the car, sound asleep. We traveled with no stops until they started waking up about seven. By that time, there was the ocean to watch. Lots of dim-out along the way, so it took nearly ten hours. We were dying for sleep, but Don had to report to the base, and the kids were raring to get out on the beach. Somehow I staggered through the day. I had slept about an hour and a half in the car.

At first the house repelled me because it was SO filthy. The water was rusty, and I couldn't bear the thought of exposing eleven month old Chuckie to all this dirt. When I remembered the house hadn't been lived in for five years, I realized that it was just an accumulation of dust and sand, aggravated by the damp salty air, so I felt better about it.

We have no idea how long Don will be here before he is shipped out. Each morning, when we kiss goodbye, we wonder if this will be the last day. Each night we wonder if it will be our last night together—ever.

The children are blissful. The only interruptions to their days on the beach are our short excursions into Carpinteria or Santa Barbara seeking food. So far no meat at all, but today Don learned of a small private meat market not far from here that gets it sometimes.

We have lovely neighbors, so helpful and interested, with an eager sixteen-year-old baby sitter. Their place is HUGE. One summer they moved into their guest house and rented the house to Bette Davis!

If you decide to come, we can easily meet the train in Santa Barbara. They call this stretch of beach and homes "Sandyland."

Love, Dody

June 12, 1943

Dear Myrna:

If you and Melvin want to share the house with another Navy family, OF COURSE it's alright with us. We feel so very fortunate to be together, and wish everyone in our situation could be as lucky. It's a break that there are beds enough. We have always wanted our home to be a "room for one more" place.

We love it here on the beach and are happy, even with the everlasting cloud of impending departure overseas hanging over us. Hope you are enjoying Springhill Road and have found the neighbors as wonderfully helpful as we have always known them to be.

Good luck and tell the Pickens for us, "Welcome to our home."—Dot

DIARY

June 13. Wonderful walk on the beach. Cold and foggy, but who cares. I love it here. We moved driftwood and rocks around and cleared a path from the back door to make a small play yard.

June 14. Lovely weather, in and out of the water all day. It was wonderful having Don home all day yesterday. Today he has the duty.

June 15. Cool morning again. Took a vacation and sat beside the fire reading. Let everything go. The kids were busy building sand castles.

June 16. Cleaned up the house and shopped in Santa Barbara. Then met Midge at the train. She LOVES the house. the kids are so thrilled to have her here. She is just like one of them.

June 17. Hot! Long walk on the beach a.m., swimming and sunning p.m. It is so terrific having Don home in the evenings most of the time.

June 20. It has been foggy and miserable most mornings, but that seems not to make a difference. The kids love to picnic on the beach no matter what. It's great having Midge here. She is such a help. Last night a lovely dinner dance in Santa Barbara. It was fun meeting Don's friends and their wives.

June 25. Don has met a sailor who has been a Prudential agent for years. He is trying to find a place so his wife can join him. He is coming today to see us and perhaps rent this place when we leave. The kids are so excited, since they are nuts about sailors. It's time to clean this place again. It's fun to live the beach life and be lazy, but the time comes when we have to "pay the piper," and today is it!

June 26. His name is Matt, and the children adore him. Me too! He brought us five filet steaks and a beef roast. It is so long since we have tasted meat. Great day on the beach. Donny loves having Matt for a room-mate.

June 27. Long walk on the beach a.m. and swimming p.m. Matt loves it here. Wonderful dinner. Yummmmmmm! The kids were all over him and begged him to stay longer, but it's nice to be alone again. Our time is so precious.

June 28. Got all five of us dressed up for a day in Santa Barbara and couldn't find the car keys! What a dummy I am. So we just spent a lovely lazy day on the beach. To see "Keeper of the Flame" at night. Terrific.

June 29. Found the keys and finally made it to Santa Barbara to shop for Chuck's birthday. Got a letter from Bernice. She has canned thirty- four quarts of apricots for us. What a great next door neighbor!

July 3. Wonderful day on the beach. It is marvelous having Don here, playing with the kids. I got a lot of housework done while they played in the waves. Then I took movies of them all in the water. Early dinner on the beach, and then we took them all to Santa Barbara to see the town, the stores, and the crowds. Santa Barbara on a Saturday night is fun. Like a small farm town. The girls were wide-eyed over all the sailors and soldiers.

THE 4TH OF JULY! Our little "Yankee Doodle Dandy" is a year old today. It's Mrs. Urton's (next door) birthday, too, but they are having her party tomorrow. Played on the beach most of the day. Had Chuckie's birthday cake out there.

July 5th. What a change in the weather, sat by a blazing fire all day and read a lot. The kids were busy and angelic.

July 6th. Yes, it's a lot of fun here, but underneath it all is the heavy sinking feeling each day, "Is this our last?" Each night, "Will this be our last night together?" We don't know how much notice we will have. It could be just a day. Lots of errands to do today in Santa Barbara and also in Carpinteria. It's lucky I finally learned to drive. I really rather like it, much as I didn't want to learn.

July 8th. In the water most of the day. Don had the duty, and the evening seemed so aimless. The kids were crabby. I guess they are getting as spoiled as I am and want their Daddy around every night. Perhaps they are scared and worried just as I am.

July 11, 1943

Dear Dody, Don, Donny, Beverly, Judy, and Chuck:

I never officially thanked you for the best vacation I ever had. I don't know why—I usually do. Perhaps it's because I felt like one of the family.

Edward Arnold was on the train! In the same car as I was, as a matter of fact. Just a note of interest—he didn't thrill me! I had the worst seat in the car with no seat in front and no place to put my feet. My seat partner was an uninteresting little fat boy of about fourteen. Phooey! So much for romantic possibilities!

Got a letter from Mac. He is in the Naval Hospital in Philadelphia with a spontaneous pneumothorax. His left lung collapsed. He said he will have to be there for at least a month. Being on a submarine had something to do with it.

My tan really created a sensation. It's pretty well faded now, but it was the cause of much envy and admiration when I first got home.

I'm a nurse's aide! Yep! I finally took the fatal step. We get two units for it, and I was looking around for a two-unit course when I realized here was my chance. I've always wanted to be one but never had the opportunity.

I must tell you about the Cal campus. All the Naval Reserve Officers are stationed at Callahan Hall (International House to you) and wear their uniforms every day. They march down Bancroft Way at 8 o'clock every morning to class. Sights like these used to give me a thrill, but now—there are all these fellows we know, walking so silently and with faces that are grim. It gives me a lump in my throat. At least twenty of the fraternities have been taken over and house Army and Marine men. The Marines, as well as the Army and Navy, will be here for one term only. They are allowed to go on with their regular courses and are required only to take two gym courses. Of course, they are in uniform. Everywhere I go there are men in uniform marching. At first, all this made me just plain sick at heart, but now that I'm getting used to it, it's not as bad. I just hope they don't close Cal to women before I graduate.

I want to tell you again what a wonderful time I had. I also want to say that it was so much fun and so interesting to find out what you, Don and Dody, are really like. Don, my big sister didn't marry such a bad egg after all (don't take the "after all" too seriously, Don).

Roy is still in Hawaii, and if I hadn't known that, I certainly would have had the whim whams when I read the headlines "Cruiser Sunk."

Love,
Midge

DIARY

July 13th. Spent most of the day cooking and cleaning. Jim Phelan home with Don. The kids adore him. In the evening we swam. It was grand.

July 15th. To see the Urton Mansion way up in the hills above Santa Barbara. WOW! To think that we have next door neighbors who own a place like that! Acres of grounds, now somewhat run down. Huge and beautiful rooms. Miles of closet space and mirrors. The kids had a marvelous time racing all over it. Mrs. Urton didn't seem to mind. She enjoys them so much. I kept thinking what a marvelous place it would be for a girls' school, or an orphanage. All that space going to waste! I wish Don could have seen it. I don't think they'll ever move back there. They love the beach so much.

July 16th. Had a great day. Cleaned house for a change and did a lot of cooking. Don came home feeling miserable. They have started his shots again, and this scares me. Does it mean they are leaving so soon?

July 17th. Don feels worse. This dampened all our spirits. The fact that Chuckie has sixteen teeth so early is very convenient. When I took him for his checkup before we left, I asked Dr. Gerow what he could eat now and he said, "Anything! Well, not hot dogs or chile con carne, but anything within reason." No more spending hours pushing food through the strainer to puree it. Hurray!

July 18th. It is dingy, rainy, and cold, and for some reason I am bursting with happiness today. It is so cozy inside with the waves crashing on the beach, my Honey at home, and a roaring fire in the fireplace. We did a lot of reading today. This has been a great time for reading. With the kids on the beach most of the time, I can watch them and read when I am not in the water, and there is a good library in Carpinteria. I have been consuming five or six books a week. What a treat.

July 21st. We are getting so hungry for meat again. Don can get a lot of our food at the commissary, but even with a front yard full of New Zealand spinach, we have a hard time making our ration points stretch. We can't feed them that every day. I do miss our garden. The kids don't eat canned vegetables nearly as well as they do our nice fresh ones. Took Donny and Bev to see "My Friend Flicka." We all loved it. Jean Urton stayed with Judy and Chuckie.

July 23rd. HOT! Great day on the beach. Then Don came home a complete wreck. More shots, and they are starting "training". Does this mean that they are leaving momentarily? This constant never knowing is killing me.

July 25th. Matt and his wife came. He is the sailor who came before. Again he brought gobs of meat. THAT is the kind of guest to have these days! He still hasn't found a place where he can have his wife with him, so they are going to rent this house when we leave. He isn't in Don's unit, so he won't have orders at the same time and will probably be here indefinitely.

July 28th. Shopped like mad in Santa Barbara all day for Judy's birthday tomorrow. Jean stayed with the kids. Don got home really bushed, and Pete came to tell him that the unit is going "dockside" tonight. OH DEAR! He had to turn around and go back, as if ninety miles wasn't enough commuting for one day! Now what? Is this it? He can't be here for Judy's birthday. DARN!

July 31st. Don got back at seven tonight. He still doesn't know what's happening. He isn't even allowed to tell me what he does know. He's pretty sure though from what they have been doing that the time is very near. I can't stand it. Early to bed, as he has to go right back and work all day.

August 2nd. Don came home in a jeep and brought Jim and Bill with him. It was fun for the kids. They all got to ride in the jeep, even Chuckie.

August 4th. Well this is it. Don got home really late for dinner, nearly eight, and was he bushed! They are to leave on Saturday. Drove in to Carpinteria to phone Rae and Harry. Harry said he would come down on the train and drive us all home after Don leaves. What a dear brother-in-law.

August 6th. Don got a twenty-four hour leave and we worked like mad packing in the morning and then had a lovely time on the beach in the afternoon. Early to bed. How can we bear this? Will we ever be together again?

August 8th. Woke up at 2:30. Don met Harry in Santa Barbara at 5:00 a.m. It was weird to see Don in all his battle gear, guns. helmet, and all, when we left to take him to the base. We had never seen him that way before. UGH! When we got back, Harry slept, we packed, and left at 7 p.m. It was a horrible drive home. Poor Donny was sitting on a box of groceries and was so very uncomfortable. Six people plus lots of stuff in our little coupe is just too many. Arrived at dawn— 5:30. DEAD!

Port Hueneme, Saturday, August 7, 1943

My Dearest Sweetie:

It was certainly tough leaving my wonderful family this morning. I know I am going to be terribly lonesome. In fact, I have started already. Part of my time today was spent censoring letters, and they sounded so much like mine.

I hear that the picnic, which I was so happy to miss yesterday because I was home with all of you, was a huge success. Alice Faye was boating on the lake, and one of the officers invited her over. She came later with Phil Harris and two other movie stars. Of course the boys were all thrilled. But how lucky I was to have that extra twenty four hours with you.

I'm going to have to rush this letter as I haven't much time. I hope your trip home is not too painful.

We certainly have a fine bunch of officers and men. I really expect this to be a crack outfit in all respects. I bought a guitar for the unit this morning, as one of the boys plays well.

Take good care of yourselves, and don't worry about me. I'll be careful. I have a lump in my throat right now. Keep your chin up and keep smiling.

I love you. I love you. I love you.

Part Four

AUGUST 8, 1943 – NOVEMBER 27, 1943

"WHERE THE FLYING FISHES PLAY"

AT SEA August 8, 1943

My Beauty:

    I've been thinking of you almost continuously. This morning when I attended church services I prayed for you and for our precious children. I thank God for all our blessings and pray that we will all be together again someday. It brought tears to my eyes to be thinking of you and praying under the beautiful canopy of Heaven.

    The weather today is marvelous. It's a beautiful sight to see the flying fish, the blue Pacific, and the ever changing sky. We are extremely busy, but whenever I have a chance, I go topside, gaze at the beauty, and think of all my precious ones.

    I am enjoying everything to the utmost, that is, as much as I can without you. The food is ample and delicious. I go to each meal ravenous. Our quarters are surprisingly comfortable, and all personnel are most cooperative.

    We just received some good war news and assume you are reading about it in the papers today. It is difficult to write when I am so restricted in what I can say. I will write my thoughts from day to day aboard ship and mail it all at once when we reach land.

    AUGUST 10TH. I am sitting in the extreme bow of the ship, topside, leaning against my "Mae West" (our name for our life jackets), and enjoying the pitch of the ship immensely. This is the first moment I have had to relax all day. I enjoy my duties, so the time passes rapidly. Fortunately we have had clouds overhead for the past two days, otherwise it would be extremely hot.

    LATER. It has turned plenty hot since I started this letter. I'm soaked with perspiration. Right now I am sitting in a nook, topside just below the bridge, where I can get an occasional light breeze. The Pacific is bluer than ever today. It's great sport to look over the side and watch the flying fish. They are about two and a half inches long with stomachs that glisten in the sun. A whole school flew at once just now. They get more numerous daily.

    This is a great way to travel and see the world (I keep telling myself) at no expense, and getting paid besides! Hugh, Bob, and I spend quite a bit of time topside, gazing at the ocean and discussing such things as post war problems, economic, political, and social. Like most such conversations, no conclusions are reached.

AUGUST 14TH. The enlisted men are excited that we will soon cross the equator and all become "shellbacks" with the usual initiation.

I'm lucky not to be seasick and to be enjoying the trip so much. Some of the fellows have been under the weather the whole time. Even our Chief with three hash marks (twelve years of service) was sick.

STILL AT SEA. August 16th. Yesterday was a very busy day and a very interesting one. In the morning I went to the church service. I spent the afternoon enjoying a program on deck. We have some wonderful talent aboard.

At last we are shellbacks. There is a definite difference in the sky and clouds, particularly at night.

AUGUST 17th. Since early this morning, I've been thinking about this date fourteen years ago—the day we got engaged.

Last night I slept topside. It was such a beautiful night with the full moon! Earlier in the evening we stood for a long time looking at the Southern Cross and the florescent fish that shine in the water from time to time. Before the moon came up the sky was so full of stars. I'd like to know more about the constellations in the Southern Hemisphere. Oh how I miss you, my Darling.

August 9, 1943

Honey:

This is the very first minute I could possibly spare, and there is so much to tell you. After we left you, we went to Ventura to find a Buick Garage. Harry left us at the Pedricks' and took the car to be checked. Mrs. Pedrick is darling, a little slip of a thing, very clean cut and alive looking. After a nice visit, Harry took us back to Oxnard. By this time things were open, so we went to the rationing board for our gas tickets, then home.

Since Harry had been up all night coming down on the train, he went to bed and slept till four. We had a hectic dinner and a mad scramble getting packed. Mrs. Leeds came over with a plate of brownies and some grapes. She asked if I would let her clean up the house and wash the dishes after we left, but I just couldn't let her. Then Mrs. Urton came over and INSISTED that I let her and her sister do it, so we did. Off we sailed with the two of them waving from our door. How lovely to have neighbors like that, just like at home.

The children kept waking up all night. We stopped twice for gas and two other times for Harry to eat. We were also stopped by a cop for going fifty miles an hour with parking lights on in a non dim-out zone. Harry was very polite to him, and we didn't get a ticket. Donny almost queered the whole thing by piping up from the back seat, "Ha ha! You thought you could get away with it, didn't you, Uncle Harry?"

We arrived home at 5:30 a.m. Everything looked so strange in the dim light. The shrubbery had grown so much, and the house looked heavenly. It was clean and lovely. We didn't wait to put sheets on the beds—just rolled up in blankets. I got to bed after six. Two hours later Donny awakened me with the news that his playhouse had been demolished. I lay there a while and finally decided I would be happier up, accomplishing things, than trying to sleep.

When Rae arrived with Stevie and three of her friends, we had a picnic in the patio, and in the middle of it, guess who else arrived? Yep, that's right. It was the Burkes! We DIDN'T feed them this time. After eating, everyone started picking pears. About that time the Wisemans arrived expecting to get free pears as usual. I was embarrassed, but they caught on after seeing the others paying. Altogether I took in $11.50 yesterday. Isn't that wonderful?

It was nearly nine by the time everyone left, and I got the children to bed in a daze. I felt as though the bottom of me was anchored, but the rest of me was swaying around in a complete circle. What a strange feeling!

I took a bath! Oh boy! What a treat after two months of showers only. I got to bed shortly after ten and slept like a log.

Can you imagine what it was like having that much unexpected company with the house in a chaotic, moving-in condition? The Wisemans brought friends to see the house, and Rae's friends had to be shown every nook and cranny, too.

The Myers names are Rusty and Mabel. She came dashing in with a check as soon as I got up yesterday to make sure they could continue to rent the rumpus room. I remarked that I hoped our children wouldn't drive them crazy. Her reply was, "Oh, I just love children,and my husband doesn't get home till after 6:30." She gave me $25, and we will arrange about utilities at the end of the month. This is certainly going to help make the money stretch. Today she did my shopping for me, and tomorrow she and Catharine Pickens are going to the commissary and will shop for me there.

Starting tomorrow Donny's duties will be: 1. Clean room. 2. Get the milk. 3. Do the breakfast dishes. 4. Water the garden.

Beverly and Judy are glad to be home again, but Beverly feels terrible because they can't play with Nancy and Lois. The polio epidemic is so bad that no one is associating with anyone else these days.

Our garden is in terrible condition. The flowers are dead. The tomatoes are dry. The strawberries are prolific but tiny, like wild ones. The lettuce and artichokes have gone to seed, and the chard is practically dried up. The things I planted over the septic tank drain are thriving. One squash plant is three or four feet high and over six feet in diameter. I picked enough for two meals and enough cucumbers to make pickles. By tomorrow, we'll have corn.

Jack and Marky fixed up their garage apartment so attractively for the Pickens. It looks comfortable and really charming. Their little boy is a dear. His name is Gary, and he is two. Goodnight my dearest Honey

August 10, 1943

Oh Honey:

Yesterday the sand came, and it was a picture to see Donny, Beverly, Judy, Chuck, Susan, Philip, and Gary all playing there under the big drooping green walnut tree, with the white sand in the green box. I am glad you insisted on making the sand box so huge.

Donny worked hard all morning hauling the extra sand and spreading it where I plan to put in New Zealand spinach. Then I packed him a lunch, and off he went. He came home at five so hot and thirsty. He had been up at the Army camp. Lindy is still there and Dahlgren too. I should think those kids would go nuts having to be there doing absolutely nothing for so long.

Beverly thought she had figured out a great scheme so you could get more sleep on the ship. She said the various officers could sleep at different times while the others worked. When I told her they do that already, she was so crestfallen and decided not to write you about her great idea. Goodnight, Honey

August 11, 1943

Honey:

The trunks came today. I have partially unpacked your sea chest, but that is all so far. I had a good day making nine jars of bread and butter pickles, twelve of plum jam, one of pear jam, and also canning twenty-six quarts of peaches.

What a time I had last night picking up those peaches. Mildred phoned to say they had the peaches for us and I'd better get them right away, as they were pretty ripe. When we left for Oakland I discovered the gas tank was registering empty. When I looked for the gas tickets, I realized Harry still had them. I was in a frenzy trying to find someone who could lend me some tickets. Finally Marky gave me some gas from their drum. It was seven thirty before we left.

They are fixing the highway from Lafayette to Orinda. We got behind fruit trucks going ten miles an hour. By the time we got home I was a wreck from driving in the dim-out, and the children were so tired.

The pear pickers came through on the last picking today. I had to rush out and pick what I needed before they got them all.

It's a lovely evening. Oh if you were only here. I love you so much.

August 15, 1943

My Honey:

It doesn't seem possible that we've already been home a week. The time has flown. I have finished canning all my peaches and made more jam. This morning when I went out to pick, I couldn't carry all the stuff in one trip. I hadn't picked for two days, and it's unbelievable what can happen in that length of time: huge zucchini, summer squash, and cucumbers. I'll probably have to make another gallon of pickles in a few days.

Last night I rode up and down the road on my bike for a while after the children were in bed. Oh Honey, I was so terribly lonesome for you. Sometimes I think I just can't stand it any longer. But then I think of how much worse it must be for you. At least I have the children. Even though they do drive me nuts sometimes, what would I ever do without them?

Donny walked up to get Donny Rogers this morning and brought him down here to Sunday School. After it was over I packed a lunch, and he went back up there. When he got home at six, he had had a marvelous time all day, including falling into the creek! Yesterday he earned forty cents picking pears. It's hard picking now with all the choice fruit gone. He also painted the sand box. Tomorrow I am going to LET him paint the fence. I've been taking lessons from Tom Sawyer!

The other day Beverly and Judy dressed up like brides, and Beverly said she had picked out a Navy officer like Daddy to marry, and "We're pretending that Grandpa isn't married already so Judy can marry him." The next day they stuffed things inside their clothes and walked around holding their tummies out, both saying, "Look Mother, we have babies growing inside of us," and Beverly added, "And mine's going to be a girl, at least I certainly hope so."

Chuckie says "Mama" now, shakes his head and says "No," when I ask him if he wants to go to the bathroom. That is not always the truth! But twice he has asked to go. He is much happier than he was, but he still thinks it's a dirty gyp not to be able to go around with the big kids. Fortunately little Gary Pickens keeps him happy for hours at a time.

I hope you are continuing to be busy and satisfied with things. I am glad you are so enthusiastic. That is one reason I can stand the separation. It doesn't seem such a waste of time for you to be away from us if you are really doing something worthwhile.

I wanted to write to you so badly last night. I got into my nice clean comfortable bed between lovely smooth percale sheets and soft blankets, with the breeze blowing through the ruffles of the sheer white curtains and the full moon shining in. I wondered if you were watching the moon on the water. You are having so many new experiences. I can't go with you in my thoughts because I know so little of what you are doing. It will be grand when I receive your first letter.

Goodnight, my precious Honey.

August 17, 1943

My Honey:

We have all been through a terrible ordeal, but everything is going to be all right. Little Gary Pickens fell from the back seat as they were driving to St. Mary's. He hit the door handle, the door opened, and he fell out. They took him to sick bay, and the doctor sent him to Oak Knoll Hospital in an ambulance. They sent Melvin and Catherine home that night at eleven, but they didn't know till morning whether or not he would live. We all went around in an awful state, especially Marky. She is almost as fond of him as she is of Susan. He is the best little fellow. Last night they learned he is going to be all right. Catherine and Melvin came home and finally had a good night's sleep. The suspense seemed interminable for all of us but was actually only two days.

You should have seen Rusty and me last night. Mabel is away for a week, so Rusty decided he had better do a washing. He had never investigated the Bendix before, and he certainly was intrigued with it. So there we were, he washing and me ironing. I began to giggle, and he wanted to know why. I said that it just struck me funny—such a domestic scene. That sort of broke the ice. We got to talking about college, and the ironing went quite fast. He was on the football team at South Dakota University, and he worked nights in restaurants. He was in the class of '33. He is crazy about dancing. I told him about the dances at the Hotel Leamington. He seems to like our kids. They think he is wonderful, especially in his blues!

Chuck and I had our second disciplinary battle today. It dawned on me that he practically never puts his fingers in his mouth any more except at bedtime. However, he still refuses to be put in his room to play alone. So this morning I finally let him cry it out. He has never cried so long in his life before. He must have yelled for at least forty-five minutes before he gave in and started playing. It just killed me to hear him cry like that. I wanted to give in so badly. The children were furious at me for being "so cruel."

Last night at dinner Donny was going on about how much he loved me, so glad I was his mother, etc. Judy insisted he should like Daddy best, but he said he liked Mother and Daddy just the same amount and best of all, even better than Chuckie. Judy was shocked. She said, "OF COURSE we should all like Daddy best because he is a NAVY OFFICER!" Donny was a regular Pollyanna all day yesterday—glad he was alive, glad he had a kitten etc. etc. Gee, it's grand when he is like that.

I am so sleepy I can't hold my head up any longer. Goodnight, Honey.

LAND AT LAST. August 20, 1943

My Precious:

The first news is that we arrived. Then I found that we did not have to pay for our meals which puts me ahead a little, financially.

No mail has arrived yet, so you can imagine how anxious we are. It is so beautiful here. The vegetation is an intense green and is terribly thick. There are coconut and banana trees everywhere. The natives are very "civilized". They ask enormous prices for souvenirs. The women wear dresses, but they all go barefoot. The men wear wraparound skirts. It rains here about 300 inches a year. Although this is not the rainy season, it has rained three times already this morning. The sun is HOT, so we perspire, too.

Last night Bob and I went for a long walk until we were too hot to go any further. I hope to go swimming tonight and also to take a freshwater shower.

I miss all of you so much and am so lonesome . . .

Something just came up, and I have to quit. Darn it! . . .

August 24, 1943

My Darling:

Yesterday I managed to find some time in the afternoon to go swimming. You can imagine how much I enjoyed it. The water is much saltier than at home and almost as warm as the air, but nevertheless is refreshing.

I'm learning more about the natives and hope to learn some of their language. They say there are only fourteen letters in the alphabet. The skirts which the men wear are called "lava lava". Anything that is important has the word repeated twice. All of the male natives are tattooed, some of them solidly from their knees to their waists. They are not considered eligible for marriage until they are tattooed; the more tattoos, the more eligible. Married women wear two skirts, one to the ankle and one about twelve inches shorter.

Even though this isn't the rainy season we are having rain four or five times a day, and the humidity makes it seem very warm.

The natives call a building a "fale." The place we live in is called a falies. Our falies is for six officers. The officers' club is very nice too, with a pool table, a ping pong table, and comfortable chairs.

The harbor here is an extinct volcano crater which has one side broken down. The mountains around the harbor are very steep. Our falies is up on the side of one of these mountains, 210 steps! The view is beautiful, as it overlooks the entire harbor.

I read parts of your letters to Hugh who is only twenty-three and unmarried. He was flabbergasted at the everlasting merry-go-round that constitutes your days . . .

August 26, 1943

Honey:

Wonderful news! Ken, Esther, and Davey are arriving from Seattle Sunday. They will be here for two or three weeks. I started figuring out where everyone would sleep, if they can spend a few nights with us. When I said

Davey would sleep with Donny of course, Beverly wailed, "Why can't I sleep with Davey? If I'm going to marry him I don't see why I can't sleep with him!"

Today I finally made the kosher dill pickles I've been talking about. They look and smell grand. How long shall I save a jar for you? Yesterday, after I finished canning applesauce, I got fed up and walked out on the whole mess—got cleaned up and took Chuck up to the Underhills. They have baby scales, so we weighed him, and he has gained over three pounds since June. Isn't that marvelous? He is now almost average and doing really well for a preemie.

I saw Ruth yesterday. She finally heard from Arleigh. His tentative orders are to a Destroyer Escort from Rhode Island. She is feeling so sunk. Linda is five-months-old now and so lovely. What a crime for Arleigh not to be with her.

Ann is spending a couple of days with us, which makes Donny supremely happy. Right after breakfast we left for Walnut Creek to shop before our appointment with the doctor. I combed the town and finally found a place where they know of a man they THINK they can get in touch with who PERHAPS can fix Donny's radio. I left my good old standby shoes to be repaired, and they promised them in three weeks.

Donny was in the money. He had $1.80. A dollar was for war stamps and the rest to spend. He said he wanted to spend the whole eighty cents on Ann. He took her into the dime store and told her to pick out anything she wanted! She found "just what I have wanted all my life," a red five-year diary with lock and key. He bought her that and a pair of sunglasses. Since he had a few pennies left they got weighed—twice!

Beverly was also in the money, since she lost a tooth Sunday night and another one Monday morning, so she got Ann a bottle of hand lotion.

When we got to the doctor, he hadn't arrived from his morning house calls. The office was jammed. Going to a new doctor is so disconcerting. If only Dr. Gerow hadn't joined the Navy! We need him here. There is only one doctor in Lafayette now and one in Walnut Creek.

The results of their examinations were quite interesting. Chuck weighs 20 lbs. 13 oz. and is 29 inches tall—taller than Stevie. Judy was vaccinated for small pox and didn't even make a face. Her tonsils are large but o.k. Her heart murmur has entirely disappeared. She weighs 46 lbs. and is 46 inches tall. Isn't that interesting? He vaccinated Chuck too, who did far more than make a face! The doctor gave us a prescription to improve Beverly's appetite and said she needs more exercise. Then he sneaked out the back door to finish his morning calls before he took his one o'clock appointment. It was now 2:15. The doctor shortage is rough on us, but how tough it must be on the doctors, too.

Mabel and Rusty had a steak barbecue for ten of their friends last night. They all had so much fun. It made me extra lonesome for you, but I looked in the mirror, made a face at myself, and told myself to cut it out! So I did.

What a thrill! My first letter from you arrived yesterday. Practically all I did the rest of the day was read and reread it.

Lady, the Halls' dog, has been frightening Marky's cow, so yesterday I took her home to Jean. She was in bed with a HEADACHE AND A SORE THROAT! That's scary, with all the polio going around. Her doctor won't say what it is but is giving her shots and pills. I talked to her from across the room. She felt awful about the dog and hoped the cow wasn't too upset to give milk.

I'm so glad you are happy and enjoying yourself the way you are. I am the same way. If we can just stay this way, it will be fine. We can be lonesome and miss each other terribly but still keep busy and happy doing everything that has to be done. As long as we have to be separated, I think we can survive if we keep handling it that way. I read an article today describing to a T the way I was last fall. What I had was "nervous depression". Golly, I hope I never get that way again. It was horrible.

When you say you enjoy the motion of the ship, I shudder in horror, and so does my Dad. I'm disappointed that you haven't been seasick at all! Just a teeny bit, so you could know that it is NOT "all in your head."

Today I tried to clean house but people kept dropping in. A friend of Mabel's came over with her little three year old boy. Soon there were twelve in Donny's playhouse, having the most wonderful time. I had seven children for lunch. After rests, they all played in the hose on Bernice's lawn.

I started digging for the lawn tonight. Putting in a lawn is quite a process. I got the directions from Bernice today and wrote them all down—soak, dig, hoe, rake, cover with peat moss and fertilizer, let it set for a month, watering daily, remove all weeds that come up, rake and level. Then add more peat moss, fertilizer, sow the seed, roll it, and then water it every few hours during the day until the grass is well established.

Oh Honey, it makes me sick clear down to my toes to think of you going so long without letters from me. I hope you have gotten some by now.

It is the biggest thrill to hear Chuck yell "Hi" at people. He tries to say "Philip" too. Oh! He just took a step and grabbed at the typewriter.

August 30, 1943

Talofa Alofa,(Hello, my Love)

I learned these words from one of the officers with whom I had lunch. He has been here for seventeen months and in the Army for over thirty years. The last time he was stationed here was in 1912. Think of the changes he has seen.

After supper we had a U.S.O. show consisting of four men. They were all part of the very first U.S.O. unit to leave the states. They think that the best song of this war is, "Don't Sit Under The Apple Tree."

Tomorrow I have to take the men to the rifle range all day. Quite a change from Sundays at home! I try to visualize your Sunday mornings now that you and Bernice are conducting Sunday School in our rumpus room instead of everyone having to use precious gas going in to the church in Walnut Creek. How many children come now? Are Philip and Susan as cute as ever?

Native villages are scattered all over this island. Each one has three to five churches—Catholic, Mormon, and Protestant. There are a few scraggly horses in each village, some very small pigs, and small varieties of dogs. All the villages are along the shoreline where the narrow winding road is easily accessible. The scenery is beautiful, as is the ocean with waves breaking on the coral reefs.

The natives are extremely friendly. Today they were all dressed up for church in their finest clothes. The women wore everything from formals to house dresses. The men were in everything from brightly colored lava lavas to white shirts, ties, and jackets. Of course all of them were barefoot.

I am still desperate for mail. We found out today that a grave mistake was made in our address, and it has all been sent to an island far away from here. From now on use only ARGUS UNIT NO 9, FLEET POST OFFICE, SAN FRANCISCO.

I'm writing this on the screened porch of our fale. The reflection of the lights on the bay is beautiful. Even though it is late at night, I am wringing wet with perspiration from climbing those steps.

If all of a sudden you should stop receiving my letters, don't worry. It will be because we have left for our new island. Don't worry about the new island. It is quite safe from war, and also medically safe.

This morning everyone was paid. I am enclosing a money order for $75. I hope this arrives in time for Donny's birthday. I'd like you to buy him a really nice present out of it. Also, since I probably won't be paid for another six months, please buy yourself a whole new outfit as an early birthday present and then save the rest for Christmas. Honey I hate to stop writing, but I must.

September 6, 1943

Honey:

I'm sitting out in the patio while Esther runs the vacuum. Pretty soft, huh? We're having a grand time together, although it's rather wearing. This is due to the fact that the children are continually bickering over who is to play with whom and who is to sleep with whom, just as they did when Ann was here.

Yesterday we flew around getting ready. They were to take the 8:10 bus from Oakland. We were just leaving the house to meet them when they phoned from the bus depot to say that the buses were so crowded with the military that they wouldn't sell them a ticket. Consequently we all went to Oakland and picked them up at College and Broadway.

Chuck seemed to think that Ken was you and kept loving him all the way home in the car. Later he seemed to feel a difference, and he was puzzled.

Of course we all had a lovely day together, talking our heads off with so much to catch up on. We had assumed that Davey would sleep in Donny's room, but he didn't want to. He said he had come to see Beverly and no one else. Finally after all sorts of shifting, Judy went up to sleep in Donny's room, and Davey stayed downstairs to sleep in Beverly's room. But after a while, Davey decided he wanted to sleep in Ken and Esther's bed, so he did. I had to hold Beverly in my arms for a long time while she sobbed her heart out.

Beverly and Davey's attachment for each other is just as great as ever. They walk around with their arms around each other and talk about when they are married! Beverly says they plan to have five children, three girls and two boys, and build a house on Springhill Road so that "You and Daddy can baby sit for us when we go dinner dancing."

She longs to go to Seattle again. I think she would actually be willing to leave us all and go there indefinitely. Esther begs me to let her come up for a while, but naturally that is quite impossible with school starting. Love ya!

September 6, 1943

My own sweet Beloved:

It is raining in earnest today. It's lucky, because the water supply was getting so low that it had been turned off. We are entirely dependent on rain.

I must tell you more about the natives here. They believe that all women should have at least eleven children. It makes no difference whether they are legitimate, or whether they are pure blooded or not. So many of the children, and even adults, are partially white. Some children are almost entirely white.

Each five falies has a Talking Chief. All the troubles and problems in these five falies are taken to him. If they are of too great importance for him to decide, he takes them to the Village Talking Chief. If he can't handle them, they are taken to the Village High Chief. If they still can't be decided, a conference of all the Talking Chiefs and High Chiefs is called. There are also District High Chiefs and District Talking Chiefs. On this island there are five of each, and they run the island under the direction of the governor. Since this has been a protectorate of the U.S. since about the turn of the century, the governor is an American.

All able bodied males have to work, or they are sent to jail (puy puy). In jail they have to work at the same thing they would be doing otherwise, except that they do it without pay.

In their language every letter of every word is pronounced and none are ever left out. However when there is a "g" the letter "n" is pronounced before it, even though there isn't a letter "n" in their alphabet. The commonest word around here is " Ua Sa". It means "keep out."

Practically all the natives can speak or understand at least a little English—when they want to. The children speak excellent English, and when they are playing "cops and robbers", marbles, and other games, you would think you were back home if you heard them and didn't see them. MAIL JUST ARRIVED!!!!!!

I received a letter from you dated the 24th of August. I AM SO THRILLED!!! But where are all the others? There were only twenty letters for this entire unit. I have already read your letter three times, but I'm going to quit typing now so I can really concentrate on it. Goodnight, My lovely lady

September 7, 1943

Dearest Honey:

Yesterday I went to the blood bank. It took just an hour from the time I got there until I left. That included the blood count, blood pressure, red tape, questions, and drinking orange juice.

When I got back, we fixed the kids a picnic lunch, and they ate in the playhouse. After dinner, much as we hated to part with them, we took Ken, Esther, and Davey back to Oakland. Chuckie cuddled with Ken all the way.

We all enjoyed having them here so much. Davey and Beverly are so sweet together, and when they parted last night, it was so sad. They stood on the corner of College and Broadway hugging each other interminably.

I think I'll have to stop reading your letters to the children. They get extra lonesome for you when I do. That's the opposite of their effect on me.

I am overwhelmed with the money order. I don't understand how you can spare that much when it will be so long before you are paid again.

I heard the Hoskins boys had a small bike for sale, so I immediately went up to find out about it. It is pretty awful, but they will put in a new axle and fix the tire. It will be $3.50. It should be worth that. Donny is in seventh Heaven over it, awful as it is, because it fits him, and he can actually ride it.

If I can get hold of a tractor, I think I'll have Donny's playhouse moved back of the garden fence as soon as the tomatoes are pulled out. Then the play yard can be there, since that soil is too poor for growing vegetables.

Pat Gibbel has been visiting since yesterday, but I would like to take her home tonight. Much as I enjoy it, having extra children overnight always upsets the routine, and it has been happening so much lately.

Chuck is crawling around the kitchen chasing an orange and shrieking with delight. I must get dinner now. Goodbye for now, my very dearest Honey.

September 8, 1943

My Dearest:

Things have started to happen. I was up till well after two this morning and up again before five. I'll be working with the Skipper all night.

Today I received a letter from you written on the 2nd. That's more like it! I gather that the ensign and his wife are named Rusty and Mabel and that you like them. I am delighted to hear that Rusty is helping you in the yard and with the gravel and the walks.

I don't believe I have ever told you what a fine doctor we have in our unit. He certainly knows his business. It is good to know he will be around when we need him. Our pharmacists' mates are excellent, too.

The news is good, isn't it? Let's pray it won't be long until both Germany and Japan follow Italy's lead, and we can soon be together again.

LATER-In fact it's two days later. I told you things were beginning to pop! I hope to get to bed by midnight tonight, as I have had less than eight hours' sleep in the past two nights put together. This is only the beginning.

The Skipper and the Exec call on me to do more and more things every day, for which I am very thankful as it keeps me busy. In the Navy, they call people like me an "eager beaver". However I haven't heard anyone call me that yet.

We are anxiously awaiting the arrival of our ship. When it comes, all hands will be plenty busy. . . . Your ever lonesome, ever loving Honey

September 9, 1943

My darling Honey:

I am terribly tired tonight. We stopped at the folks for a few minutes on the way to the dentist, to take them some vegetables from our garden. After the dentist we started hunting for jeans for Donny. There aren't any! I phoned all over Berkeley and Oakland, even neighborhood stores. No one had any jeans or any kind of school pants, only little boys' bib top overalls!

When we looked for socks and panties, we went into store after store and finally found panties with drawstrings instead of elastic.

Thanks to the money order you sent I let the children buy defense stamps at every booth they saw. They bought $6 worth. Then I let Donny have an extra birthday dollar to spend. He bought a complete camp with tents, jeeps, flags, and cannons, for $1.12. He got a huge kick out of spending that much money on stamps too, and intends to write and thank you. The girls bought perfume, as usual. It was disguised as a tiny grandfather's clock, rather cute for twenty- nine cents, but oh, how it smells!

TWO DAYS LATER. If I had written last night, it would have been a terrible letter because it was one of those days. They delivered alfalfa instead of peat moss. When I went for the peat moss, it more than filled the car and trunk. With the trunk lid up I could barely see to drive. Getting home was scary. Then Judy poked a hole in the sack of grass seed and tried to hide all the seed she had spilled, in a box of ironing. Don't ask me why there! Last night when I ironed, I had to shake out each piece carefully and then vacuum the kitchen three times before I got it all. The whole day went that way.

Today was a different story. Donny was so excited about his birthday that he woke up seven times during the night and started the day at 5:30. I had put your gift and several others beside his bed. He was thrilled with everything.

Nancy and Lois came for a birthday lunch, also Betty Jean and Philip. It was quite a messy affair with lots of spilled milk and cake, but they all had a good time. I insisted on naps if they wanted to go to the movies tonight. After that they all went up to the Browns to play in the sprinkler.

We had a quick dinner before going to see "Cabin In The Sky" with Ethel Waters. Remember when we saw the musical in S.F in 1941 and how we loved it? Ethel Waters is so terrific. I would love to know her as a friend. It was definitely not for children, but they enjoyed it immensely, gathered the good from it, and their minds skimmed the bad completely. Afterwards Donny explained it to me. I was amazed at how well he grasped the meaning of the Negro personifications of God and the devil. . . . Goodnight Honey.

September 12, 1943

Dearest Honey:

Today since it started out cool, I phoned the Stocktons to come out for a picnic. I figured I could use the help of Milburn and Bobby. I'll bet you never knew I was such an opportunist! By the time they got here it was boiling hot, but they hauled eight loads of gravel, and Milburn fixed the Mixmaster and the sliding door. We had a grand lunch on the patio.

Tomorrow will be a big day—first day of school, and I'll be registering Judy at play school too. I also have to take Chuck to the doctor for his rash, Donny to the barber shop, Judy home from play school, and pick up Donny from the barber shop after he has spent A FEW HOURS waiting his turn. I AM NOT KIDDING. Lafayette has just one barber now. The Army took the others.

While Donny was pasting $8 worth of defense stamps into his book last night he gave Donny Rogers a pep talk about how we must buy lots of stamps to get the war over and bring his daddy home. Besides it is a good way to spend your money because you get it all back plus interest. I couldn't hear what D. R. was saying, but apparently he is not enthusiastic about defense stamps from the way our Donny was carrying on. Goodnight my very dear Honey.

September 13, 1943

Dearest:

We are having a terrific storm. I got thoroughly drenched this morning. The rain appears to be falling horizontally in waves. The wind has felled six trees on the path up to our fales and knocked off oodles of coconuts. I mailed one to you this afternoon. When it arrives, the best way to open it is to drive a sharp stick into the ground and drop it with heavy blows on the point. I'm not very good at it but you should see these natives, even small boys of six.

I see they are trying to defeat or defer the draft date for fathers. I hope they do and that Harry doesn't have to go. I'm glad though that I went in when I did. I know I couldn't have stayed out much longer without regrets.

Everything grows so abundantly here. The insects are huge, and the leaves of plants and trees are enormous, except for "mile a minute". It actually grows about that fast. You can cut a path one day, and the next day it is filled with the stuff. It is a small plant that grows all over the ground.

Tonight I saw "Meet Doctor Christian". Remember when we saw it together and how much we enjoyed it? It made me so lonesome for you but I enjoyed it more than any other I have seen here. . . . Good night, my Love.

September 13, 1943

Dear Mr. Fibush:

I must say that I am getting rather tired of the one-sided correspondence I have been carrying on for the past five days. Maybe you have moved on. Maybe you are mad at me and my daily letters that never reach you. Maybe you broke your right arm. Maybe I'll get a letter tomorrow.

When we got up this morning Chuck was covered with large runny sores. When Mabel looked at him she said, "smallpox!" The whole neighborhood went into an uproar! I talked to the doctor and took Chuck to see him. I was scared to death it was impetigo. It is actually cowpox—a reaction from his vaccination. Dr. Beede had never seen such a bad case of it before and didn't recognize it at first. He gave me a prescription for some salve to put on him which cost $1.75. That is highway robbery! Chuck feels a little better, but he looks horrible.

It took me practically the rest of the day to do the washing and clean things up a bit. After dinner Rusty and Mabel worked with me on the lawn, and we got it all raked again and the peat moss spread. We worked the last half hour in the dark with all the lights we could muster and the moon coming up behind the trees. After that I made cookies and took some out to them.

Tomorrow Judy starts to play school on Tuesdays and Thursdays. I am to help out on Tuesday mornings. If I find that I can't do it, it will be $3 a month, otherwise only $1. She is so excited about going on the school bus.

I actually talked the old fellow in Walnut Creek into fixing Donny's shoes while I waited today. The ones you had soled at the base were losing their soles again. Oh I almost forgot, Dr.Burns' bill was $3 for me and $5 for Donny. That is $1 a visit for Donny . . .

I finally received another letter from you today written on the 9th in answer to mine of the 2nd. Not bad! But where on earth are all the others? Isn't it maddening not to be able to carry on an intelligent conversation because of all the gaps?

After I took Judy to play school this morning I picked up your letter at the P.O. and kept reading it over and over. I suppose future letters will explain what is meant by "things are starting to happen." I thought you told me that where you are, it is a case of "It Can't Happen Here."

When I picked Judy up she was bubbling over with excitement about play school. She loves everything about it. . . .

September 16, 1943

Dearest Honey:

Yesterday I received the letter you wrote September 3rd. Don't you know I would have sent you cookies long ago if it was permissible? Anyhow think how stale they would be after traveling for weeks.

Today for the first time, Judy went on the school bus to play school, and great was the excitement. They all looked perfectly darling as they walked down the road to catch the bus. The girls wore the dresses I got them for Judy's birthday, with white shoes and socks, green ribbons in Bev's hair and red ones in Judy's. Donny had on a white shirt and the sweater Aunt Nettie gave him. His hair looked slick. I was bursting with pride, they looked so grand.

When I picked up Judy she was radiant. She had made a picture out of things she had cut out and pasted on paper. She hung it proudly on her door when we got home. We also took home a young mother and her little boy. Her car had broken down, and they were walking along the highway.

Monday is shakeup day at St. Mary's, and everyone is holding their breaths about where their husbands are to be assigned. The gal I picked up is a friend of Mabel's. She is expecting in February and is petrified that her husband will be shipped out and not be here then. The maddening thing about their baby being expected right now is that they have been trying for this pregnancy for over four years. What timing! She says everyone kids them and says, "Well, the Navy certainly made a man out of you, Steve!"

Today was better than Christmas—five letters from you. To answer your questions. Due to the polio epidemic, there is no swimming. Susan and Philip are cuter than ever. Sunday School is now held at the Condits' because of our rumpus room being occupied. I can well imagine how that paragraph about Gary must have had you puzzled.

I forgot to tell you we saw Una Merkel on 17th St when we were in Oakland. We noticed an exquisitely dressed woman, and Beverly said, "Did you see that pretty lady, Mother? Wasn't she dressed cute?" I said, "Yes, and she looks so much like the movie star Daddy likes so much, Una Merkel." When we turned the corner onto Broadway, I noticed that she was billed at the Orpheum in person. Beverly was ecstatic when she realized that she really HAD seen a movie star!

Tonight when dinner was ready, Donny was nowhere to be found. Just then, he came tearing down the road ON HIS BIKE! He had talked the Hoskins boys into fixing it today. Was he ever thrilled! He could hardly bear to come to dinner, and I didn't blame him. He bolted his food, and we both went outside and rode our bikes up and down the road for a while. We each gave the girls a ride, then they all helped me crumble peat moss until dark.

After putting on a new axle, fixing the tires and brake, they charged $7.50 for the bike. I think that's all right, providing it holds together.

NEXT DAY. Forgive me, Honey, I didn't get this mailed. This morning flew as we straightened the house and got ready to go to the folks. John was giving a party for all his young friends. After leaving them there I went to see about bricks. The type we bought three years ago for $13 a thousand are now $48!

By the time I got back the party was almost over. When Edie came to pick up Ann, she asked if Beverly could go home with them, so reluctantly I agreed. The house seems so empty without her.

Midge was in her nurse's aid uniform this afternoon and looked so cute. She had just come from seeing a baby delivered and was very excited and awed by it. It's hard to realize that my "baby sister" is so grown up.

Be sure to save these letters, and we can have fun reading them after the children are grown. We can relive the "merry-go-round" of our present lives.

If you can think of anything you need PLEASE let me know. People are always asking me what they can send you. I would like to send you SOMETHING for Christmas that is a little more interesting than a shoe lace or a razor blade!

I wonder how you will celebrate your birthday. I hope not with fireworks!

September 18, 1943

My Wonderful One:
Yesterday I had the thrill that comes once in a lifetime. I was more than Santa Claus. When I went to the P.O. I had two enlisted men with me. The long delayed mail had just come in. We spent over an hour just sorting it. There were about 2500 letters for the unit. When we distributed them, you should have seen the men's faces. What a thrill! Many of them had received no mail in all this time. One of the men, for example, had a wife who was so sick that she couldn't even finish the letter she was writing to him. That was on August 2nd. Recently I had gone to bat for him and gotten the Red Cross to send a dispatch to find out about her. Six letters in that bunch were from her.

I received five from you. I'm in seventh Heaven with all this on top of yesterday's. First I'll answer yours.

No, Argus Units are entirely different from Acorn Units. That's all I can tell you. The only reason I sleep well is that I am so tired I can't help it. So many things in your letters refer to things in letters that I still haven't received that I am constantly puzzled. Why is the piano in the garage, for instance? We don't have our "Mae Wests" with us on shore. However we are required to have them with us at all times when we are aboard and next to us when we sleep. I am afraid I will never acquire a mad passion for gardening, so don't raise your hopes, and I won't expect you to learn to love playing bridge. I just dote on everything you tell me about the children. Please continue to read my letters to them even though they seem to get more lonesome for me when they hear them. It will be such a long time before I see them again and it is the only way that I can be kept real to them. When will this nightmare end? When will we all six be together again? Goodnight from your lonesome Honey.

September 19, 1943

Dearest Honey:

It is the loveliest evening, all full of crickets and good smells. I just came in from having a luscious piece of chocolate pie loaded with whipped cream, with Mabel and Rusty. It is fun to break the monotony once in a while with a binge like that.

Today was blazing hot. After Sunday School, I pulverized peat moss and started putting it on the lawn. I plugged in Donny's radio on the patio and listened to music from "The Student Prince" and "Porgy and Bess". Wonderful!

Donny took a lunch to picnic under the walnut trees with Nancy and Lois. I rested while Judy took her nap. Later while I was tying up the rose bushes, the folks arrived with Beverly. It's so good to have her back.

They sat on the patio while I continued to work on the peat moss. Chuckie took an immediate liking to John. He called him "Unka John," quite clearly. After they left, I continued working until dark, and that is when Mabel invited me to come in for the pie.

Oh dear, I just remembered I have to iron something for Donny to wear to school tomorrow so I'll have to quit now. I love you to pieces, Honey.

September 20, 1943

Hello Honey:

We are all a little up in the air tonight because the school bus had an accident this morning, and Beverly got bumped a little. She has a patch on the bridge of her nose, and her eye is swollen, but that's all. It scares me to think how much worse it could have been with three of our children on board.

It seems that a black convertible containing five high school boys came tearing around the corner and crashed headlong into the bus. Donny said the car "just shrank right up," and a seat flew out. One boy had his clothes torn off, and his back was bleeding. I heard that they have an assortment of broken legs, arms, and noses. Poor kids.

The bus was smashed in front, a headlight was broken, and the battery wouldn't work. Beverly was the only one injured. She was taken to Dr. Fieler and most emphatically does not approve of the kind of shoes he wears! Leave it to her to notice that he was wearing barefoot sandals! Joe, the driver, was sick afterwards, which distressed Judy more than anything else. All through dinner she kept saying, "Poor Joe, I can't stop thinking about poor Joe."

Donny's bike is the most wonderful thing that ever happened. He is glued to it every minute and is an expert on it already. He can even come down that steep hill from the Ingrams'. It terrifies me when he does. For some reason, Laddy bit him tonight. He was in our driveway when Donny came zooming in a mile a minute yelling, "Look out, Laddy," and Laddy took a nip out of his knee. Marky was terribly embarrassed, and Donny cried as though his heart would break. It hurt his feelings, he loves Laddy so much.

Midge's boy friend is a censor and says he can skim a letter for censorable material without knowing the contents of it. Are you that way yet?

We had quite a wash day at our house today. First I washed, then Leslie, back from two weeks in Washington with a huge collection of laundry. When she finished, Mabel started. The Bendix was going from 9 a.m. until after 3 p.m.

Rusty has been having trouble with his appendix, and today he went to Oak Knoll. They told him he must have it out next week. I guess we had better work hard before then, as no telling how long it will be afterwards before he is able to dig and load gravel.

We are having a heat wave, and I dread going into town all dressed up in girdle and stockings. I really can't put off going any longer though. I am destitute for clothes, and I must also do something about our bare bedroom. It looks so stark now that the rug and the chair are in the rumpus room. . . .

September 20, 1943

Dearest:

Sunday we explored the island. It is about 17-18 miles long. The road follows every bend of the shoreline—about thirty six miles. It goes only on this side. A pass over the middle leads to a short stretch on the other side.

We took our ponchos and put the jeep top down. We no sooner started than it began to pour. We were like a bunch of kids just out of school, enjoying every minute of it. Every little bend in the shoreline has a native village, some with only a few houses and some with as many as thirty-five. I should say "fales" rather than "houses."

The churches are nice buildings of stucco or wood, some with stained glass windows and altars beautifully decorated with flowers. Some of them have seats and some don't, since at least 90% of a native's time is spent sitting on the ground with his legs crossed, tailor fashion.

The villages are amazingly clean and well kept, with outhouses built on little wharves out over the ocean. They are all right at high tide but not so good at low tide!

Their lava lavas are all colors of the rainbow, and the adults keep themselves well covered. However the children up to about age five are usually naked. Speaking of children—there are oodles of them, and about every third woman you see is pregnant.

The scenery is especially beautiful along the shoreline and the edibles prolific —papaya, mango, kava, pineapple, banana, and coconut.

In the afternoon we took the trip over the pass through the middle of the island to the other side. Never have I been on such a steep and treacherous road, but we enjoyed that too. There is a beautiful harbor over there, and the native villages are even more interesting than the ones on this side. When we returned, we wangled a ride on a cable car to the top of the mountain—an 85% grade. It was quite a thrill, and the view at the top was magnificent.

NEXT DAY. Yesterday Bill Dennis and I learned where there is an efalelee tree. They are extremely scarce. The wood is very hard, and is beautifully grained. The natives use them to make kava bowls. Usually they won't part with them because they are a part of one of their most important ceremonies. If they will sell one, it costs about $80 or numerous expensive trading items.

We are going to have natives make us each a bowl from the wood we cut today. It will be ideal for serving large salads. We cut five pieces, each about two feet long and about two feet in diameter. The wood is so hard and so heavy that each piece weighed about 200 lbs. After cutting it, we had to carry it about 300 yards up steep, narrow, winding paths.

There has been another delay in the unloading and loading. It looks as though we won't leave before my birthday. I am so anxious to get going.

I saw two of the cutest little girls today, just about the ages of Bev and Judy. They were dressed alike and had wreaths of flowers in their hair and also necklaces of flowers. I wanted to stop the car and talk with them, but couldn't because I was driving down a very steep hill.

The children go to school here all year around. There is also a Catholic school to which the girls wear middies and skirts (and go barefoot). The men natives are very muscular, but the women are mostly on the buxom side.

The mosquitoes here carry only one disease, and that can't affect you until you have been here about seven months or longer, so it doesn't worry me.

God bless and keep all of you, my Love.

September 23, 1943

Hello, my Honey!

Today I asked the children how they feel about having Navy people around constantly. Donny said he likes it. It makes him less lonesome. As long as you have to be gone, he wants the Navy people around until the war is over. Beverly says she wishes they would go out and win the war so you could come home. Judy says she loves having them around. I enjoy them too.

This morning I took Chuck to the barber for a G.I. haircut! He looks so cute. Bernice has been cutting his hair because the waits in the barber shop are so interminable. Afterwards we bought your birthday card. Chuck "helped" me sign, address, and mail it. The people in the P.O. got a kick out of him. He stood up on the ledge and yelled "Hi" to everyone. He thinks he is perfectly wonderful when he stands alone. (So do I!)

I envy you your rain. This time of year it would be such fun to sit in a downpour, listening and watching it. After spending seven hours watering the garden today I would especially appreciate a good rain!

What a terrific thrill that must have been distributing all those hundreds of letters to the men. How lucky that you were the one who got to do it.

The heat has been terrible. The house is 89 degrees and seems quite cool compared to the outdoors. After I watered, I canned green beans and prepared a special dinner for "my baby brother". He picked up the children, bought them ice cream cones, and played with them all afternoon. They had a glorious time. Oh how they love their Uncle John. Goodnight from your oh so lonesome Honey.

September 23, 1943

My wonderful Hearthrob:

Someone predicted the Nazis would be defeated by the first of the year and Japan within six months thereafter. It is almost too much to hope for, but maybe a miracle will happen. Oh Honey, I hope we won't have to wait much longer to be together.

This morning was very busy and went by rapidly. This afternoon Bill Dennis, and I went to a talking chief who is an expert wood carver. He is going to carve the bowl and also a war club for nothing, in exchange for half of my wood. It was so interesting talking with him. He does marvelous work. While we talked the women all stood around giggling, young and old alike.

A very sad thing has happened. Three men took a hike in the jungle and mountains behind our barracks. The men didn't return, so we had a search party out all night. Two of them came back and said that when they became lost, the third man went for help. When the search party finally found him, he had fallen off a 100 foot cliff and was dead. He was one of the best men in his outfit and was well liked. It is a real tragedy. . . .

September 24, 1943

Honey:

I've been cross as a bear all day. After sleeping from midnight until six, with three interruptions, I woke up like a rag and continued to feel worse all day. They phoned from play school that Judy was sitting on a chair doing nothing and asked if I thought she was sick. It worried me because Chucky had awakened with a dilly of a head cold. However, it turned out to be just a case of the famous Judy sulks.

When I went to buy milk, they would let me have only one fourth the amount I needed. "That is only enough for one meal. I have four children. What am I to do?", I asked. They said they were very sorry, but I could get more tomorrow. Does that make sense, when we are supposed to be saving gas and tires, to expect a person to drive six miles to get enough milk for one meal?

The bright spot of the day was that the new chair and the rugs for our bedroom were delivered. They are simply heavenly. I am so glad I got them. I have to walk in there every few minutes just to look at them and enjoy them.

An insurance man came today to see if Beverly was all right and to have me sign a statement that I wouldn't expect any more money after they have paid the doctor bill. That insurance company is also taking care of the five high school boys. None of them were licensed drivers. He had been in Dutch before for his driving. He jumped out of the car and was hardly injured at all. His father is a physics professor at Cal. The others are in pretty bad shape, particularly Commander McPherson's son, who had to have plastic surgery.

I have reams of papers to fill out tonight for the Navy so that we can be reimbursed $26.22 for the trip down to be with you. What a bunch of red tape.

I hope poor little Chucky has a good night. He was so miserable at bedtime. I put drops in his nose, then held him and rocked him. The trouble is that while I was doing that it got too dark to work outside. But I guess I have to stop being a gardener and be a mother sometimes.

You should have seen him today. I let him out of the pen while Mabel and I dug. I figured the sunshine might do him good. First he got wet, then he sat in mud and peat moss. Then he crawled up the steps and sifted dust off the door mat. His nose was running like a house afire. All we needed at that point would have been a surprise visit from the adoption worker! PLEASE come home soon.

September 26, 1943

My dearest Honey:

I have been waiting all day for a chance to talk to you. I worked on the lawn all day from 6:30 a.m. until dark. I was too tired to do anything but take a bath, and BOY did I need it! You should have seen me—peat moss in my eyebrows and black all over me—what a bathtub ring! But it's in at last!

I am waiting for a call from Harry with the news about Rae. Grandma Caplan called about three to say Rae had gone to the hospital, and the nurse had just told her it would be six or eight more hours.

At five o'clock Mary Cohn phoned and asked if we had a spare room for them tonight! I started flying around like mad to clean up the house. The kids had gone to the Springhill Road picnic with the Condits, and when they got home they all pitched in and helped make up beds.

Poor Mary was so tired and disappointed she wanted to cry. They moved to Lodi today, and when they got there, the house they thought they could have was not vacant after all. They couldn't find even an auto court or a place to eat. That's when they called me. We fixed some soup and sandwiches and got all the kids to bed. Now they are unpacking while I write to you. I wish Harry would phone. It is 10:30.

OH JOY!!! IT'S A GIRL!!!!! Harry just phoned, and he sounded so happy. Rae had a fairly easy time and is just fine. They named her Frances Caroline for her two grandmothers, and they hadn't even weighed her yet when he phoned. Signing off at 11:45 P.M.with oceans of love. . . .

NEXT DAY: In spite of the fact that I didn't get any letters from you today (you snake-in-the-grass!), it has been a grand day. It is such fun having Mary and the kids here, and Mary is so much help. I don't know what I would do without her now that we have Stevie too.

Right after lunch I had to go to a meeting at play school so I picked up all six children from school afterwards, and they had a marvelous time the rest of the afternoon.

Dinner was pretty hectic with nine of us to feed at once. After that they all had baths and were in bed by seven. We have Mary and Stevie in the spare room, her girls in Donny's room, and the rest of us downstairs.

Harry had arrived with Stevie about ten. He is such a darling and so good. He was very subdued all morning but opened up after lunch and was positively hilarious after dinner. We are running a three-ring circus around here—no fooling. I imagine things will calm down in another day or so. Goodnight Honey.

Dear Daddy:

I am telling this to Mommy so she can type it and I can say more. I read good. I got my identification tag today. I wish you would come home.

Rusty had his appendix out. Rusty helped plant our lawn. Rusty and I talk together. I like him. He likes me. I'm his girl friend.

I do my spelling good. We change partners to correct it. I play with Shirley. I eat lunch with Ann and Betty Jean. I love you. Please come home.

Love, Beverly

September 26, 1943

My own sweet Dearest:

I have been very busy for the past four hours censoring mail and doing other work in the office. Starting tomorrow my writing will be limited, as I will be working at least sixteen hours a day. Don't get worried if my letters stop for a while, as we will be on the high seas and won't be able to send mail. This afternoon I decided to play hooky from work, so Howard and I left for a native wedding. Howard is our official photographer and the only one allowed to take pictures or even have a camera. The natives are crazy about pictures of themselves, and they wanted him to take a picture of the bride and groom. As it turned out, everyone else who possibly could squeezed into the picture.

When we arrived we were taken over by the ranking officer. He ranks as high as a high chief and is the brother of the groom. We were treated royally and given the best seats at all times, next to the bride and groom. It was held in a large fale about fifty feet long and twenty-five feet wide. Everyone sat on the floor except the bride, groom, best man, and maid of honor.

The bride was dressed in white with a long flowing skirt, long flowing veil, and beautiful white flowers all over her head. She carried a huge bouquet of artificial flowers and was barefoot. She was tiny and quite cute. The groom wore a white satin lava lava, a white shirt with a very loud tie, and a white dinner jacket. He is the ranking officer in the military organization here. The best man was dressed the same way, and the maid of honor was in a pink evening gown with short sleeves. All were barefoot.

The fale was simply beautiful. Each post had palm leaves braided around it solidly. There were festoons of flowers running the entire length of the fale. Some were orchids, and there were many different shades of hibiscus.

The ceremony was very simple and quite short, with the ring going on the right hand instead of the left. The bride and all the women relatives wept.

Howard took the picture outside the fales, and then we all adjourned to a fale across the road for the "seva". This is a dance where everyone dances individually, just jumping up when they feel like it. Usually not more than eight or ten dance at a time, and sometimes only two or three, preferably one woman and two men. The seva involves loose motion of all parts of the body. It also includes a lot of slapping the hands on all parts of the dancer's body. The steps are all the way from lively jumping, to steps similar to the fad dances we have at home. Their rhythm is beautiful to watch.

The music consisted of a guitar and singing, harmonizing, humming, and clapping by all who weren't dancing at the time. Their harmony is wonderful, and after a while you get right into the swing of the various pieces and recognize them. My favorite was one in praise of these Islands.

After an hour of this they called us by groups back to the original fale for the feed. We were seated on the deck cross-legged opposite the bride and groom. Before each of us was a large platter made of braided coconut palm. In the platter were two enormous pieces of raw pig, several pieces of raw squid (octopus), a piece of boiled chicken, and three cans of sardines. We were petrified that we might have to eat it. Fortunately we were hardly seated when they picked up our plates and told us that they would cook the pig and squid for us and also open the sardine cans. The chicken was delicious, the first we have had since we left the states.

We had to go see the man who is making our kava bowls, so we made our excuses and said we would be back. Much to our surprise eight of the military men got up and left with us. We couldn't imagine why, but we soon found out.

On the way they had us stop at a plantation and gave us the best-tasting bananas I have ever had, my first since arriving. We went to see the talking chief who is working on my bowl. When I turned around the men had disappeared and Bob with them. In a few minutes Bob came back and said they had all gone up to a nearby girls' school on the hill.

Having never heard of it before we went up to see it and find them. There are fifty native girls from eight to eighteen. It is a boarding school and is run by the London Missionary Society. All of the teachers are natives. One of them took us through the school. It was certainly clean and interesting. They all speak fine English, and the teacher laughed at Bob's attempt to speak their native tongue. They are certainly a happy people—always laughing and smiling. We had a hard time trying to tear the young men away from the girls. It was a real treat for them to get a ride out there.

At that point the people at the wedding were all resting from the afternoon seva so they would be in good shape for the Big Seva that night. We went back to the base to have our dinner, and at about 7:30 we returned for the evening festivities. These lasted until about midnight and consisted primarily of the Big Seva of the bride and groom.

There were three regular American dances mixed into the seva. They tried to get us to dance, but we didn't, as it would have been too hard in our stocking feet, on mats with rocks under them.

Before they had the Big Seva, one of the elders talked for ages. When we asked what he had said, our friend told us he had merely said this would be the dance of the bride and groom. When they came on the floor, they were in new costumes, and their bodies were shining with coconut oil. They danced until they were ready to drop, and the poor little bride had to be carried off the floor. Incidentally the bride wore two complete outfits in the afternoon and three in the evening. At one point all of the natives sang, "Don't Sit Under The Apple Tree" for us. What a surprise. Tofa (good bye) until tomorrow. . . .

TWO DAYS LATER. Yesterday we spent the afternoon firing our 45s at the range. It was the first time most of us had fired a pistol. On the way back we stopped and swam for about half an hour. It was good, but I do have a hard time getting used to water that is so warm.

This morning I had office work to do. I spent the afternoon working in the blazing sun, taking inventory of part of our gear. Some of the boxes we had to move weighed over a ton. I spent this evening selecting the seamen who are to be advanced. It is quite a problem when you have such diversified activities.

*Just before mess I went over to see the man who took such good care of us
at the wedding. He gave me a ring which he had made and told me that he is
going to send one of his native uniforms to Donny and also a ring which he is
having his uncle make with Donny's initials on it. He is very intelligent, well
educated, and hopes to come to the U.S. after the war. Wasn't that nice of him
to give me presents? I wish there was something I could do for him.*

*I have enjoyed the moon so much here, but when we get to our next island,
we will be anxious for it to disappear as practically all Nip raids are made
when there is a moon.*

*This morning it started to pour and hasn't stopped since. This delays our
work, since the natives simply will not work in the rain. They will play, swim,
fish, walk miles, or do anything else. But if they are working when it starts to
come down they quit and run for shelter.*

*Today I celebrated my birthday. Why? Because I got scads of mail and have
been floating on air ever since. I know I can't receive any more mail for a
while so this is the day to celebrate. I must stop now to do censoring. . . .*

September 29, 1943

Dearest Honey:

What a wonderful time I had today reading your three letters.

Mary thinks I should rent the spare room upstairs to someone, in
exchange for help. I might be able to get a service wife and baby who need
free rent. I undoubtedly need someone. Mary and I both work continually
and never get done.

It's lucky we got to bed early last night because Stevie had a bad night.
He kept waking and crying for Rae and Harry, and also had diarrhea. He
had it when he came, and now Chuck has caught it. What a day we had. We
mopped up after them all day, gave them three baths, enemas, and boiled
milk with rice.

Art phoned tonight. He still can't find a place for them to live and can't
even find a decent hotel room. I am urging Mary to stay here until the job
is done, since the girls are in school and she can at least see Art on weekends.

This has been a rather long and wearing day. The part that gets Mary is,
"Why can't two strong, healthy, able bodied and apparently intelligent
women ever get all the work done?" She says it all day. We worked so hard
and so constantly, including knocking and peeling a whole wheelbarrow of
walnuts.

Mary made apple pie, and the children downed their dinner in a hurry
with that as an incentive. The girls have been waiting all week for a chance
to sleep together, so we said they could tonight. Judy and Boopsie were going
to sleep in Donny's room upstairs, but after a little while, they got cold feet,
and Boopsie got in Mary's bed. Judy got in mine because Punky was going
to sleep in Judy's bed with Beverly. After their baths, they decided to sleep
in Donny's room. However, Punky was soon yelling to get in her mother's

bed, so Mary put her in there. By that time Beverly was sound asleep. Now we have to move Judy from my bed to hers and Boopsie from Mary's to Donny's. Such a business! . . .

October 1, 1943

Happy Birthday, Honey!

I celebrated your birthday by leaving everything to Mary while I went to a baby shower for Mildred. The luncheon was delightful, and Mildred received some lovely things. Mine was the seventh gift to be opened, which means I will be the next one to have a baby! If only we could count on that!

We had candles and flowers on the table tonight in your honor but no cake, apple pie instead. Art arrived, and Mabel joined us. The ten of us made a happy occasion out of it even in your absence. We all sang "Happy Birthday."

SATURDAY. Art and Mary left for the day. I tried to do nothing unnecessary because I needed to devote as much time as possible to the sick babies. Stevie eats enormously, seems perfectly happy but is still far from normal. Poor little Chucky is in bad shape. Bad diarrhea, poor baby. Lots of wash, poor me!

When Art and Mary got back, they had traveled over four hundred miles and still hadn't found a place to live. Punky asked me today if I don't get awfully lonesome, sleeping all by myself. Little does she know how lonesome it is.

SUNDAY. When we got back from church I worked on the berry fence. Finally it is finished. Fastening together all the pieces of wire that came around the bales of peat moss was a job. There was just barely enough to do it. Oh for the good old days when you could buy fencing instead of having to make it!

The Woods were here today. They finally sold their beautiful big home in Orinda and got their price—$14,500. Isn't that remarkable? Their daughter-in- law had a horrible experience this morning. Someone came to the door asking for Mrs. Charles Wood. She thought it might be someone who knew her husband and could tell her something about him. He said, "Are you Josephine Wood? I read in the paper about your husband being killed, and I thought you might be lonesome and might want to get married. I have a good Job. Do you work? Do you make a good salary? You are the third one I have interviewed, and you are the youngest and prettiest so far." Imagine how she felt. She was so upset she forgot to get his license number.

You write such marvelous letters, but when you rave about me—well, to be realistic, you know, when you get home, I won't seem quite so wonderful. There will be days when I won't always have a clean shirt for you. I will have to iron it at the last minute, and you will be wearing a damp collar. Undoubtedly, I will do all sorts of annoying things like that. . . . Goodnight Honey.

October 2, 1943

Dearest Mine:

I won't be mailing this for a while, as we are at sea. You will recall when I last wrote, my native military friend had just taken me around to see his relatives in different parts of the island. You would have thought they had known me for years they were so cordial. He told them I was leaving, so each of them gave me presents, which I have mailed home to you. I hope you like them. I certainly learned the native word for "thank you" in a hurry—"fa fa tai".

Yesterday was hectic. Just when I thought I had everything squared away, I received a letter from Washington notifying us that one of our enlisted men was transferred to the Naval Academy at Annapolis. Isn't that wonderful? I am so happy for him, but I had a real rush to get the approval of the admiral, make out his orders, and effect all of the transfer papers.

October 6, 1943

Dearest Honey:

I certainly laughed about your exuberance in one of your letters over seeing a white woman. The children couldn't grasp that at all. They thought you meant white like notepaper and wanted to know what made her so pale!

Stevie has such a good time in the sandbox. Just like Chuckie, he is crazy about the outdoors. Chuck gets a little better each day, but it's slow going. He is weak from getting so badly dehydrated. He calls me "Mama" now, and the other day he called to me from the sandbox, "Hi, Ma!"

Donny was especially lonesome for you tonight. He asked for a picture of you to keep in his wallet, so I promised to find one for him. As a result, when I got out the drawer devoted to pictures, scrap books. etc., I spent the whole evening sorting them out and working on Chuck's baby book.

NEXT DAY. I actually fell asleep at the typewriter as I wrote that last line! Today when Art arrived from Stockton, they all left for Aunt Nettie's for four days. We will miss them. Mary has spoiled me. She is such a help. But it's not just that. We all have so much fun together. Today I put all four girls in the tub together, and what a splashing good time they had! Afterwards Donny read to them. He can be so dear, and he is such an excellent reader.

Rae just phoned. She was crying. Frances is vomiting and has diarrhea. The doctor says Stevie must stay here until she is in better condition. Worst of all, Harry's notice to report for his physical on Tuesday just came. He has already been to his draft board and will probably have to go in November. I want to cry every time I think of how she must feel. Oh Honey, I miss you so.

October 9, 1943

My Honey:

I have been looking forward to this for hours. It is almost midnight. I just finished hanging out the washing by moonlight, cleaning five pairs of little white shoes, taking a bath, and now I am in bed with the typewriter on my lap. Romantic Saturday night, huh?

Today I went to work on the flies, spraying each room separately and thoroughly with DDT. Then I vacuumed up the dead flies, hundreds and hundreds of them. How on earth did we get along before we had it?

Rae phoned. Frances is still vomiting and has lost seven ounces. It's just awful for Harry to be leaving for the service on top of all that worry about her. I made a date to go and help her a few days while Mary is here.

NEXT DAY. Oh what a day this has been! The children had just changed from their Sunday School clothes to their play clothes and gone outside, when the Woods phoned to say they and the Alkires would be over shortly.

Needless to say, the children were not thrilled about having to dress up again and come in to sit in the living room with your Prudential cohorts and their wives, but I felt they must. I could just hear the grapevine buzzing (do grapevines buzz?) about how "the Fibush children are just running wild since their father is gone," and I didn't want to disgrace you!

I hastily got Chuck and Stevie dressed up in their cutest rompers and their spotless white shoes and socks, slicked down their hair and put them both in Stevie's crib so they couldn't possibly get dirty before being shown off.

Our guests were here in no time. I just barely made it. Bev and Judy had a fit of the giggles when they greeted them. Donny put on the charm at first and then kept asking if they could go play now.

When I went to get our beautiful little boys I encountered a disaster area. Stevie had diarrhea again in a big way. They were having a glorious time walking back and forth through it, painting each other's faces and arms with it, painting the crib rails, and laughing their heads off. Can you picture what it was like trying to get them stripped, cleaned up, finding fresh clothes, scraping their shoes clean, and trying to do it as quickly as possible, knowing everyone was wondering what on earth was taking me so long? I was a quivering wreck! I could only hope that the children were changing their behavior and being good little hosts in the meantime.

Apparently they did rise to the occasion because everyone appeared to be having a good time when I brought our little monsters down. I've noticed our children do tend to put their best foot forward, not always, but often.

Having done their patriotic duty to help the war effort by visiting the bereft wife and children of our hero overseas, the Woods and Alkires left after a couple of hours. By this time the day was pretty well shot.

For the balance of the day I didn't even try to accomplish anything. I just did the things that had to be done and enjoyed the children. Perhaps I should encounter disasters like that more often. NO! NO! A THOUSAND TIMES NO! I'd much rather work hard all day and have something to show for it.

ANOTHER DAY LATER! This morning I was tempted to start canning but decided to get everything all neat and pretty first. Was it ever lucky I did! Mabel had guests from Lancaster and brought them in. They had no sooner left than Edie arrived with her new boss, who also had to have the grand tour!

The latest news is that we are going to quit holding Sunday School at home. Walnut Creek Presbyterian has decided to have just one combined service in order to save everyone's gas. Everyone will go at 10:30. We are hoping we can get everyone into the Condits' car and ours. Goodnight, Honey.

October 12, 1943

Hello, My Honey:

Today I received your letter of October 1st. The coconut arrived, too. It looked so cute all in the raw with the address and stamps on it. Judging from the amount of postage on it, it will cost a fortune to send the Kava bowl.

Today I went to the P.O. to get Donny's bond and another one for us, and then I picked up Bernice's oil heater, bought groceries for her, Marky and us, got some incidentals at the five and ten, then picked up Donny's bike.

By the time I picked up Judy and got home, Art had arrived from Stockton, and they were packing up. I was floored because I had planned on leaving here at seven tomorrow morning to go help Rae for a few days. Mary was embarrassed because she had assured me she would stay long enough for me to do that. But Art had finally found them a place, so it couldn't be helped. It's a converted shed with one bedroom and only a little plug-in heater for warmth, but they plan to use the breakfast nook for a second bedroom. It was a sad parting for the children, and I will be lost without Mary.

The children hustled through their dinner and to bed, inspired by the offer of a prize to the one who dawdled the least. The prize, a piece of candy to be awarded next morning, was earned by all of them, bless their cooperative little hearts! While we were eating Rae phoned. By the time we had finished doing the dishes, they had all arrived, Uncle George too.

To make a very long story short, we all decided that Rae and the children will move over here when Harry leaves. She and Frances will have the spare room upstairs, and Stevie will have Donny's room. Donny will move downstairs to share Chuck's room. This is what I want. Harry will feel much better knowing that they are here with us, and I know you will too. Poor

Rae. Right now she doesn't feel as though she could be happy anywhere. Naturally she hates leaving her own home, but she is afraid she will be stranded over there, not having the wonderful neighbors we have and not knowing how to drive.

A DAY LATER. My evening has been spent in a huddle with Jack, trying to figure out how to have a bathroom put in upstairs for Rae. I got forms from the War Production Board, and are they ever complicated! There are ten of them, each four pages long. There must be an easier way to get a wash bowl, shower, and toilet than that! I am required to prove this is necessary for the advancement of the war effort! My thoughts all day have been on how to make everything as happy and comfortable as possible for Rae and the babies. There are so many things to be considered.

Donny came home from the Army camp just in time for dinner with an identification bracelet, dog tags, and stripes of all kinds. It more than made up for his disappointment yesterday when the young man who invited him had gone on leave before he got there. He is quite enthused about renting his room to Stevie. I told him he would get $5 a month. $4.50 is to go for defense stamps, and the rest he can spend.

Mabel's brother was here today. Rusty gave him all the details about your island and the natives there. He thinks you must be in Samoa. Is he right?

I'm extra lonesome lately. Goodnight, Honey.

October 15, 1943

Hello, my Honey:

I have had a sore throat all day. I'm going to take aspirin, ephedrine, silver nitrate, soda, and a good hot bath. That should knock it.

Chuck's appetite is enormous, but he gets the food down with difficulty while gasping for breath. He has acquired a funny little mannerism rather like Stevie's "I do, I do." He goes around saying "Thank you" all the time. He sits in his high chair and whines it anxiously as he waits for his food. He stands under the cupboard where we keep the crackers and screams it. His favorite game is to hand me something and say, "Thank you." Then I say it, then he says it, and that can go on ad infinitum!

Last night I went to the show. It was Deanna Durbin in "Hers To Hold". I hope you get to see it. I was delighted that Mabel and the other Navy wives invited me. It was such fun to go out at night for the first time since July, except for the times I have taken the children somewhere.

This typewriter ribbon is still giving me so much trouble. Oh for the good old pre-war days when you could just go and buy a ribbon when you needed one.

The mail lady is concerned because I haven't received any mail from you for a few days. But knowing that I can't hear from you as long as you are at sea makes the waiting less difficult than when I just wait, wonder, and worry.
. . . Goodnight Honey

October 15, 1943

My wonderful Heartbeat:

So many things have happened. I think you will get the general idea when I say that today we had our first meal NOT on K rations in some time. Spam, cold canned tomatoes, cold canned string beans, canned peaches, and coffee, seemed like the best meal I had ever tasted, and I had seconds. K Rations! Ugh!

We have a marvelous beach here, and I have been swimming for about half an hour each day. We use salt water soap, and do our bathing before we get out.

I finally received mail and am so pepped up as a result. I was relieved to hear about Rae and little Frances. I have been so anxious. Having to wait this long to hear caused me a lot of worry. I expect that is because she had such a hard time when Stevie was born. I am so anxious to get all the details. My mail consisted of seven letters from you, two from Ken, one from Rae, several from people in the office. I took time off and spent over two hours reading them, then reread yours.

During the past thirty-six hours I have had three catastrophes. First, the sea chest containing all the important papers and files for the unit, fell in the drink and had to be fished out. I'm sure you realize the seriousness of this. Most of them will have to be rewritten, and as quickly as possible. Secondly, when we went swimming last night, I dove into the water with my wrist watch on for the first time in my life. I have it soaking in kerosene and will send it to you by air mail as soon as possible to be repaired—hopefully.

The third catastrophe was that in handling my sea bag they broke a bottle of ink which I thought I had safely wrapped. It was a full bottle, and it ruined two pairs of pants and two shirts. However in spite of all this, none of it really bothered me because of my wonderful mail.

I am so happy that you have Mary and the children with you. It sounds as though you are all getting along famously. I am anxious to hear more.

We have a fine bunch, both officers and enlisted men. They are real workers and fine company. I hope you will get to meet some of them some time.

I have the duty for this twenty-four hour period so probably will get very little sleep. I perspire even more here than I did on the other island. Even my eyebrows drip! The water we are drinking, and I usually drink about a gallon a day, is generally about eighty degrees and tastes like iodine. What I wouldn't give for a glass of good old ice cold "East Bay Mud". [1]

OF COURSE I am saving all your letters. I am certainly mad at myself for having lost most of those you wrote from January to June.

You asked what I want besides a watch so here is the list—ice cold root beer, ice cold coke, ice cold FRESH milk, fresh eggs, and most of all some loving from you. Since I don't think anyone can supply me with those, I'll settle for the wrist watch. Oh—and some snapshots, especially of you. . . .

---

[1]The name we usually used for our water company—East Bay **M**unicipal **U**tility **D**istrict.

October 16, 1943

Honey:

I was sitting disconsolately on the steps today when the mail came. What a thrill! We are all in deep mourning for those mildewed Hershey bars. That certainly happens rapidly in your humid climate, doesn't it. The whole neighborhood feels terrible! Also no one can believe you don't have Coca Cola where you are, since every other place in the whole world seems to.

Today I had to spend a lot of time showing Donny how to do the watering properly instead of just any old way. At that point a phone call from Helen informed me that there had been a tomato throwing episode with the Brown girls, and Donny is not wanted up there from now on. I picked two of the largest, most rotten tomatoes I could find and threw them at him so that he would realize how it felt. Of course then he had to take a bath, wash his hair, wash his clothes, and clean out the tub. All of this was very harrowing for both of us and left me on the point of tears. After that I sent him up there to apologize. So much for being the "fun person" in his life.

The girls had a nice peaceful day. I actually managed to keep from saying "hurry up" to them all day. Beverly has become such a bookworm, and they sit around for hours with Bev reading to Judy. They had only been out playing for a few minutes when they remembered I promised to "let" them polish their new maple beds and scrub their woodwork. They did a beautiful job.

October 17, 1943

Dearest:

I just had the pleasure of reading the mail I received during chow, eight of which were from you written from August 15th on. What a feast I have had!

Now to tell you a little more about this island. There are mosquitos but no more than we have at home. We have homemade fly catchers all over the place, and some are full already. It takes about five minutes to ride from one end of the island to the other over a very rugged road. The highest point of elevation is about ten feet, but the coconut trees tower as high as sixty feet. There is a wild rooster and a wild hen which the natives must have left here.

We don't have electricity yet, so we use lanterns. Our present "heads" are two- seaters in the open! Within another week we should have things running smoothly at headquarters. We now have the washing machines set up. The colored mess stewards will do our laundry for us for $2 a month.

This climate is hard on teeth. Everyone's are getting very dingy looking. No matter how much they are brushed, it doesn't seem to make any difference.

NEXT DAY. Today I worked like a trooper, since I am now in charge of all the work for the communications department except for the duties of the radio officer. The interruptions are frequent as I write. Everyone including the Skipper and the Exec. come in constantly to ask questions.

So, according to "tradition", you are supposed to be the next one to have a baby. Please do me a favor, and wait until I come home! Your loving Honey.

October 19, 1943

Dear Mr. Fibush:

Did you hear about the lady who rode to San Francisco and back by bus, and the transportation was so slow that her baby learned to walk before she got home? Yep, that's what happened today when I took Donny to get his glasses.

I decided to take the bus from Lafayette instead of driving to Berkeley to catch the Key train. It seemed like a foolish waste of gas to drive in when the bus was arriving any minute. Well, I certainly learned my lesson. We stood all the way to San Francisco, which was O.K. It was the return trip that was a nightmare. We were through at Rhine Optical by ten and had plenty of time to catch our bus. When they called it we stood by the door as soldiers kept filing past us, and they kept repeating, "Antioch and Pittsburg, military personnel only." Buses continued to leave jammed with soldiers and when I inquired inside what the score was, I was told "Next bus 12:40."

I was frantic. Chuckie was with Bernice, who had to leave for S.F. by noon. Judy had to be picked up from play school. Donny's lunch was in his locker at school. I phoned Bernice who said she would somehow make arrangments for Judy and Chuck. We found a cigar store nearby, where we got some chocolate cake, cokes, and peanuts, which was the only "food" they had.

Back we went to the bus depot and edged our way through the crowd. When they called our bus we managed to push our way through, only to run into a solid wall of soldiers. The bus driver kept taking soldiers' tickets, and as he turned away I started to cry. I didn't mean to, but it certainly worked! He punched our tickets and let us on. We were the only civilians on the bus, and the most amazing thing happened. After we had stood for about twenty miles, a soldier got up and gave me his seat!

Bernice told me that Chuckie had walked seven or eight steps several times. When we got home he repeated the performance for us. He gets so excited and pleased with himself.

Yesterday after Sunday School, we picked up Allen Stanley. He and Donny, taking bag lunches, had a wonderful time hiking in the hills. I wish they could get together more often. He is a delightful boy, the youngest in a large family. I believe he has three sisters and two brothers, and as you already know, his parents are the salt of the earth.

I mowed the new lawn yesterday. It was quite an event. I felt as though I was about to give my first baby its first bath! When I finished I was delighted to see how good it looks.

Children's clothes are so poorly made now that I'm constantly mending. The socks are knit so skimpily that they are hard to get on and off and wear out very fast. I felt so sorry for Beverly today. She cried bitterly because she didn't want to wear her "tie-on" panties to Sunday School. She wailed, "But it's not polite to tie your pants in public, and I always have to keep tying mine." She just broke my heart.

Two of the fellows at Coast Counties Gas are certainly burning their candles at both ends. After they get through six days' work there, they work until midnight at the cannery. One of them is also harvesting walnuts on top of that. Somebody has to do it, and I guess they must have been classified 4F.

Good night, Honey. I wish you were here so we could listen to the radio together and cuddle.

October 20, 1943

Dearest Honey:

I received two grand letters from you today. Your new island has a homey sound as though it belongs to you. You seem to take pride in it.

I forgot to tell you about Bernice's trip to S.F. Her bus broke down, and all the soldiers got out to push it up the hill. It crept through the tunnel, then acted as though it was going up in smoke before they got to Oakland. They all had to get out and thumb rides. Bernice had a terrible time getting one.

They are sending the children home at noon the rest of the week because of rationing. No heat for the school.

I phoned Mrs. Edgar today to see how things were coming along, and she was so delighted to hear from me. She is dying to come see us but just can't. The load in the Probation Department gets heavier daily. Being head probation officer while Arleigh is in the Navy is a heavy responsibility. She has everything set to have Chucky and several other children declared legally abandoned and ready for an adoption petition but no time to go to court and have it done.

I finally met Mrs. Hoffer, whose husband is a dentist at St Mary's. Donny has been dying to play with their son Jerry. She brought Jerry over, and he and Donny had a marvelous time. When I took Jerry home, we discovered they live in a little cabin down below the highway. It must be very hard for her to have to live like that, but "C'est la guerre". Families who want to be together have to take what they can find. How lucky we are to be in our own home while you are gone and also have room to share. . .

October 24, 1943

My Dearest Honey:

What a series of *catastrophes* you had! Everyone tells me it is impossible to find a shock proof watch, even at Ship's Service or the P.X. Vanette finally succeeded in getting one for Bunny. He dropped it on a cement floor, and found it was not shock proof! However, we will see what we can do.

Yesterday Duane (the little Okie[1] kid) arrived on his bike to play. He lives in a shack behind the Richfield Service Station. His parents work in the shipyards. It was quite an experience having him for lunch. He looked around, said "Where's the bread?", grabbed two slices and began stuffing. Apparently no one ever told him about breaking up his food. When I showed him how to break it up with a fork, he said he thought that was "a very good idea." I told the boys I would pay them each a quarter to fill the wheelbarrow with walnuts and peel the skins off. Donny wanted to ride his bike, but Duane said, "I can ride my bike any day. I want to earn that quarter."

Later I took the children to Walnut Creek so they could shop. They had saved money to buy birthday gifts for Grandpa and me. Beverly is saving for a bride doll in the Sears catalogue and had $1.49 towards it. She spent a dollar on defense stamps and a quarter on a diary for Grandpa's birthday.

Donny had thirty cents to start with. He took back eight coke bottles and some broken phonograph records for which he received a total of sixty-eight cents. This made him a plutocrat in comparison to the others.

NEXT DAY. After we got home from Sunday School, Catharine, Bob and Douglas arrived and we had a weeny roast. Then Bob helped me haul gravel. I'm afraid he'll have some aching muscles tomorrow.

I have to write to the War Production Board tonight. I wish you were here to negotiate with them. The plumber gave me a price of $163 but can do nothing until I get permission from them. . . . Goodnight, Honey.

October 24, 1943

Dearest beautiful lady of Mine:

In some ways it is terrible that Harry is to be inducted, and I understand how Baby feels. On the other hand, she should be happy and proud that he is physically able to go. As long as his country needs him, it's an honor and privilege. I'm so glad they will be with you.

The new plan for Sunday School and Church sounds excellent. It was a fine idea having it at home, but this will have so many more advantages.

It makes me mad that you are going to be even more strictly rationed on gas. There is so much waste in the military. By the way, Ken wrote that Seattle is no longer blacked out. How about the Bay Area?

---

[1]The poor but hard-working people who came from Oklahoma by the thousands to work in the shipyards, their big opportunity to better themselves financially.

Finally I have time to tell you a little more about this island. There are thousands and thousands of lizards and rodents. The ants are huge and outnumber the flies. Sand crabs and land crabs cover the entire beach at night.

We now have a telephone exchange in headquarters, also an electric light here and in the Skipper's office. Tomorrow they start on a screened-in mess hall. That will be a joy. It takes clever manipulation to get food into our mouths without also ingesting flies. We are gradually getting the underbrush cleared away. It will be about a two-month job, since we can spare only a few men to work on it each day. . . .

October 25, 1943

Honey:

Donny is sitting in the kitchen with me, surrounded by trucks, jeeps, planes, guns, chess men, and tents, carrying on a campaign. He gets so much satisfaction out of staying up until 8 o'clock now, after the girls are in bed. It's good for us to have some time together, just the two of us.

We have been out of milk since yesterday. The Schneiders' cow is dry. We are hoping Betty Imrie or Rusty can get milk for us somewhere.

Our sheltered children were horrified at your description of your outhouse! What is a refer? Some kind of refrigeration?

Remember those pictures we were given of Judy at eighteen months, playing in the snow? Today she was telling me about when she "played in lots and lots of snow and lived up the hill. And I wore a snowsuit—not like the one I have now. It was all blue, all over, every bit of it." That is the first memory she has ever pulled out of her past for us. And to think that it goes that far back. Isn't that amazing? I wish we knew more. We might be better able to cope with her problems.

This has been the craziest day. It started out cold, dingy, and dreary. Then the sun came out, so I hung out the washing. Soon it got black and lowering. The wind began to howl, and the leaves were driven in gusts. Before noon it was pouring and has been ever since. The washing had to be taken down and hung in the attic. Then I had a wonderful time running around in the rain picking up things that must be brought in, including the six lugs of walnuts sitting on top of the play house which I almost forgot.

Last night at about ten there was an earthquake that lasted nearly two minutes. I was scared stiff. It was the strangest sight to watch the sink go writhing around. No damage was done here, however.

Marky just this minute dashed in with the most exciting news! Bunny arrived home on Saturday. In case you have forgotten, he is her sister's husband and a Chief in the Seabees. He flew from Guadalcanal and has eighteen days leave. The Navy finally decided to overlook his red green color blindness and have given him an ensign's commission. Goodnight, my Honey.

October 27, 1943

Dearest Precious:

This morning I had a new experience. I took a fresh-water shower in the rain. I was working hard in the Skipper's tent when it started to pour. I went over to my tent, got my soap, stripped down, and lathered up. Wonderful.

Bob and I spent most of the day opening boxes of office supplies. Some very poor judgment was used on some of them. For example, we got four dozen pens, but no pen points, so I guess we will have to use the pens to play pick up sticks! We got two calendar pad holders, but no calendars. We got enough sealing wax to last ten years and enough typing paper to last about two months. We use at least six reams of mimeograph paper a month. We got none. We received no tables, so are using boxes.

We started a new system about our foxholes today. As you know there are always some men who are reluctant to put out and who are willing to let someone else carry their load. Well, digging fox holes is VERY hard labor. One of our petty officers, who is a good slave driver, is now in charge of a group of men in that category. He has them making foxholes for the whole outfit.

We have been having lemonade made from powdered lemons. We have it cold right out of the refer for dinner, and it is very refreshing. Usually I drink at least four glasses. We also have canned fruit juices, and each man was allowed to buy one a day until today when we began to run out.

Bob and I have turned out to be fine carpenters. Did you ever think you would see the day? We used the crates in which our office supplies came and made dressers with separate compartments for clothing and other things. Our tent now is so much more livable.

I missed writing you yesterday. I reached the end of my endurance and flopped into bed the minute I finished my day's work at 9:30. I had been going hard since 5 a.m. after having had only three hours' sleep the night before.

Tonight a lot of package mail came including the Sept. 26th Oakland Tribune. What a treat. Pete went to Cal too, and we were both so excited to have news about the first football games.

I was happy to hear you actually went somewhere for a change. Please try to do it more often. I want you to do something besides work, work, work.

Please give each of the children an extra kiss from me, Honey.

October 28, 1943

Dearest Honey Presh:

Today I made the Halloween costumes. I got half masks for the girls and a pirate mask for Donny. I painted a black patch over one eye and made a vicious looking cutlass of heavy cardboard dripping with gory red paint. Bob Underhill contributed high boots, and they were the making of Donny's costume.

NEXT DAY. At that point I conked out. This has been quite an evening. The school Halloween party was tonight. Betty Imrie drove us. Betty Jean looked perfectly adorable as Bo Peep. Our girls went as Jack and Jill. Bev was lovely with a turquoise ribbon tied around her softly curling red hair and a full skirt to match. Judy was cute as a bug's ear with her hair tucked out of sight under a boys cap.

Betty let us out by the Standard station where the parade started. We were late and ran to catch up. We acquired a tiny ghost named Margaret who dashed with us. I have no idea who she was. It was quite a run from there to the school. Margaret kept falling. I could see she was on the verge of tears, so I picked her up and ran with her in my arms.

Mr. Ellis was having the time of his life as he ushered each child onto the stage. There were some very clever costumes. One child wore a dirty old riding habit and was labeled "The Filthy Habit".

Everyone was there. All our friends were asking about you; the Ruckers, Ongs, O'Neills, Warburtons, Iversons, Duncans.

They had a couple of appropriate movies which the children loved, gave out the prizes, and everyone went home tired and happy. I'm still wondering who that little Margaret is.

So our prices shock you. How do you like two cents apiece for carrots? Remember when we paid a penny a bunch? I remarked to the sales clerk that the price of twenty cents for baby socks didn't jibe with the ceiling price of fifteen cents printed on the rack. She said that didn't mean anything.

Our girls have new beds just like Midge's—Jenny Lind spool beds of maple, and we just love them. Sears had a special for $10. However, the "Victory" mattresses are awful. I have to turn them over every few days, and then they immediately turn lumpy again. These days anything that is produced for civilians is labeled "Victory", "Liberty", or "Defense" and is of very poor quality. I love you to pieces. Did you know that?

October 31, 1943

Dearest Honey:

Mr Edwards and the girls from your office just left after a grand day. The weather was perfect. We had frost on the roofs this morning, but the sky was blue and the sun was dazzling by the time they arrived. They brought a gorgeous array of food and also toys for the children. They left all the extra food here, so we are really going to enjoy our meals for the next day or so. They just surged through the house. All the girls who had been here before were eager to show it to the ones who hadn't.

They were all nuts about Chuck. He was passed from one to another all day, and he loved it. They also helped Donny make the ships and other things in the cardboard set they had brought.

They were tickled to death to get walnuts from the Wooleys for ten cents a pound and also enjoyed the Woolleys' animals immensely. However we discovered somethng so sad as we arrived there. A young doe had died in childbirth. The Wooleys were shocked when we told them. She was apparently all right when they fed her early this morning.

I read the girls parts of your letters and picked out a few particularly insteresting ones to pass around. The children and I had a very good time, and it was obvious that they all did too. . . .

November 1, 1943

Dearest Mine,

Today for the first time in months I was able to wear my glasses for three or four hours because I wasn't constantly dripping with perspiration. Now that we have almost all the underbrush cut out clear across the island from our camp to the ocean and to the lagoon, the breeze gets better daily.

So you think our island sounds homey! That's a laugh. When we first arrived it was like the proverbial island upon which a person is shipwrecked. The land crabs, rats, mosquitos, and flies came down on us in droves. Even tonight at supper I just missed swallowing flies with my food three times. Last night I didn't have a chance to take my sponge bath until after ten o'clock. It was quite an experience as I had to do it in complete darkness and had only half a bucket of water.

I have the duty tonight but will at least get this started. The boat just arrived with mail and I can hardly wait for them to get it sorted. Did I tell you that all the water we use is either distilled from ocean water or caught in buckets and barrels when it rains? Speaking of rain, we have had over six inches in the past twenty-four hours.

THREE HOURS LATER. Nothing but interruptions, but what can I expect when I have the duty? Soon I have to go out in this downpour and inspect all the outposts and the change of guard. It is a two-hour job. I shouldn't kick. The enlisted men are in the same boat. They have their guard duty every four nights besides their full day's work. They are great sports and pitch in without complaint.

NEXT DAY. Good News! The assignment I wrote about went through, and I will leave this island tomorrow for another one. The Skipper has given me our Chief to go with me, and he should be a big help since he has been in the Navy for many years and has been on duty on five different battleships as well as a flat top. (airplane carrier) I will be in complete charge of the installation, operation, and setting up of a system for which I was trained and it will be the hub of all such set-ups in this area. DON'T DISCUSS THIS WITH ANYONE!

I had quite an experience on my trip to the other island yesterday. First they lost the anchor when we were getting started, and it took two hours to find it. On the return trip, instead of having to wade ashore as I usually do, two of the enlisted men insisted on making a hand seat for me and carrying me ashore. I felt like a king! Wasn't that nice of them? Also since my hair is finally long enough to comb, I put some vaseline on it. As a result, I had droves of flies around my head all day. Never again!

When I got to bed the moon was so beautiful shining through the coconut palms, I started thinking of you. . . . Before I knew it the moon had disappeared over the horizon. Goodnight Honey.

November 1, 1943

Oh Honey:

This morning the roofs and fences were beautiful with frost. What a time for Jack and Marky to be out of butane and consequently out of heat!

Tom Slaven took Donny and me to S.F. to pick up his glasses. We parked in that gorgeous new Union Square parking garage. Donny just loves his glasses. He looks good in them too. They are comfortable and don't bother him at all. I am so glad he doesn't feel self-conscious.

Tomorrow I have to push Bernice to Lafayette to get a new battery. Their car has been standing by the fruit stand on the highway for two days.

While I was gone today, the gravel was delivered. Marky and Bernice asked the driver to try to spread it along the driveway as he dumped it. He did a beautiful job. They said he drove back and forth dumping it very gradually. That is certainly a relief and will save me endless hours of hard work.

I am worried to death about the bathroom again. The plumber didn't read the application carefully and didn't fill in all the necessary details. Then he mailed in only one instead of both of the forms. I hope that won't put us on a poor footing with the War Production Board. . . . Good night, Honey.

November 2, 1943

Dearest Honey:

Your Commissary Chief left about an hour ago. When he phoned and said it was Berkowitz, I told him I knew right away who he was, and he wouldn't believe that I could possibly know. He had rented a car and was coming right over.

By the time I straightened up the house, the children were home from school, and we all worked on the gravel. There ARE advantages to the short day at school! It was soon time to fix dinner, and he still wasn't here. At that point he finally arrived. He had gotten lost.

After we finished eating, the children played marbles with him for a while before they went to bed. Then we had a chance to really talk. He found your islands on the map for me and explained the ARGUS responsibilities. Now I can understand why you keep the hours you do and what a pleasure it must be to be the head Communications Officer. I can readily see why you are enthusiastic about the spot where you are—not geographically speaking. He had to leave fairly early because he was afraid he would get lost again. He has to report in every morning early, to see if he has his leave yet. What a waste of precious time when he could BE on leave! I feel so sorry for him and his wife, having such a short time and then having to part again.

When I stopped by the P.O. this morning, Mrs. Harter looked perfectly terrible. I'm afraid she may have had bad news about her son. When she handed me my mail she forced a weak smile, which was not like her.

Chucky has been walking all day, over to Marky's and back several times, over to Bernice's, and up and down our driveway. He enjoys the lovely fine white gravel. Today he climbed out of his potty chair and performed in his bed instead! When I came in he had a "I shouldn'a done it" look on his face.

NEXT DAY. When Mrs. Harter brought the mail today, I told her that yesterday I was afraid she had bad news. She said it was just one of her down days. Sometimes she can stand it, and sometimes she can't. She is trying very hard to think that "No news is good news".

We accomplished a lot today at Red Cross. We really had a production line, with three sewing machines sewing seams as we worked on hospital gowns. The rest of us were turning, basting, pressing, and handing them to stitchers to be stitched again.

It has been a perfectly gorgeous fall day. It smells so good—like football and burning leaves. Rusty went to be checked yesterday, and the doctor won't let him go back to work yet. Today he helped me instead. Pretty nice! He cleaned out the garage and stacked things neatly on the shelves. Then he fixed my bike, finished graveling the front path, did the clothesline path, the back path, and all around the back door. It looks simply grand.

It seems so very long since I last heard from you. Good night, Honey

November 4, 1943

Honey:

I have spent most of the evening going through your recent letters to find the one in which you requested that the Tribune and the Lafayette Sun be sent you. The P.O. has a new ruling that no newspapers can be sent without a written request from the addressee.

I started celebrating my birthday today. Like you, I decided that as long as so many nice things were happening, I had better call it my birthday. To begin with Marky did all my shopping and came home with some BANANAS! These are the first to arrive in our area since last April. When the mail came there was the package from you and also the OK on the bathroom from the W.P.B. I just couldn't believe it! Shortly after that Rusty came home with some film for us.

There was great excitement when your package came. The girls are ecstatic over their hand-carved rings. Donny is just dying because I won't let him wear the hat to school. That uniform slays me. The idea of a khaki lava lava had never occurred to me, nor had I ever dreamed of a Marine in a long wraparound skirt! The tapa cloth is beautiful. I haven't decided yet where to hang it.

My last treat of the day was reading in bed till midnight. It felt so good to take time out like that.

Jack came over tonight to advise me on materials I need for the bathroom. There is enough of your electrical stuff left so all I have to get is one box and a fixture. I need 200 feet of 2x4s and 3 4x8 sheets of whatever I can get for the walls. I may be able to get Grandpa Underhill to do the carpentry.

Two fellows escaped from San Quentin last night. They caught one of them, but the other is still at large, and it has been reported that he has been seen around Lafayette. Mabel made me promise to lock the doors tonight.

NEXT DAY. Today I received two wonderful letters from you. My birthday letter made me cry, it was so beautiful. Aren't you smart getting it here exactly on my birthday?

It is such a comfort to be able to picture at least vaguely what you are doing when you say, "Today has been such an interesting day," and all those things that pique my curiosity. I was so completely blank before.

I wanted your watch to be a surprise, but I may as well tell you I mailed it today. Rusty got it at St. Mary's. He had to give them the letter in which you requested it and also point out that you asked that it be sent insured airmail. Mrs. Harter said she couldn't guarantee it would be sent airmail.

We no longer have dim-out. We drove home last Sunday night with the regular lights on, and what a pleasure it was. No large illuminations are allowed, but porch lights can be turned on.

Since we were going to the folks today for my birthday dinner I did lots of errands. We looked for stepping stones and finally found some at a nursery on Broadway. I bought eight of them at ten cents apiece to put across the lawn from the gate to the patio so the lawn won't be ruined by the constant traffic.

At various stops we picked up a huge variety of items for the Berkeley scrap drive, and the car was loaded to the hilt. When we reached the folks', Midge and I unloaded, sorted, and stacked it.

It was a keen dinner, and the children ate well. The folks weren't able to find me a clock so gave me a $5 gift order for books. I'm delighted. My head is nodding, and it's time to stop. Goodnight my very dear Honey.

FRIDAY, NOVEMBER 5, 1943, THAT SPECIAL DAY

My Precious:

Of course you know that today my thoughts have been with you even more than usual. All day long I tried to picture what you were doing. . . .

I just had an extra good bucket bath, and then mail arrived. At that point the Skipper came in. I don't know how he knows that I had been having such difficulty sleeping, but he brought the pharmacist's mate with him and some sleeping powder. So I must get to bed and see how well it works.

SATURDAY. I guess it worked pretty well. That was as far as I got! The next thing I knew it was this morning. I'm a new man today! The Skipper had told me to sleep as long as I wanted, and I slept clear through for twelve hours! On top of that, he phoned from the other island about noon to tell me my assignment is on again. I hadn't unpacked, so I'm ready to leave any time.

Tomorrow will be our first day of rest for many weeks. I tried to get the chaplain to come from the other island for a service, but he won't be able to come until next week. He hopes to make it every other week from now on.

Well, what did I tell you about the military? The Skipper just phoned to tell me that a Marine major has arrived to take over that assignment of mine!

Last night I sat outside my tent, gazed at the moon and stars through the palms, then looked at the reflection of the moon on the water. It was so beautiful. The more I looked at it, the more I thought of you, and the more homesick I got. I was just on the point of breaking down; then I realized it was useless to go on feeling that way. So I took a walk and, much to my surprise, fell asleep as soon as I hit the sack.

I'm writing this on another island as I wait for the Skipper. In addition to my other duties, I am now on the coding board here, on a basis of eight hours on and thirty-two hours off. That gives me a chance to accomplish quite a lot at our own island between shifts.

I must quote you a paragraph from Miss Carlson's last letter about the day the staff from my Prudential office spent with you. "I thought you might like to hear about your family from an outsider, Mr. Fibush. You don't have to worry about them. They are fine, and everyone agreed that they are the best-mannered children they had ever seen. Your wife is fine too and, aside from the fact that they all miss you so much, they seem to be very happy." Her little sister wrote, "I was afraid at first that I wouldn't get to go for lack of space in the cars, and I wanted to go so badly. We all had a wonderful time. You are so lucky to have such a nice family. Your wife is so nice, and your children are so good. That in itself is worth fighting for, isn't it?" It looks as though our children do put their best feet forward sometimes.

The big news is OUR MESS HALL IS FINISHED! What a pleasure to be able to eat without flies. The mess hall also makes a fine officers' wardroom with comfortable chairs and space to sit around and relax.

That beautiful new wallet which Ken gave me is getting moldy from this climate. I could use a new one any time. I hope you can find one. . . .

November 6, 1943

Hello, Honey!

Mabel and Rusty took me to a show at St.Mary's tonight. What a treat it was. I think you said you saw it—Olivia De Haviland in "Princess O'Rourke." We just about killed ourselves laughing.

The St Mary's campus has certainly changed since that beautiful spring day in '29 when we went there for the Cal baseball game—our third date. Instead of just one building and a playing field without bleachers, there are several of them now, all beautifully landscaped with acres of lovely green lawns.

Today, right after lunch Leslie came to wash, and the mail arrived at exactly the same time. After reading what you said about airmail sometimes having to go by ship, I can see why the P.O. is adamant about not sending unnecessary things.

I received a note from Rae today which said that Harry's induction date is the 28th. They'll be moving in here on the 27th.

Judy misses you so much. She always asks for an extra hug and kiss from Daddy when I put her to bed. I could use a few of the same myself!

I just finished paying the bills, including the taxes. I wanted to be sure how I stood before buying materials for the bathroom. It will be a pretty tight squeeze until I get that paid for. However, I think I can do it without letting the bank account go below $100.

As soon as Sunday School was over this morning, I got all the children into sleepers, tacked up a silvery "Merry Christmas" sign and four stuffed socks over the fireplace. Dan took their pictures for our Christmas card. I think it should be good.

I saw Bunny for a minute this morning. He said it sounds as though you are on an atoll. He said to be sure to ask you to send us some of the lovely shells and "cat's eyes" you find there. It is time to say, "Goodnight, my Darling."

November 8, 1943

Honey Dearest:

We got a kick out of your description of the contents of the boxes you unpacked. Donny was slightly horrified at the idea of your taking a shower right out in the open with nothing on! Beverly is rather distressed because you haven't "gotten any Japs[1] yet." She wants you to "get some Japs and Hitler and Hirohito. Is he as tough as Japs? Tough as Hitler?" They thought it was a good joke for you to be talking about Halloween coming soon, when it's already over.

---

[1]This may sound crude and racist, but in the frenzy of war no one ever thought of calling our nearest and most dangerous enemy anything else.

The plumber came this afternoon. He hopes to start tomorrow, have it all roughed in by Wednesday. Then the carpentry work can start on Thursday. The materials came to $23.32. Latest news bulletin! We have a mole in our new lawn!

November 10, 1943

When I wrote that date I suddenly remembered what date it was. I felt terrible that I forgot to celebrate with Donny this morning the fact that it was nine years ago today that we brought home our adored, eight-weeks-old first son. Also it is a year-and-a-half today since we brought home our bubbly, dancing, dimpled, and smiling all over but scared to death little Judy. What wonderfully exciting and happy times we have had.

Donny brought Duane home from school and wanted him to stay all night. They insisted that Duane's mother said it was ok, if it was all right with me. They had a wonderful time all afternoon and were late coming to the table. It turned out that Donny had been coaching Duane in table manners! Also Duane had suggested that one must always comb one's hair before going to the table. So here they came all slicked up. It came out in the course of the meal that Duane hadn't had anything to eat all day. He certainly enjoyed the dinner, and it seemed to make the others eat better, just seeing how much he enjoyed it.

After dinner we dressed Bev for the Fathers and Daughters party. She wore a pale blue frosted organdy trimmed with insertion and lace. It was to have been a banquet, but at the last minute (yesterday) they sent home notices that the Office Of Price Administration would allow them less than a ration point per person, and they couldn't get a meal on that. It was too late to get parents to donate ration points. So the Dads' Club just had entertainment and cookies.

George Brown had phoned to see if he could take Bev, so had Bob Underhill and Gary Brown, but I had already arranged for her to go with Tom Slaven.

NOVEMBER 11, 1943, ARMISTICE DAY

Honey Dearest:

Jack just told me he'll stay home from work on Saturday and work for me for $1 an hour. He said that by the time he got dressed, drove to Berkeley, paid income tax, social security, and all that, not to mention the gas, he would save by staying home and working for me. Grandpa Underhill will work here both Friday and Saturday with Jack. I'm in luck!

Donny had a happy holiday with Duane here. He wants to be Donny's brother so badly, which thrills Donny to pieces. He keeps us all amused with his droll way of talking. He started one of his tales with, "The time we lived in the house that had a bathtub——." We were all weeding the lawn together, and I was telling them about four-leaf clovers being lucky. He said "I gotta find a four-leaf clover. Then maybe I can get to be Donny's brother." Goodnight, Honey.

November 14, 1943

Dearest Mine:

Perhaps you would like to know a little about this island. Compared to the one on which we are living, it seems almost as crowded as New York City! It is crammed with tents all very close together. There is so much noise, constantly, that it is hard to get any sleep even if not on duty. The water supply here is even less satisfactory than at our island, both in quantity and quality. However the tents are decked and screened, which is a big plus. No creepy crawly things and I was able to sleep undisturbed for four hours after twenty-two hours on duty. The work we are doing here is very fatiguing.

We had a real treat at dinner—real honest to goodness ice cream. It was given to us by one of the ships that came in.

"An extremely interesting evening," doesn't necessarily mean a raid, and I couldn't tell you if it did. We still can't even say where our last island was.

Today was a fairly easy day and a very interesting one, since I was getting all the news hot off the wire in the coding room. I worked on my Navy regs for several hours, and after that Doc gave me my annual examination. He says I am in perfect health, even better than a year ago. My chest expansion is one inch greater, my blood pressure is perfect.

I have just finished cleaning my 45. Did you ever think I would be having one of those things, the way I feel about guns?

Our sick bay will now be a quonset hut, and we will have one for our office, too. Remember at Port Hueneme how terrible I thought they were? Well, here we consider them the last word in luxury, and in fact they are.

A fond goodnight from your loving Honey

November 15, 1943

Dearest Honey:

I just learned that all the pictures we have taken for the last three months, including our Christmas card pictures, are blanks. I could die! Rusty can't get more film for us yet. He is allowed only one roll a month.

Rae and I have made the following arrangement. She will pay $50 a month for room and board for herself and Stevie. She will buy Frances' formula and baby food separately. She plans to use her Prudential check, plus the profit she makes from subleasing their house, toward a down payment on a house when Harry gets back. She should be able to put nearly $50 a month in the bank.

The room you built upstairs for Donny will be perfect for Stevie. You did a wonderful job. Right now Jack is upstairs finishing the bathroom. I plan to put on the flat coat tomorrow and the enamel the two following days. The linoleum man can't come until the day after Thanksgiving, but we'll have it all done JUST in time if all goes well. What an accomplishment!

Mrs. Harter has had wonderful news. Her son David is in a German prison camp, and she is so relieved. Jack just told me Stuart Wade heard that Chuck Wood might be alive. A friend of his who was supposed to have died in that same camp has turned up in another camp.

Shopping gets more and more wearing. The new ration books are a labyrinth. I have given up trying to figure them out. I buy what we simply have to have if I can find it, and hope for the best. So far I have gotten by all right.

We have a new system at mealtime. Only those who eat all their dinner and do it without dawdling interminably can go out to the rumpus room and kiss Rusty good night. Beverly was the only one who made it tonight. Her appetite has improved considerably with this incentive!

We had roast lamb today! That leg of lamb was a real splurge—$2.65. I should have saved it for Thanksgiving or some other splendid occasion, but I hadn't seen one for so long that I couldn't resist. I roasted it at low heat, and the house smelled wonderful all afternoon. Oh Golly! I miss you Honey.

November 17, 1943

Hello my Honey:

The children want to know what a bull session is. They were so tickled with your description of a bucket bath. Beverly was very upset because you cut your leg and couldn't go swimming. I nearly got killed in the rush when I gave them their extra hugs and kisses from you.

I talked to Donny's teacher yesterday. She is delighted with the way he is improving. Apparently she takes a certain amount of mischief for granted, but she is as eager as I am to break up the two Donnys. She says D.R. is always distracting him and trying to get him to start something.

This morning Rusty asked me where the switch to the furnace is and I said, "right by my bed." Mabel said, "Now he'll know just where to go when he wants to get warm, won't he?" Tsk! Tsk! Disgusting conversation, isn't it my darling? You had better come home and protect my honor!!!

It has been a dark and windy day, with leaves falling fast and furiously. About six this morning it started to pour, much to our delight. Donny put on his rain things and took a flashlight to go for the milk and eggs.

Chuck kissed your picture tonight. His idea of a kiss is to open his mouth very wide and flatten his nose against the object being kissed. He loves the flag we hung in his room and asks for it several times a day. He just wants to hold it a minute and then put it back. We always march around with it singing, "It's A Grand Old Flag." He gets so excited.

News flash! Bernice's mother got some film and is mailing it. We'll be able to get pictures on Sunday. Now just watch it rain all weekend!....

Dear Daddy:

I have been very busy. Please write me every Monday. We had a good time at Marge and John's ranch. We also went on two fairy boats.

How are you, I got some new shoes. When we got are report cards my teacher wrote on the back Donny's work has been improving and he has made much progress in adjusting socially. Keep em flying Daddy.

Love, Donny Fibush Jr.

November 19, 1943

Honey Dearest:

Today I went to Oakland for towel bars, light fixture, shower curtain, and linoleum. I stopped at every radio place in town. Each one said they are positive there are no more tubes of that number to be had anywhere. I guess we'll have no more music or news until the war is over.

On the way home I picked up a lady whose car had stalled. She had gotten stuck in the mud near the Army camp, had left her baby and a friend in the car, and hitchhiked to Lafayette to get a tow car. They had to send for one, and she had been gone for over two hours. She had been thumbing for an hour, and no one would stop for her. She was so thrilled when we took her back to her car.

NEXT DAY. Today I received your letter of Nov 9th. I really needed that letter. This was not a great day! After getting to bed at midnight, I heard someone creeping past my window at 5:30 a.m. I called out to see who it was, very quietly at first and then louder. As I had suspected, it was Donny and Billy Nagler, who was here for an overnight. They were dressed and ready for adventure! I was furious. I sent Billy back upstairs and Donny to Chuck's room, with orders to stay in bed till nine! Fortunately they went back to sleep, but I didn't. I got through today in sort of a haze of tiredness.

We have a dog, darn it! The army camp was ordered to get rid of its dogs. Donny was sick over little Blackie because they were going to shoot him. So I weakened, and we went after him just before dinner. He was lonesome and shivery tonight, so I let him sleep with Donny.... Goodnight Honey.

November 21, 1943

My own dear Sweetheart:

I have been sitting here in a hammock suspended between two palm trees, facing the setting sun. As the sun approached the horizon, the color of the sky, clouds, and water kept changing. They took on almost all the colors of the rainbow. It was beauty at its best—indescribable. The stars seem even more beautiful and numerous here than they do at home on a night without a moon.

The quonset hut for the enlisted men has been completed, and they expect to start on the one for the officers tomorrow. We should be pretty well fixed by the time the heavy rains come. If what we have had so far isn't considered heavy, I am wondering what is!

It's amazing what has been accomplished in six weeks. I think the boys deserve a a big hand for getting so much done in such a short time.

I have the duty tonight and just wasted an hour playing ping pong. Bob and I spent the afternoon fixing up the officers' wardroom so we can all enjoy it and relax there, as well as having our meals. When we completed it, he wanted to break in the ping pong table we had made out of sheets of five ply.

First we cut and nailed Masonite tops on the chow tables. We broke out eight comfortable chairs, put in light fixtures, set up a table for magazines, books, radio, and a small Victrola. After that we made the ping pong table and then took a quick swim before chow.

As I finished posting the watch the mail arrived, so I came over here to read in luxury and ease without insects of any kind.

NEXT DAY. Right now we have a little lull so I am going to get this started. I am all in because I spent a very strenuous hour in the dentist's chair this afternoon. He found about four hours' worth of work to be done, but he has to crowd so many men in, he didn't even have time to polish my teeth after he cleaned them. He found a cavity, took out a filling and part of a tooth in order to fix it. He seems to know what he is doing, and he certainly works fast but with total disregard for all pain.

How I wish you were here with me—or rather that I was there with you. I'm in love with you, Honey. Did you know that?

Dear Daddy:

I love you. At play school we couldn't go out in the rain because it was so wet and we'll get our shoes so wet and dirty, so I played with clay and we colored and I made a pretty doll with bells all over and stripes and all colors. And I worked and worked and worked. Then I went at the school and I came home with Beverly on the school bus. And we had fun. And the bus was so crowded and I stand up and Beverly stands up.

Leaves are dancing as the autumn winds go by, and Humpty Dumpty— but you know that one. Do you know about birdie with a yellow bill? You love Judy don't you Daddy? Please be careful not to get killed in the war. I love you.

Judy

November 23, 1943

Dearest Honey:

You won't be particularly interested in the letter when you see what else is in the envelope. I am pretty thrilled about the way the pictures turned out. I'm hoping we can print the Christmas cards next week. I have gone through our list and hope to get it down to 125.

Donny went up to the camp after school and brought Blackie back again. He came eagerly, and though he still won't eat, he certainly is devoted to Donny. He is lying here in the kitchen as I type, and occasionally gives a whine.

You should have heard the conversation Donny and I had about some dirty expressions he picked up from Billy. Honestly—I can't even bring myself to type the words. He started in by asking me, and ended up by telling me, what things meant, bringing in girls' anatomy and everything imaginable. I was floored. Most of the words I had never even heard before.

I'm hoping that Harry can do something with Donny's radio so that we can at least have that to use. I guess we may as well accept the fact that our radio-phonograph is out for the duration.

What a marvelous day! SEVEN letters! It was like Christmas, opening them, getting them in chronological order and reading them over and over.

The children got their report cards today. Donny got "Satisfactory" in all his subjects except P.E. in which he received "I" for Needs Improvement. In his "Attitude" grades he received "Satisfactory." His teacher's comment on the back was that he minds other people's business too well but that he was improving greatly and showing much more interest in his work. Oh, I forgot the most important part. He received an O (Outstanding) in spelling. He thought it meant zero and was very upset. Beverly got Satisfactory in all her grades and in her attitudes.

Almost all the leaves have fallen now, and everything is carpeted in gold. I have been thinking all day and all evening what a very lucky person I am to have someone I love, who loves me so much and writes such beautiful letters. It's very cold tonight, and the owls are busily "hoo hooing." Since it's already past midnight, I guess I had better say "Goodnight" or should I be saying "Good Morning, My Darling?"

November 24, 1943

Dearest:

Poor little Blackie didn't want to sleep on the back porch last night, and it was after two before he finally settled down. Then, the minute the linoleum man opened the back door this morning, he was gone. I guess we'll leave him up at the camp until Friday, since we will be gone all day tomorrow. He would be so miserable here alone.

The linoleum is laid, and it looks beautiful. The pale turquoise ceiling, walls, and door look lovely with the white fixtures and the shower curtain and waste basket in a soft yellow. When I get the fluffy white curtains up again, I think Rae and Harry will be very pleased with it.

After dinner tonight Rusty brought their turkey in here so the children could watch him clean it. They were fascinated.

McNeils' Dairy started delivering milk to us today. I explained the whole situation to them, and they said they would do their best to let us have a gallon every four days. They only deliver that often now. As soon as some other customer drops out, we can get more. That's a help anyhow. Of course with so many of us, we really need that much every day.

I feel all jumpy and jittery tonight. I'm dying to go somewhere and do something, and I am tired of having no one to lean on. Oh what a clinging vine I am going to be when the war is over. Let me warn you right now, you'd better be real nice to me when you get home and take good care of me. You and a few other people seem to think that I was a pretty good sport to let you join the Navy, but when the war is over, I am all through being a good sport! PLEASE don't ever consider accepting a big promotion to the Home Office in Newark if you should be offered it. PLEASE let our life settle down to normal on Springhill Road. Let's raise our children without any more disturbances.

I wish you were here calling to me to, "Hurry up and get done with your hair and face and come to bed sometime!" Oh well, I guess I'll go fill up the hot water bottle instead. Good night, my Very Dear One.

November 25, 1943

Dearest Honey:

This morning Mrs. Ingram phoned to say that she had some bad reports on our children. She said they went over to their old garage by the creek, broke into it, took stuff, broke a jug of motor oil, left broken glass all over the place, and took their son's football. They were away at the time, but Mr. Summers saw them. I thought I would die! I started to cry as I hung up, and I couldn't stop. I didn't see how I could face the day. It turned out that it was Donny and Billy last Saturday. Donny claims that Billy did it, even though he told him not to, and they both ran when they saw Mr. Summers. However, he was absolutely blank about the football.

As soon as he was dressed to go into Berkeley, I had him go up to the Ingrams' to explain it to them and tell them that, since Billy was his guest, it was his responsibility, and he would do whatever they wanted. He also told them he didn't remember seeing a football. It turned out that the football was not in the garage, but in their son's closet! They warned Donny that if anything like that ever happened again, they would call the police.

As a result of all this, I was a wreck and had a splitting headache the rest of the day. Donny behaved beautifully at the folks' and stuffed himself with two helpings of everything, just as a boy should on Thanksgiving Day. The girls enjoyed themselves immensely but had a hard time finishing everything their Grandpa had put on their plates.

We loaded everything into the car, including John's old Victrola, with the help of a young sailor they had invited for dinner. Then we went to get gas, since the gauge was registering "empty." I went to eleven gas stations before I found one that was open. I was getting pretty nervous by that time.

After we got home, Dan came over to help me carry the Victrola upstairs, and the children had a wonderful time playing their records for the first time in ages. So did I! Goodnight, Honey.

THANKSGIVING DAY

Dearest Sweetheart:

Well, we certainly had a real Thanksgiving dinner. It lasted over an hour, and we have all been trying to talk and walk it off ever since. Our cooks stayed up most of the past two nights preparing it, and they certainly did themselves proud. We had large helpings of everything one could possibly have on Thanksgiving, and seconds of anything we wanted. It was all excellent.

Some of the officers came up from the other island, and we had quite a gathering. Afterwards the enlisted men had the Victrola hooked up to a loud speaker, and we had a community sing, plus an excellent quartet of our colored boys, and a talk from the Skipper.

NEXT DAY. This morning I worked steadily at the office, then two of the colored boys swabbed the deck of our new headquarters so we could move in. We worked hard all afternoon but have barely started. It will take at least two more days to unpack everything and get settled. I am going to make a storage cabinet, since our carpenters are all too busy.

Did I tell you that the natives all come over to this island about once a month to get coconuts and taro? These natives aren't nearly as clean as the ones on our first island, and they are much more primitive, but they are even more friendly. When they spear a fish, they eat it raw, head and all, not even cleaned. Little boys smaller and younger than Donny, as well as the men and older boys, climb right up the coconut trees, just like monkeys. The trees are slick and straight like telephone poles and usually around sixty feet tall. They weave buckets out of the palm branches, sling two of them on each end of a stick which they carry over their shoulders. This enables each of them to carry about four dozen at a time. I guess that's all for tonight, Honey.

Part Five

NOVEMBER 27, 1943 – MAY 31, 1944

TWO'S COMPANY, BUT TWELVE IS
VERY DEFINITELY A CROWD!

November 27, 1943

Dearest Honey:

Am I tired! And imagine how tired poor Rae and Harry must be. He and his friend Walter arrived at noon with Stevie and the first truckload. They had a bite of lunch and were gone again by one. It was after six when they arrived with Rae, Frances, and the second load.

Our dinner was catch-as-catch-can. It was obvious that Rae was completely worn out, and I wanted to get her to bed, but she refused to go. When Harry and Walter went after the third load, the truck stalled on the San Mateo Bridge. It was needed at 11 p.m. to transport shipyard workers to the graveyard shift, and they barely returned it in time. All they could bring in the car was the chickens!

NEXT DAY. Harry rented a trailer this morning so they could go after the last load. At the end of the day they arrived exhausted.

It's raining, and it sounds delightful. However, it's not so good for Harry, since he plans to start building the chicken house tomorrow.

I must tell you how cute Chuckie was today. I put him out in back, tied to a tree by a very long rope so he could watch Harry work on the chicken house. For two hours he sat watching Harry's every move. It was fun to watch him with a rapt expression on his uplifted face, his head moving back and forth like a spectator at a tennis match. He would jabber away in his own special language, and Harry would answer him.

While this was going on, Leslie was washing clothes. They are buying Rae's washer, but Harry didn't have room to bring it yet. Eight families are using our Bendix now. If the time ever comes when people can buy machines again, or even get theirs fixed, our poor Bendix will certainly have done it's "war duty"! It does an average of thirty-five loads a week.

I got the plumber's bill today and nearly collapsed. It was $289.50! He had originally quoted me a price of "about $163." His itemized bill listed every hour of labor and each piece of material. He said he had to pay his helper $18.50 a day! He charged six hours labor for each of them for going to S.F. to get the shower stall instead of getting it over here at Sears and having it delivered.

I tried to get Beverly's new shoes repaired. She has had them only a few weeks, but they need new soles. There's no chance of getting them back in less than a month. I don't know what to do. We are out of shoe ration stamps.

The children are enjoying Rae's good cooking and are eating well. Me too! Today she cooked a tongue and also baked a lemon pie and some apple dumplings.

I forgot to tell you an amazing coincidence I just discovered. My Dad gave Donny another bunch of boys' second hand books. One of them, by William S. Hart, had YOUR signature on the flyleaf. Isn't that amazing? Can you figure that one out? Weren't you still living in Wyoming when you were that age? No one in your family can figure it out either. It's like the fairy tale about the tin soldier who fell out the window into a stream, was eaten by a fish that was finally served at dinner to the family where he had originally lived. . . .

November 29, 1943

My Love of My Dreams:

You mentioned a woman checker at Safeway. Have you seen any others? Can you imagine Prudential hiring a woman? That reminds me, I hear that some of the Prudential wives are pitching in and taking their husbands' places now that they have been drafted. I wonder how that will work out.

Today, because we were so anxious to move into our new headquarters, Bob, the two yeomen, and I worked like Trojans. First we shortened sixty table legs and arranged fifteen desks and chairs, then made cabinets out of the crates. I was afraid we might have a tidal wave from all our perspiration.

The Skipper arrived again in the middle of the night. Starting very early this morning, he and I worked hard and fast. We cleaned up a lot of details that needed attention badly. Then I took the boat to the other island to transact a lot of the end-of-the-month business of the unit. While there I picked up mail, which included three letters from you and my birthday gift from Ken and Esther, a small compact chess set ideal for shipboard, and the Oakland Tribune for September 26th. The program from the Cal-U.S.C. game also arrived.

It's surprising that I get such a thrill out of a newspaper that old, but in a way it makes me feel at home. The program was passed around to each of the fellows here, and everyone read it avidly. We noticed that practically all of the players were Army, Navy or Marines.

This morning they finally decked our tents. We have the best location of all. It's right on the point where we get whatever breeze there is and is handy to the wardroom, the office, sick bay, and the head. Next they are going to put on screen doors. Then we will be living in the lap of luxury.

Please let me know how much it would cost to have the driveway properly paved and whether you could get it done. I think I could pay for it in two or three months, if I am very careful.

Last night I went to bed for the first time in our new and luxurious tent. Not only does it have screened windows and door, but also awnings, an electric light, a double socket for shaving, a small table, and individual lockers. . . .

CHRISTMAS CARD TO DADDY

DEAR DADDY

I HOPE THAT YOU HAVE A NICE MERRY CHRISTMAS
AND A HAPPY NEW YEAR.

I LOVE YOU.

BEVERLY FIBUSH

December 2, 1943

My Own Sweet Big Boy:
I was so happy today to receive another letter from you. You are writing better letters all the time, and I enjoy them so much.

Tell me all about Blackie. Mother says he likes you very much. She also says you're getting along much better in school, and that makes me very happy.

Thank you for sending the paper you wrote about Sir Frances Drake which was marked 100. I'll bet you were tickled. I'm so proud of you. . . .

December 2, 1943

Honey Dearest:
This morning we had a heavy frost, and our Butane froze again. Stevie and Rae have colds, and we need the heat so badly. The butane man was furious when he got here, and he wanted to know if we kept the house at ninety degrees twenty-four hours a day. He said he filled it two weeks ago and couldn't continue to come that often. When I told him it was being used by three families, he said Coast Counties Gas would have to put in another tank.

This morning the girls missed the bus, so I drove them and then stopped at Sally's to talk about our boys and the Ingram episode. She sort of laughed it off. Maybe that is why Billy does so many irresponsible things. Personally I don't think it was anything to laugh about. I know "boys will be boys," but when it comes to other peoples property, that is definitely out of bounds.

I am so mad! I have a date at the blood bank tomorrow, but I have a cold, and they won't accept me.

Tonight Rae and Harry are developing pictures in the kitchen and also doing Mabel and Rusty's Christmas cards. As a result, we have quite a houseful. People keep breezing in and out—Dan, Bernice, Philip, Mabel, and Rusty. Your box of coconuts arrived, and everyone was excited. I decided I had better distribute them immediately before the milk got dried into pulp like the other one did. Right now Harry is having fun drilling a hole in a coconut with his electric drill. I spilled all the milk out of the one I tried to open. He says he wants to do this one very "scientifically."

That darned mess of Navy papers about our travel pay to join you last June came back AGAIN, asking for another bunch of signatures. . . .

December 6, 1943

Dearest Mine:

We have now improvised a shower behind the officers' tents. It consists of a scaffolding about seven feet high with a shower head and an on-off switch. The pipe attached to the head is also attached to the bottom of a bucket at the top of the scaffolding to feed it by gravity. The colored boys fill it every day, and we can each have about a bucketful of rain water.

This has been an exceptionally busy day. We had to send one of our chiefs back to the States because of severe arthritis. Also, we finally received orders for flight training for one of our enlisted men and are happy for him. These things require inordinate amounts of paper work. That one demanded three complicated applications, each one taking six hours of my time.

You probably think I spend a super-abundance of time talking about insects and other wildlife. Well, I do. The latest oversupply we have is lizards. They are everywhere, in our beds, lockers, shoes, clothes, desks, wardroom, the head— you name it. They are about the same size as those at home and come in a great variety of colors and stripes. We also have ants that can hop and fly, not termites, ants. Also thousands of moths in all sizes and colors.

Honey, please write a letter telling me all about you—just you—how you look, how you feel (aside from lonesome) how much you weigh, what color nail polish you are using, how you are fixing your hair. I feel as though I have been gone so long, I don't know you any more.

DECEMBER 7TH. This is quite an eventful date, isn't it? Four months since I said goodbye to you at Port Hueneme and two years since Pearl Harbor. All day long my thoughts have been on those two days. On that "Day of Infamy" little did we dreeam that two years later we would be thousands of miles apart.

I have a feeling we will be leaving about two weeks before Bev's birthday. There's lots of scuttlebut as to where we will go. The prevalent guess is, it will be where Charlie was. Did you get that clue? Being forced to give you only clues, rather than just saying, "We will be leaving on. . . . and going to . . . .", is so DARNED frustrating!

I keep thinking about the Baby and how blue she must be feeling. I'm glad she and Harry were to have those few days together at the last. How do you like having the six children you have always said you wanted?

According to your letter you would like to go places and do things. So would I—the place I would like to go is HOME! Goodnight my love.

December 8, 1943

Honey:

It is the strangest night for December. The moon is beautiful, not quite full, but pretty super-deluxe just the same. There is also a howling wind, a warm wind. It was such a lovely day. Our green carpet is finally coming up under the pear trees, giving the impression that we are living in a huge park.

Already the narcissus and the crassifolia saxifraga are saturating us with their color and fragrance. By Christmas who knows what may be blooming.

When you talk about "decking the tents," my mind starts singing, "Deck the halls with boughs of holly fa la la la la, la la la la." Then I remember you are talking about putting in floors, not hanging garlands of greens!

The two Donnys and Duane had a fight today which took them all over the backyard, kitchen, through the hall, out the front door, into the garage, and up to the attic. It was over a sailor hat which D.R. claimed they had taken from him. Duane claimed D.R. had taken it out of his locker. They finally got him to admit it wasn't his.

NEXT DAY. You should see us. Rae and I are sitting here in the kitchen wrapped in robes and blankets writing to our husbands by the light of a Coleman lantern and one small candle. Last night due to the storm, the electricity went off and is still off, twenty-three-and-a-half hours later.

That was SOME storm. The wind continued to blow a gale. The trees and shrubbery were stripped bare. The leaves were blown in huge drifts several feet high against the house. The garage door wouldn't lock and kept going up and down all night. Now the inside is banked solidly with leaves.

Rae and Harry had taken our car to San Francisco and had very considerately filled the tank at a service station, instead of from our tank. Apparently the attendant didn't fasten the hood securely when he checked the oil, because while crossing the bridge the wind blew the hood up, and it was badly battered by the time they were across and able to stop and fasten it.

We didn't know when to wake up this morning, with no clock operating. Donny went upstairs with a lighted candle to look at the cuckoo clock and discovered it was 7:15! What a mad scramble! They made the bus at eight o'clock, but I don't know how on earth they did it. We kept our babies warm around the open oven door. Thank goodness our stove and water heater are on butane gas.

When I took Rae to the train to see Harry off, the lights in the tunnel were off. Fires were raging in Montclair and East Oakland, and quite a number of people were evacuated. Schools were dismissed. Driving was very difficult. The wind was coming in such strong gustss that my speed went from twenty to fifty-two miles an hour without any change in my acceleration. It was disconcerting and nerve wracking to say the least.

When I got to the folks', I called Mrs. Wood. They have finally received official word that their son Chuck died last February. They weren't even notified until March that he was missing! All that terrible suspense and hope, and now this. How my heart aches for them. They also found out from friends that all of the other boys in his unit are in the prison at Cebu and alive.

When we got home I discovered the wind had blown the window and the screen out of the back door.

OH! OH! OH! What a thrill! The lights just went on. We were beginning to feel as though we might spend the rest of our lives living like this. . . .

December 10, 1943

Dearest Mine:

For the past twenty-four hours we have had gale winds which have almost reached hurricane proportions. Every fifteen minutes or so a torrential downpour coming from every direction hits the ground almost horizontally. When I drove to Headquarters this morning the wind carried fine particles of coral which stung my face and hands. At one time it was so bad I had to stop the car and turn it in the opposite direction. The tall palm trees swayed as much as twenty to thirty feet. Strangely I didn't see one branch come down, although in one place I saw the telephone wire fall across the road just as I had driven past it. The palm trees serve as telephone poles.

We have no tops on the jeeps and don't have the windshield up, as it gets so muddy we can't see. I was completely exposed but was prepared with my pith helmet and poncho. Consequently I really had an enjoyable and exciting trip.

We have reached the stage I have been dreading—all caught up with our work. We're anxious to receive orders to move on. We do have a definite job here, but the Army could take it over now that we have it established.

Last night Doc, Ted, George, Bob, and I had a picnic and bull session. It lasted until almost 1 a.m. Since it was way after lights out, we had to use flashlights. Our feed consisted of crackers, American cheese, club salad, chocolate, ice water, and coca cola. After that I slept like a baby in spite of the storm that was raging.

TWELVE MORE SHOPPING DAYS UNTIL CHRISTMAS! That's the headline today in the paper from the other island. That is just one of the crazy things they do out here. For example, you should see the signs. One fale has a sign, "Peaceful Inn, Hot and Cold Running Maids." The main road through our camp, which is completely filled with water from the storm, has a big sign, "Riverside Drive."

I read an article today about freezers for the home after the war. Can you imagine that? It certainly would be wonderful.

Thirteen days since I received a letter from you. All of us are getting pretty low. Even Bob said this morning, "If this continues much longer, you and I are going to have to get plastered" and, as you know, he never touches a drop, nor does he smoke or swear. Burying ourselves in books is wearing thin.

Since my Schick is giving me so much trouble, I gave up and used my safety razor. I hope my face won't start breaking out again. If you can possibly get a new head, please send it insured airmail.

December 11, 1943

Honey:

Harry planned to paint our car, clean the gutters, fix the screens, and do some of the heavy digging, but he didn't have time. It was disappointing.

Your screening sounds fine. I didn't intend that to be a pun, but there it is!

Rae has been terribly low, so that makes me feel low, too. She took charge yesterday while I dropped the girls at school, had my hair done, and mailed the fifty Christmas cards which I had addressed while my hair was drying.

Since it was Friday, I had told the children we could have movies after dinner. First we had the new reel showing Chuckie from five to sixteen months. Oh how I wish you could see it. After that we went through some of the older movies, and everyone got such a kick out of them.

Today when Betty Jean arrived, the girls watched Rae make cookies. When she tried to light the oven, it exploded. I don't understand how she managed to remain intact. Her eyebrows and lashes are singed. The explosion moved the stove almost an inch off its base, threw the tea kettle across the room, and blew open every window in the house except the ones upstairs which have double hung sash. It knocked things off the walls and scared us all to death.

I am so tired of all these colds that everyone keeps getting. Today Mrs. Hoffer said she has read that after the war (there's that old familiar phrase again), there won't be any more colds.

The moon is beautiful tonight. Everywhere I look I see a picture, the white sand framed by the green sand box, glistening in the moonlight, the winding path to the Condits' sparkling like snow, the moonbeams filtering through the bare branches of the pear trees. It's lovely.

Yesterday we took Stevie to Dr. Beede since his croup is still so bad. By some miracle he was able to take us right away. When he examined Stevie, he told Rae that apparently he has inherited her bronchial tendency, and the pollens in Lafayette are bringing it out. Rae liked him very much in spite of the fact that she had gone feeling that he was "just a country doctor."

I tried to Christmas shop today, but it is hard to find anything at all worth buying. I did find a dress for myself. It's the kind that will make me wonder how I ever got along without it. You will love it.

Poor Rae. Harry phoned to say he was leaving Monterey in an hour, going by bus to Salinas, then by train to Mississippi. So much for her plans to spend a weekend with him occasionally. When she asked him if he was lonesome he said he hadn't had time. She said he could have at least lied about it!

Jack brought us a beautiful Christmas tree from his folks' ranch. I hope we can put it up tomorrow. . . . Good night Honey.

December 15, 1943

My precious Honey:

Tonight Mabel and Rusty took me to a grand vaudeville show at St Mary's. The show was one of those traveling shows put on by Shell. There was a female ventriloquist with three darling little dummies, all children. It was amazing the way she threw her voice around those three. Next was an excellent and very pretty magician, with a knockout figure and a personality to match. A very clever pianist gave an impersonation of Ethel Waters singing, "My Handy Man." The words were rather suggestive but kind of cute. The music made me miss you unbearably, especially, "I've Got Rhythm," which reminded me of the day we got my engagement ring and went dancing at Roberts-At-The-Beach. When all the boys sang "White Christmas," I thought I would die!

Today we walked up to the Imries to see if Johnny had any outgrown shoes for Chuck. I tried yesterday at twelve stores, without success. Unfortunately Betty didn't have any the right size either. She finally received a letter from her parents who have been in a Jap prison camp near Manilla for two years. This is the first she has heard. Her mother, who is very petite, has lost thirty five pounds from having sprue, which is a form of dysentery.

It was an extremely good letter, written very objectively without making the place sound too wonderful or too horrible. Her father has a cute little sense of humor which Betty says is unmistakably his, so she is sure it is authentic. There have been cases of people receiving fake letters.

I think your suggestions for the children helping me more are unrealistic. They have a long hard day themselves and little time for play. They leave home at 7:45, getting back around four. They spend over two hours a day on the bus. I think for a nine-year-old to tend to his room, the trash, the cans,[1] the chickens, and help with the dishes occasionally is plenty. I don't think I should expect more of girls of five and seven than for them to tend to their room, help with the dishes and with the care of Chuck and Stevie.

NEXT DAY. This noon, just as I sat down to eat, I saw that the chickens were out again. Soon both Marky and Bernice noticed them and came over to help. Those darn hens! They are smart enough to know that we can't get at them when they are way back in the thick growth on the creek bank. To make a long story short, it was nearly six when with the combined efforts of Marky, Bernice, Donny, Mabel, Rusty, and Rae, they were finally back in their pen.

I hope to put up the tree tomorrow and decorate the whole house. I hate Christmas this year. Did you ever dream you would hear me say that?

---

[1] It was required that all cans be washed, peeled, and completely flattened.

December 18, 1943

Dearest Honey:

When we were ready to leave this morning, I realized that I no longer have a winter hat. The day that I got drenched in the cloudburst, the lady I picked up sat on it! I hate to go to church without one, but my other is white straw.

We sat up in the church balcony to have a good view of the children. Donny looked like a picture of a perfect little boy. If he acted that way all the time, my troubles would be over! Beverly and Judy were in the front row, mothering Philip and Susan and seeing that they stayed where they belonged. The music was especially lovely today.

After lunch Uncle George and Aunt Gertie arrived unexpectedly. We asked them to stay for dinner, figuring that somehow we could make it stretch. Uncle George took the children to Lafayette, bought them ice cream, candy, and potato chips (all of which made me furious) then gave them each a dollar. They also gave Rae some extra money, but she wasn't supposed to tell me because they were afraid I might get jealous!

Rae managed a sumptuous meal, using half a pound of hamburger to make a delicious meat loaf for eight, and ending with gingerbread with ice cream.

Don't feel like a heel when you tell me how lonesome you are. I hate to have you be that lonesome, but I love to hear about it!

NEXT DAY. This has been a bad day. Bev was feverish and fretful all night, and first thing this morning she started vomiting. This afternoon she was delirious. It seemed as though all I did was fly from Beverly to Frances and back to Beverly again to hold her head while she vomited. She was so weak and tired. This is a terrible time for her to be sick. She has been looking forward to so many holiday events.

Rae and Donny went to Oakland for the day with Marky and Susan. Donny did all his Christmas shopping, and Rae bought some lovely trims and braids for the dresses I'm making for the girls. You know what impeccable taste she has when it comes to things like that. She also brought me a darling little philodendron plant. It is green and chubby and so healthy looking. I am delighted with it.

The flu epidemic is getting really bad. The paper said there are now over a million cases in the U.S. Twenty six of Daddy's Chung Mei boys[1] are down with it, running Daddy and all the house mothers ragged.

---

[1]Chung Mei Home for Chinese Boys was established in Berkeley in 1922 by Dot's father, Rev. Charles Shepherd. For a variety of reasons there was an increasing number of young Chinese boys with inadequate supervision who were in danger of becoming delinquents. Because of prejudice against the Chinese they were not acceptable at the existing orphanages or other childrens' instutions.

Daddy phoned to tell me he actually found someone to fix my typewriter and is getting it completely fixed up for me for Christmas. Isn't that grand?

Rae received a telegram from Harry today and finally has his address. So she was able to send his Christmas box plus forty-three pages of letters she has written since he left. That lifted her spirits considerably. . . .

December 21, 1943

My Precious Dearest One:

Yesterday I received a wonderful Christmas package. It contained walnuts, raisins, and marvelous gifts. Donny sent lotion to keep me from getting more fungus. My precious Poochy sent what I needed so badly, razor blades, and my Honeybun sent something I need right now—air mail envelopes. I was almost out. Lucky me to have such thoughtful children! Thank you all so very much.

I also received a letter from Marky. She says she is a poor correspondent, but I don't agree. Please thank her for me for the letter and especially for taking care of my Christmas shopping. I hope all of you are surprised. I know it will take a lot of conniving on Marky's part.

Yesterday morning I was extremely busy at headquarters. After chow I REALLY went to work. Bob and I decided something must be done about the many cracks and holes in the floor and ceiling of our wardroom. As a result, it is now designated "Fibush Hall," but more commonly called "Firebrush Hall!" Shortly after I started, Bob joined me. When we were almost finished, several other officers helped. We put five ply throughout the place—decks, bulkheads, and under the eaves.

NEXT DAY. We are running out of paper and don't know when the next shipment will be here. I'm going to write this in one paragraph to save space. I received oodles of mail today, including seven letters from you. So I think I'll celebrate Christmas early as I did my birthday. You should have seen the rain this past twenty-four hours. It topped anything we have had so far. In two hours it filled a fifty-five gallon drum sitting under the eaves of one side of our fale. The lightning flashed throughout the night and day. Shortly after I arrived here this evening, it hit the corner of this building, but did no damage. The building is nine-tenths underground and is supposed to be bomb proof. It has coconut-palm logs for walls, and has a second roof on top of the regular roof, with sand bags on top of that. I can't get over that William S. Hart book turning up. I must tell Ken about it. It was one of our favorite books. It's really one for Ripley's " Believe It Or Not." As I recall, the last time I saw it was about the time of the Armistice—1918, while we were still in Utah. Yes, I remember the story of the tin soldier. It doesn't seem as far fetched now, does it? . . .

Please try to take things easier, Honey.

December 22, 1943

Honey:

Bev's flu has been really bad. Then yesterday morning, when Rae asked me if I would like an egg for breakfast, I made a face and replied I felt that I might be joining Bev. She made me go to bed so I could nip it in the bud. I got into Judy's bed to keep Beverly company. The only work I did all day was to carry weak and shaky Bev to the bathroom to heave. As a result of the enforced rest, I feel fine now. I guess I really did need that day in bed. It certainly was marvelous of Rae to make me take it.

I had Judy and Donny take naps so they would be in good shape for the party at church tonight. Bev was feeling better, so I helped her wrap and label her twelve packages. When Donny and Judy got up, we worked on theirs. The tree looks much more festive with thirty-six gayly wrapped packages under it.

I expect to finish the girls' corduroy jumpers tomorrow. They are absolute dreams, and I am so proud of them. It cost me $2.75 for the two of them, and they look as though they would cost at least $8.95 apiece in a store.

I bought each of the children a fifteen-cent record today and also a record of "Jingle Bells," and "Santa Claus is Coming To Town," sung by Bing Crosby with the Andrews sisters. Finding things for the stockings was hard.

I'm so glad you enjoyed your storm. It sounded absolutely fascinating. Isn't it nice we both enjoy that sort of weather? Because I do and make it so apparent, the children are the same way.

In the evening we had fun setting the table for Christmas dinner and putting more packages around the tree. Rusty laid a lovely big fire for us to light on Christmas morning. Tomorrow we cook and clean.

Oh, I forgot to tell you. Mrs. Summers came this morning with a bag of candy she had made for the children. Wasn't that sweet of her? (Ooops! Did I just make another pun?) I love you, I miss you, I want you, Honey.

CHRISTMAS NIGHT 1943

Honey:

Yesterday was a rather harrowing day. Rae didn't get a letter from Harry and was sunk in the depths of despair. Then we discovered Stevie's temperature was 103.2. There went the only thing she had been looking forward to—seeing him with his wagon and other toys on Christmas morning. She tried to send Harry a "Merry Christmas" telegram, but the operator, who was "only following orders, Ma'am," wouldn't accept it.

Hanging the stockings, reading "The Night Before Christmas," and the Christmas story from the second chapter of Matthew, gathering around the piano to sing carols, and tucking them all in bed were accomplished with anticipatory delight by all of them and a choking loneliness for me. The minute they were tucked away, I started to assemble the dollhouse which took two hours but was thoroughly enjoyable.

Tom Slaven picked up the radio tube which Miss Carlson finally succeeded in getting for us. THE TUBE WORKS! Now we can have Christmas music. What a difference that will make.

I am using my all-fixed-up typewriter, and it certainly feels good. Daddy and Mama gave me a $100 war bond, too. It has been a good day in spite of my dread. I finally completed everything about one this morning. Shortly after that, and again at 4:30, Donny came in to see if he could get his stocking, and I sent him back to bed. By the time I got up at 6:30, stocking contents were strewn everywhere, and I wondered why I had bothered to clean.

The children quickly downed substantial breakfasts, since we were all going wild with eagerness to get at the tree. I let Donny give out the presents. He got a blue polo shirt from Rae and a fort full of plastic soldiers plus a cowboy suit which he adores, from us. He also received a very nice looking coat sweater from his daddy! He couldn't understand how you could possibly have gotten it. It was certainly clever of you to have packages under the tree for us. They looked so pretty, and it was so exciting.

Your other gifts were: badly-needed slippers for me, a blue sweater for Beverly, for Judy a rose-colored one, and for Chuck, blue corduroy overalls.

Donny received defense stamps and books from the folks. They gave each of the girls a Storybook Doll, defense stamps, and nurse's kits. The four-room dollhouse, which I had made from two orange crates, was darling. I papered it with remnants from their room and ours and crocheted rugs for each room.

As soon as he saw the tree, Chuck spotted a huge brown teddy bear and started tugging at it. He finally got it and lugged it around with him all day.

The table looked beautiful with red candles and a centerpiece of greenery and silver balls. Besides the eight of us and my folks, there were John, Midge, Grandma Caplan, Babe and Mitch, Uncle Bob, Aunt Barbara, and Michael.

Stevie was pretty miserable, but he joined us for opening presents. Then Rae put him back to bed. Frances was a dream in a frilly little dress, with ribbons in her hair. She captivated everyone with her smiles. It was nice having such a big family, eighteen of us.

I wish you could have seen the living room last night. Six socks hanging on the mantle covered with greenery, a big red satin bow hanging from the center, and fat red candles at each end. The recessed window is piled with pine branches sprinkled with Christmas cards, a fat red candle in the center. The Christmas tree, about seven feet high, stands in the big window, and on the window sill, we have the little snow houses interspersed with tiny Christmas trees. The tree looked wonderful with the paper chains and strings of pop corn the children made, the ornaments, the lights, all the packages, and topped with a tiny pink teddy bear for Frances. As usual our Christmas cards are hanging in festoons all over the hall, and Rae made a lovely arrangement of narcissus in a white bowl for the carved Chinese table in the entry.

Well, I got through Christmas! Now the next thing is to get through New Year's Eve. It will seem strange to be doing nothing for the first time in fifteen years. Remember the Rose Bowl in 1929 when Cal played Georgia Tech, and Roy Riegels ran the wrong way for ninety yards? He was in my Econ class, and we all wondered how embarrassed he would feel and whether to look at him or not when he came to class on Monday morning.

I ache with fatigue after three-and-a-half hours sleep and wearing high heels all day. I wish you were here RIGHT NOW. Good night, Honey.

December 25, 1943

Dearest Mine:

I must describe the sunset tonight. Each night it's different and seems more beautiful. This one surpassed any we have seen previously. In every direction, beautiful rich colors appeared in the cloudless sky and reflected on the water. Each direction offered different colors and different shades of colors. Then, as clouds began to form in the east and north, the colors and reflections became even more spectacular. The entire western sky became a deep deep indigo. We were all fascinated and dropped everything to watch.

It seems unnecessary to tell you how I felt today. I keep praying this will be our last Christmas apart forever. My heart yearns for you.

DECEMBER 27th. When I started to write this it was Monday. Now it is Tuesday 12:45 a.m. That's the way it goes. We have only one typewriter now, and with two yeomen each working nine hour shifts, it isn't often available.

It's high time I described our Christmas for you. Our biggest celebration was on Christmas Eve. The stewards' mates decorated with palm branches around the walls, with colored lights shining from behind them. On one table was a Nativity scene made of coral, with figures beautifully carved out of soap. Across one wall was a streamer on which was painted, "Merry Christmas."

There were quite a number of officers from the other island. Some of us hadn't seen each other for several months, so it was a real reunion. After dinner we had fun presenting the Skipper with a package containing sheets. That must sound funny, but they are a real luxury here. Doc acted as toastmaster. He did a fine job. Then the colored boys entertained us with Christmas songs and Negro spirituals. They are really marvelous. Our applause was long and enthusiastic. We finished off with community singing.

The next day everyone slept until noon. Our Christmas dinner was even better than the one the night before. I wish they had given us less all at once and saved some of that marvelous food for other meals. We have had Spam and canned meat ever since then. I am certain the Spam people will go out of business after the war. No serviceman will want to see or hear of it again. I'm sure the man who invented it will be as universally hated as Hitler!

December 31, 1943

Dearest Honey:

I made the mistake of telling Donny he could stay up as late as he wanted tonight. It is now after eleven, and he is still holding out, trying very hard to keep me from knowing how sleepy he is. He is lying draped over the ottoman with his head on the floor. Twice his eyes have completely closed.

I spent hours today trying to get food. Many of the meat points were expiring, so the shops were crowded. I started standing in line at 7 a.m. but everything was gone by the time my turn came. A lot of our points were wasted.

It has taken most of the evening to take down the Christmas tree and the other decorations. That reminds me, I completely forgot to write you anything at all about putting up the tree. How could I DO that? What a time we had!

First we couldn't find a way of making it stand up. Then when we thought we were finished, we realized we had wound the strings of lights too tightly. It looked as though it was wearing a hobble skirt! So we took it all apart and started over. Finally, when we turned the lights on, we were delighted. At that point sleep overtook us, and we quit, leaving the living room strewn with wood, paper, greens, hammer, nails, ribbon, you name it!

By now, Donny is so sleepy that he has gotten a blanket and pillow and asked me to wake him up at midnight, in case he falls asleep.

Well, here it is—HAPPY NEW YEAR, HONEY! Donny just got some pot lids and went outside to bang them and shout greetings to the wide open spaces.

After an intermission for a hilarious celebration and a glorious repast of chopped olive sandwiches and ginger ale, Donny is still trying to stay awake. Why did I ever do such a dumb thing? He is sleepily chanting, "It's one o'clock, and I'm still awake. It's one o'clock, and I'm still awake." I am going to desert him and go to bed. I'll finish later.

NEXT DAY. I left Donny very much impressed with the fact that he was the only one up. At three I got up and found him asleep in front of the typewriter with his head on the keys! He had been trying to write a letter to you. I gathered him in my arms and carried him to bed. Today he is bursting with importance over having stayed up so late.

It's pouring now, and the wind is howling, but I must get out on my bike and get some exercise. That's what I need to lift my spirits. I'm extra lonesome.

Dear Daddy

I hope we win the war. Mother made dresses for us green and red jumpers.

I got a story book doll. Thank you for the sweater. I got a Doll house and nurse set. Do you think my printing is good? I love you. Please come Home.

Beverly F.

~

ILLUSTRATIONS
AND
PHOTOS

~

Laying bricks is a back breaking job! 1944

Home Sweet Home, 1945

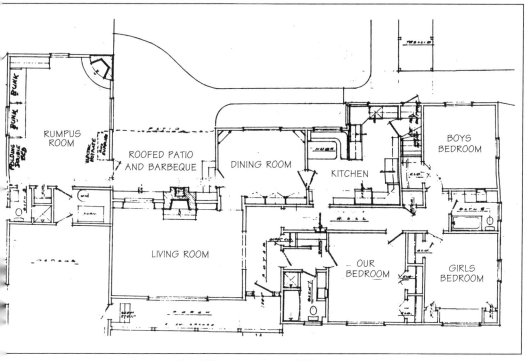

Our Home — Ground Floor

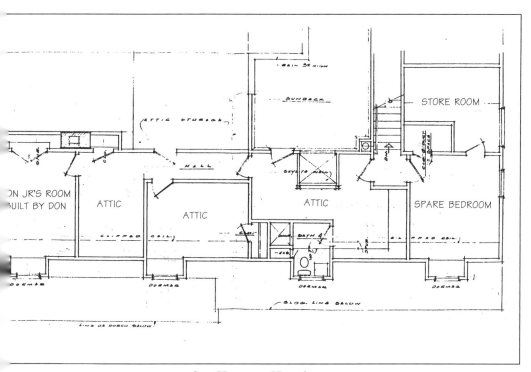

Our Home — Upstairs

March 1943, Don with Dot, on leave
after graduation from communication training.

Picnic, 1944

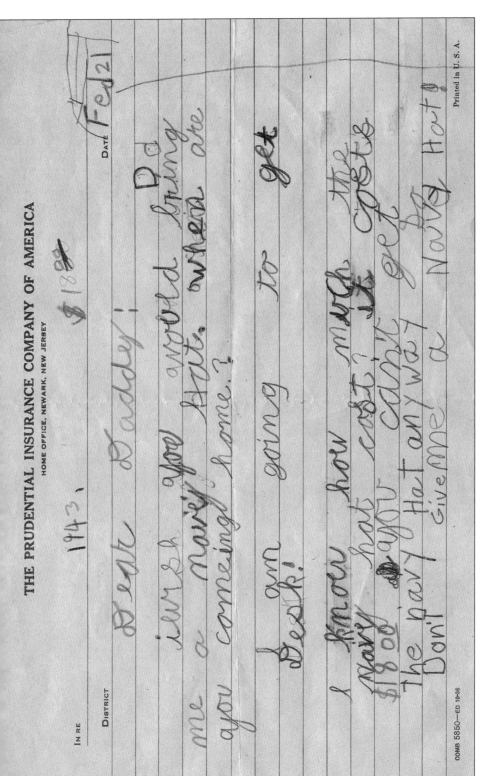

Letter from 8 year old Donny to daddy.

The 'Thank You' note.

The Stamps contained in this Book are valid only after the lawful holder of this Book has signed the certificate below, and are void if detached contrary to the Regulations. (A father, mother, or guardian may sign the name of a person under 18.) In case of questions, difficulties, or complaints, consult your local Ration Board.

Certificate of Book Holder

I, the undersigned, do hereby certify that I have observed all the conditions and regulations governing the issuance of this War Ration Book; that the "Description of Book Holder" contained herein is correct; that an application for issuance of this book has been duly made by me or on my behalf; and that the statements contained in said application are true to the best of my knowledge and belief.

[Book Holder's Own Name]

_____
(Signature of, or on behalf of, Book Holder)
Any person signing on behalf of Book Holder must sign his or her own name below

and indicate relationship to Book Holder _____

_____
(Father, Mother, or Guardian)

U. S. GOVERNMENT PRINTING OFFICE : 1942   16—29853-1   OPA Form No. R-302

UNITED STATES
OF AMERICA
War Ration Book One

WARNING

1 Punishments ranging as high as Ten Years' Imprisonment or $10,000 Fine, or Both, may be imposed under United States Statutes for violations thereof arising out of infractions of Rationing Orders and Regulations.

2 This book must not be transferred. It must be held and used only by or on behalf of the person to whom it has been issued, and anyone presenting it thereby represents to the Office of Price Administration, an agency of the United States Government, that it is being so held and so used. For any misuse of this book it may be taken from the holder by the Office of Price Administration.

3 In the event either of the departure from the United States of the person to whom this book is issued, or his or her death, the book must be surrendered in accordance with the Regulations.

4 Any person finding a lost book must deliver it promptly to the nearest Ration Board.

OFFICE OF PRICE ADMINISTRATION

No. 239550 -39

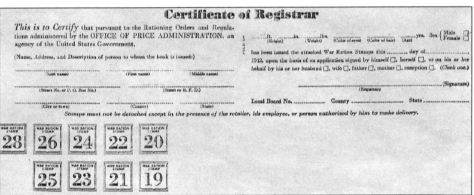

Sample of War Ration Book and Stamps.

From: _____

_____

_____

V ···—MAIL

To: _____

- -

V-mail service provides a most rapid means of communication. If addressed to a place where photographing service is not available the original letter will be dispatched by the most expeditious means.

INSTRUCTIONS

(1) Write the entire message plainly on the other side within marginal lines.

(2) PRINT the name and address in the two spaces provided. Addresses of members of the Armed Forces should show full name, complete Military or Naval address, including grade or rank, serial number, unit to which assigned or attached and Army Post Office in care of the appropriate postmaster or appropriate Fleet Post Office.

(3) Fold, seal, and deposit in any post office letter drop or street letter box.

(4) Enclosures must not be placed in this envelope.

(5) V-Mail letters may be sent free of postage by members of the Armed Forces. When sent by others postage must be prepaid at domestic rates (3c ordinary mail, 6c if domestic air mail service is desired when mailed in the U.S.)

Armed Forces sent mail free of postage costs.

ON NUCAFATAU ATOLL

Don, (front row) Bob Pedrick, his assistant and closest friend, and the skipper, a W.W.I. Navy veteran, (back row) with the "beauties of the tribe."

Officers of ARGUS 9.

Loading LST at Pago Pago to transport ARGUS 9 to the atoll where they will operate.

Ocean water desalting machine, Nucafatau Atoll.

"Doc" and his emergency operating room and hospital (sick bay).

Native dancers entertaining ARGUS 9 before it's departure from the atoll.

Daddy's home!! Happy New year, 1945.

December 31, 1943

Hi Babe! Hey Babe!

This is the first time in fifteen years that I haven't been able to kiss you into the New Year. Honey, I miss you so much.

My bath last night was a luxurious experience. Due to the rain, the drum was full—fifty five gallons. That's a lot of water, after being accustomed to a bucket bath. It was just the right temperature, and being rain water, was nice and soft. By this morning it was full again, and it only collects from one fourth of the roof of our 14x14 pyramidal fale.

We now have a flag pole. It's about fifty feet high with a concrete base. Somehow the presence of "Old Glory" makes a lot of difference to all of us.

I finally had a chance to reread my mail of yesterday. Aunt Bertha's letter was so cute and included a $1 money order in a folder and a note, "Just a bit for candy." If I get to be eighty-seven, I hope I'll be as much fun as she is. The box the girls from the office sent contained a large box of candy, which I am devouring avidly and keeping in the refer away from the ants. It also contained a large fruit cake, caramel bars, almonds, and cookies.

JANUARY 1st. When I tell you about our celebration last night, you will know what nuts we have become. The Skipper told me he wanted a cordon of eight officers, including myself, to perform a very important mission. I collected the officers specified. We marched goose-step to Doc's fale and ordered him to come out and stand at attention. Then we ordered him to take two steps forward, which put him right in the center of a large juicy mud puddle. We ordered him to continue standing at attention while we put leg cuffs and arm cuffs on him. We then ordered him into the fale and held a court of inquiry. Everyone refused to take his case as counsel, and we proceeded to specify every charge imaginable. Just as we were about to bring him to trial, the Judge (the Skipper) decided we had a more hardened criminal in our midst. We removed the cuffs and put them on Bob. After his inquisition, we went to Pete, then we cuffed Bill, our Exec. Officer, and so on.

We moved to the wardroom where we would have more space and then cooked up charges against the Skipper. We constituted the wardroom as the court. I was the prosecuting attorney, Doc was the medical expert, Dick was the judge, and we had three jurors who swore to convict the accused. He was convicted of having leprosy. An argument ensued as to whether we should hang him, banish him to X island for life, or both.

Just before midnight we went to the enlisted mens' mess hall to sing "Auld Lang Syne," and to wish them the best of luck for the New Year. Suddenly someone realized that Bill hadn't come with us. The Skipper instructed us to get him out of bed and throw him into the lagoon. We went to his fale and found him asleep. When we got him down to the lagoon, the tide was way out. The three fellows carrying him had to get soaked themselves in order to get him drenched. They couldn't throw him in, or he might have been injured on the coral. When we returned to the Skipper's fale, he said we must do it all over again because he hadn't seen it! After we followed his orders, we went back to the wardroom, had a bull session until after 4 a.m. Are we nuts? Or just stir crazy?

Our meal today was just about the same as the dinner we had for Christmas. For supper, what do you think we had? Yep, you guessed it—Spam! Which reminds me, the other day we had a dessert with coconut on top. The coconut came in cans from San Francisco! Good night My Love.

January 3, 1944

Oh Honey:

I just received the revised plumbing bill and realized I forgot to tell you what I did about it. When the original bill which gave me such a shock arrived, I asked Jack to go over it. He found several flagrant overcharges. I sent the bill back with those items checked and a note saying I had consulted with an expert who felt the charges he had circled would not be acceptable to the War Production Board and should be changed. Obviously there were three other items which he (Mr. Big Shot Plumber) was afraid might get him in trouble, because they were dropped from the revised bill. It is now $30 less than Jack had figured it should be—almost the original figure quoted. That rotten war profiteer, supposedly a pillar of the church and a community leader!

Today has been bitterly cold. The ice that formed on yesterday's puddles didn't melt until mid-afternoon,and there was snow on Mount Diablo.

I had a lot of trouble at the blood bank this morning. They must be using inexperienced volunteers. First they couldn't find my pulse. After several attempts, they finally succeeded. Then it took several tries to get my blood pressure. Next they attached all the paraphernalia, but the blood wouldn't start flowing. I was beginning to feel like "the little man who wasn't there." They fooled around much longer than the entire process usually takes. When they finally got it to start, the pain was awful. They said that was because they had the tube against a nerve. They finally got the pint, thank goodness, then put a large bandage on it to stop the bleeding and told me to use hot compresses. I was so shaky I could hardly drive home. I'm thankful that didn't happen the first time or I would have been scared away forever.

We just got back from a basketball game at St. Mary's. Donny did the dishes tonight, and never were dishes done so quickly, because he wanted to go along. I am so glad we took him. He was absolutely entranced. The colored Jazz band, which I heard the other night, played. Since I hadn't seen one for so long, I enjoyed the game tremendously.

Your Christmas Eve sounded interesting but certainly not Christmasy. And sleeping till noon on Christmas? Unthinkable! I'll bet you hope you never have a chance to do that again! Your New Year celebration certainly was a kick. I didn't know a bunch of OLD MEN like you could do such crazy things. I'm glad someone thought up all those ridiculous antics to relieve the boredom.

SUNDAY NIGHT. After Sunday School today, Rae made the girls happy by giving them a dancing lesson. She showed them the first principles of ballet—the five positions, etc. and they loved it. Now they are begging for toe shoes!

While Rae prepared an exceptionally delicious dinner we went for a walk in the rain. After DINING in the dining room, with candles and flowers, we did the dishes together and had fun singing silly songs. . . .

January 7, 1944

Hi Ya Beautiful!

Our heated war against the wildlife here still waxes relentlessly. We have cleared all the underbrush for at least sixty yards from the nearest buildings. But Doc says we will never get rid of the flies, lizards, and rats. We caught sixty-four rats yesterday.

Tell my sweet Poochie that today I shaved with the razor blades she gave me. I am saving Donny's hand lotion for a special occasion, and I have already used up the envelopes my Honeybun sent.

I am so fortunate to be free of infections. I don't know of anyone else here who is. That's why I bathe daily using plenty of soap. Sometimes it's after midnight before I do it, but I don't dare let even one day go by.

This morning I went to the other island for the first time in nearly two weeks. I was amazed at the improvements in the road. It can now be driven within one hour of high tide. While there, I drew some pay and am enclosing a money order. I wish it was larger, but I only had $40 coming. I want you to spend every bit of it on yourself, except for using some of it to buy a birthday present for Bev from me.

I will be rather busy for a while as our educational officer went to another island for two weeks, and I volunteered to attend to his duties while he is gone. I am also to give a course in a new radio procedure, starting Monday evening. I'll be instructing and organizing the entire course. . . .

January 10, 1944

Dearest Honey:

I had hoped to finish hauling gravel for the chicken yard today,but hauling wet gravel through the mud is getting to be too much for me. After three loads I quit. Then I raked out the pile in front to form a parking area for at least five cars. After that I carried all the leftover scrap lumber up to the attic, then put fifty pounds of sheep manure on the strawberry patch.

I can't think of anything I do outdoors that could be left until after the war. As it is, I didn't get the fall garden in. We are spending a fortune in money and ration stamps for our vegetables.

Judy was so delighted to start back to play school. I am going to be cooperating on Tuesday mornings, so it will cost just $4 a month. You will probably write that I shouldn't be taking on something more, but this will be good for me. I'll be doing something I thoroughly enjoy.

Chuck came running with one of Rae's cigarettes tonight, and when he reached me, put it in his mouth, holding it just right. He looked so funny. We can't let him get away with not learning right from wrong, so he had his hand slapped for getting into things that don't belong to him.

NEXT NIGHT. Rae and I just got back from seeing "Stage Door Canteen." I am still so disappointed we didn't see it together when it was playing in Santa Barbara. I just LOVED it! Every time they played "Good Night Sweetheart," I died a thousand deaths.

The Imries have been trying for a year to get a phone and learned today that they still can't. Existing phones can be transferred, but new ones cannot be put in. Life would certainly be simpler for us if they had one.

Chuck and Stevie had quite a time outdoors today. They went round and around the house lickety split, jabbering away. Chuckie was going so fast he kept falling down. Suddenly he was down the driveway and onto the road. Now THAT is a danger situation. For that I spank!

January 10, 1944

Dearest Love:

I just finished my first class. I think it went over well. They all seemed interested. A number of men stayed to ask questions. I am really enjoying teaching. They are so eager to learn and feel I am helping them. Imagine me being a teacher. But in a way, it does remind me of my educational meetings at the office. Incidentally, Bob, who is a teacher, says my teaching technique is fine. I hope I can sustain their interest and enthusiasm.

The fellow I picked at Hueneme to be a master at arms for us has turned out to be excellent. Everyone is enthused about him. He recently requested submarine duty, and today his orders came for the transfer. He is so thrilled, as we are for him. He should go far in the Navy.

TWO DAYS LATER. Today I gave my class an examination. I have corrected the papers and will interview each of them tomorrow, with appointments a half hour apart all day long. It's time consuming, but I think that's the best way to handle it so they can get the most out of the course.

After class the Skipper wanted to talk to me, so we walked to "Sunset Point," which is the westernmost tip of the island. He had a lot of confidential matters to discuss with me about the possible future location and work of our unit. We will probably be here for several more months, even possibly through next winter. However he sees the possibility of my having a leave and a plane ride home unless things change drastically. Along with my future duties will go much more responsibility. He is anxious to see me become a Lt. Commander as soon as possible and will do all he can to expedite it.

Your difficulties at the blood bank made me sick. Please don't go again. You have done more than your part and are doing your share every day.

I'm so glad Rae was planning on a few days across the bay and hope all went well. It would be good if you could get away for a day or two some time. It's a shame she gets so terribly depressed. . . .

January 12, 1943

Dearest One:

Tonight Donny was trying to figure out time. He asked the length of a year, a century, a thousand centuries, and then asked, "How long is a duration?"

My right wrist has been bothering me for some time. When Mabel goes to Oak Knoll Hospital next week, I think I'll go along and find out what's wrong with it. I am getting so I can hardly pin a diaper or tie a hair ribbon.

Your terribly lonesome letter of the 4th depressed me. I felt so sunk. I think I know exactly how you were feeling. You had that horrible feeling I had for several months last year. It's awful. I hope neither of us ever experiences it again.

Sixty-four rats in one day? That is appalling! It even beats Jack and Marky's record of fifty field mice in one night when they first moved here.

Rather than have Donny feed the chickens in the morning, he lets them out before he leaves for school. They have a wonderful time getting worms and fresh grass and weeds. Then I feed them. That brings them in quickly. They were out when it started to rain, so I quickly fed and watered them, and was soaked by the time I got in. But that was ok. You know how I love rain.

I just listened to something beautiful on Kate Smith's program. It was Martha Scott ("One Foot In Heaven" and "Our Town") doing a play about a mother talking to her baby about his daddy who is overseas and telling him about how they met, etc. It was all in verse and so beautifully and dramatically done. I just sat here and sobbed. Even telling you about it now chokes me up.

Chuck had a haircut today. Afterwards, he had a perfectly wonderful time walking the streets of Walnut Creek. He was so excited about dashing along the sidewalk. It must be a treat for him to have something smoother than our rough orchard, walks, and road for his little feet. He can find a mud puddle quicker than you can wink, and he has a passion for walking in gutters.

He had a wonderful time outdoors this morning while I hung the clothes, took them down, and tended to the chickens. He stayed out until I finished, even though it was raining. He thinks the chickens are wonderful and leans over and talks to them constantly. Goodnight from your ever loving, lonesome Honey.

January 15, 1944

My Dearest Poochie:

It made me so happy to receive such a nice letter from you this afternoon. You print very nicely, and I love to receive letters from you.

The dresses Mother made for you and Judy must be very pretty. I am glad you like the sweater I gave you. Were you surprised to have a present from me under the Christmas tree?

Mother tells me that you help her a lot, and it makes me very happy to hear that. Do you have fun with Chuck, Stevie, and Frances?

I love you very much and miss you terribly.

Loads of love,

Your Daddy.

January 16, 1944

My Honey:

Thanks so much for the lifesaver in the form of a money order for $30. The money disappeared fast this week, in spite of my optimistic report on our finances. Since you asked me to, I really will buy myself some clothes if any are available. I'll get Beverly a Storybook Doll from you for her birthday.

Perhaps what we have is not REAL rain in your estimation, but it does produce REAL mud and plenty of it. In spite of all the rock and gravel I have spread, we are constantly beset by muddy shoes and clothing.

Donny was so ambitious this morning. He did his room, washed and squashed the cans, burned the trash, got the milk, fed the chickens, and was ready to leave at 9:00 for a day with the Burke boys. Every once in a while he gets inspired and races through his jobs in record time, doing them well. I wish I knew which button to push to make it happen more frequently.

This has been quite a day, starting at 4 a.m. when Harry phoned. He and Rae talked for ages. Rae is scared to think what the call will cost.I have no idea what he had to say. Rae did most of the talking, mostly commiserating with him over his terrible fate. She seems to think he is being persecuted by having to do K.P. and clean toilets and all the other menial tasks that must be done.

Nursury school is a workout, a constant procession of sweeping, scrubbing, dusting, toileting, hand washing, etc. I could just eat up some of these darling children. There are at least four girls and three boys that I would love to kidnap!

Daddy is terribly tired. On top of his regular heavy schedule, he writes long letters to all his Chung Mei boys in the service, over seventy of them.

NEXT DAY. I have had a grand day. I stopped at the P.O. and picked up two letters from you on my way to Estelle's. The first thing we did was to find a hat for me. It's navy blue, cute, and exactly what I wanted.

After that we shopped all the dime stores and then went to Capwell's, where I bought material for fixing up "Judy doll" which we gave Beverly for Christmas several years ago. She will be a bride doll with a new wig, fresh "makeup" and all new clothes from top to toe. She has had a lot of loving and a lot of wear and is ready for refurbishing. It is such fun doing it.

I am now at the folks, where I have been tieing and quilting a comforter for Donny. He's going to love it. It's a transportation print with sail boats, river boats, stage coaches, trains, etc. on a blue background.

I am staying here tonight and have orders from Daddy to sleep late in the morning. I wonder if I still know how to do that. . . .

January 17, 1944

My Sweet:

I never knew before that chickens eat their eggs. How do you stop them? It must have been harrowing having to haul all that rock and gravel when you were so miserable. Isn't there a high school boy you could hire to do some of the heavy work? If only I could be there to do it myself.

Just before noon chow today someone discovered fish in the tidal break. Before you could say "Jack Robinson," four of the officers were stripped and in the water with a huge net. Two of them dragged it, and the other two tried to scare the fish in their direction. The natives, would have gotten a big kick out of their "inexpertise"! They did catch two fish about five inches long.

As a result, we spent chow time tonight making plans to build a dam to catch them, also a maze to see how intelligent they are, then build another maze on land for the rats. However we decided that the officers would probably get lost in the maze, thus showing that they were less intelligent than either the fish or the rats, so we abandoned the idea! You see what nutty things we do to try to occupy our minds? Oh Honey, I miss you so. . . .

January 17, 1944

Honey:

I went to Oak Knoll today with Mabel and Ann Dingus to see a doctor about my wrist. When we got there, since I didn't have an appointment, I had to argue at length with the fellows at the desk until they finally took me in to see the head nurse. She wouldn't make an appointment for me. Finally Mabel located her orthopedist, who arrived about noon, and explained the situation to him.

Four mothers, three babies, and a little girl were waiting for him, and he wasn't even supposed to be having office hours yet. He breezed in, remarked on what a lovely crowd, seemed very glad to see Mabel, hugged the little girl, told her she was too thin, and got a sailor to take her over to the mess hall. He told the mother of the darling little four-weeks-old baby to go in, and they would remove the cast from her hip. Then he took care of Mabel.

I went in with her, and while the nurse washed her back, he asked me why I had come. He was extremely annoyed at the outpatient department.

After examining me, he called another doctor to come look at "this very interesting wrist." They tossed off all sorts of long words and decided that it was something with a very long name, which I can't remember, but it was at least five syllables and unheard of in anyone my age. That made me feel better. I had felt like such a fool bothering anyone with my silly little wrist when everyone was so busy with babies, club feet, and all sorts of really important things. He told me he had never heard of anyone less than fifty years old who had this. He said the pain and weakness are caused by the fact that a deposit has formed over the tendons, making it almost impossible for them to move. They don't know what causes it. He says it will get worse in time but is nothing to be alarmed about. He was amazed and delighted that I had come in with it so soon, because most people wait until they have completely lost the use of the thumb, and nothing can be done. I can have a slight operation on the tendons just above the thumb, providing the X-ray shows his diagnosis is correct. At this point I can't tie a hair ribbon, insert a bobby pin, change a diaper, open a can or—well you name it. Anyone in this household who can't do those things is a total loss. Aren't you proud of me for going in right away? . . .

January 23, 1944

Dearest Mine:

Today we had a doctor and a dentist as guests at supper, and there was a lot of fun throughout the meal. About half the fellows were from the southern states, so there was constant ribbing between the North and the South. Two or three fellows would start singing a song from their state, and the rest of us would join in, if we knew it. Someone asked Doc for the Montana song which, they said, had gained nationwide attention. It seems there is none, and they knew it. A motion was made that Montana be admitted to the Union provided Doc could give a good reason for it. He said Montana should be in the Union so that it could turn the rest of the states upside down and make a Republican platform out of them for 1944. This brought down the house. A bunch of us started singing "California Here I Come" (there are more of us from California than any other state). All the rest shouted and booed but couldn't drown us out.

After the tables were cleared, we asked the colored boys to sing for us. We joined with them in singing anything we knew. When they came to "That Lonesome Valley," they harmonized it beautifully and sang it at each one of us, individually by name. It was very moving and something I will never forget— a fitting climax to the evening.

After censoring letters for four hours today, I typed one to send you, changing the names to preserve privacy. I couldn't resist. You'll see why.

TO MISS FLORENCE BROWN

Dear Florence

It is indeed a pleasure to write you, especially someone that i have not been fortunate enough to cast my eyes upon. knowing that you are the most ensentious one. knowing that you have treasured the idea of such a person but to you i must express myself clearly.

My name; Reginald W Washington. I am between the age of nineteen and twentyone. not handsome but a lover of your name. i could not relieve my self of this panic unless I write you, and evidentualy try for a chance on love at first sight (or of letter). What chance do i have.

Receiving your name from Morris and your adress I could not resist the chance for which it could be more facinating if you want it. I cannot say darling as I would like to, but with your permisson, darling. (smile)

Can I say that you are my most invisable friend or say it or inaminate.

Love is a great thing. If I could only compare my love and proceed, we could live like it or we would like for it to be.

Morris is a swell friend and he said you are a very nice girl for which he did not have to tell me because I know a Florence would be. I imagine you are as beautiful as Mrs. Roosevelt has political knowledge.

How can I continue my work without writing a girl I imagine has ability, glamor, personality. It is rather impossiable for me to monopolize a word from my vocabulary that will express my thoughts about you. for which you may think that I am formubigating, but darling this is strait from the heart. I am very much a fellow of my word and I just can't indure in any forth activity.

To be true & serious I am looking forward to a photo of you in the answering letter. your invisable lover

REGINALD W. WASHINGTON Stm 1c.

January 25, 1944

My Dearest Beloved:

This was a great day because mail arrived. I don't think you really know how much your letters mean to me. I'm sure if we were having an air raid, I would read one before I dove for the foxhole, or at least take it with me!

Whenever you describe your meals, my mouth waters. Which reminds me— there is another item besides Spam you had better not ever serve me when I get back, and that is BEANS in any form, except green beans from our garden. We have beans at least six times a week. Now I know why they are called NAVY beans!

It certainly is grand the way Uncle George wants to do so much for Rae and the children. I don't know how on earth other privates' families manage on the pittance they are paid. It is hard enough for us to make it on officer's pay.

Well I finally got it—FUNGUS! After I have been so careful. It is all over my body. Doc is treating it, but so far I don't see any improvement.

We spent most of today examining the men for advancement in rates. Tonight and tomorrow night I have lectures to do. The subject is very dry, and I have been wracking my brain to think of ways to make it interesting.

Just before chow I had a wonderful bath in the rain. It's marvelous not to worry about the quantity of water I am using. Can you picture taking a shower in the open, with a forty-mile wind blowing, the water quite cold, and still being nice and comfortable and enjoying it to the utmost?

Now about Harry—I don't know much about the workings of the Army, and I am not qualified to give Harry advice, but I do know that if a man does his work well, it will be known by his officers. He can then make any reasonable request, and they will usually endeavor to obtain favorable action for him if it is at all possible. Requests must be made through the chain of command. However a man has to put out before he makes a request. I know Harry will put out, so it's just a matter of time until he is can make a request.

Your descriptions of Chucky's doings and his and Stevie's comings and goings are practically the most precious parts of your letters. I want more!

January 25, 1943

Hello My Honey:

While we were shopping at the dime store yesterday Beverly stole a pack of gum! Our angel child did that? I led her back into the store. With her head bowed and her eyes streaming she told Mr Jenson what she had done and handed him the rest of the gum and money to pay for it. He wasn't much help. He started to tell her that because she had paid for it, it was hers. I gave him a high sign behind her back, so he dropped the subject and accepted the nickel. However he told me later that legally it is what he is supposed to do. I think that's a ridiculous law!

You asked about St. Mary's. There are three hundred officers there. Two hundred sixty-seven of them have their families with them. The Officer's Club is nice, but the one at Mare Island is the one everyone is crazy about. It's a beautiful place and serves a lovely dinner with dancing to an excellent orchestra, all for $1.

My difficulties at the blood bank are not going to keep me from going again. It was uncomfortable, disconcerting, and time consuming, but I have heard since of several others who had the same trouble.

It is strange the way no one is getting any rain. I wonder if there is going to be a world-wide drought. It will be pretty serious if we don't have more here. Remember how high the mustard used to be, with the children hiding in it, completely out of sight? Right now we have exactly two mustard blooms in the whole orchard, and they are less than five inches high. Leta writes that in New England, where they are, they don't have enough water for baths. Ken and Esther said Seattle is dry, too.

When I left home yesterday morning it was bitterly cold, not frosty, but dark, windy, and miserable. It was even colder in Berkeley. Catherine had made an appointment for me to have my hair cut by a MAN, one of those extremely rare creatures one hardly sees any more. He was doddering with old age, but it was a treat to have someone who knew what he was doing. He cut it just the way I wanted it. He's expensive, but it was worth $1 to get it just right. It was wonderful to have a nice relaxing day. But at home there was bad news.

Mabel and Rusty are moving. I am crushed. They have found a three-room place for $37.50. We are surely going to miss them. Mabel knows someone who wants to move in here, but I hate to think of renting to another couple. . . .

January 28, 1944

Hello, My Dearest:

I am SO LOW. Probably it's because I am not busy enough. The hours I spend censoring sometimes make me so sad. So many men are writing to people they don't know and have never seen. What will happen if these lonely strangers eventually marry? The copy I sent you is typical of hundreds. Also, hardly a day goes by that someone doesn't receive news that his girlfriend is getting engaged or married. Sometimes it's a wife leaving.

These poor kids (the enlisted men) have had very little education. I feel so sorry for them, and it makes me mad when so many of the officers treat them like trash. I don't mean they are mean to them, just treat them as though they don't exist. Waiting for a haircut is one example. Most officers automatically go to the head of the line, leaving the enlisted men to keep moving back. . . .

This past week several natives came over to this island to help with the camp clearance. They are marvelous workers and accomplish a lot. We learn so much from them. They are introducing us to the edibles and teaching us which things are poisonous, which fish are the best to eat, and how to catch them. As a result we have had several delicious fish dinners. They even showed us how to make butter out of coconut oil.

I have become so emotional lately that last night and on several previous occasions I have lain awake with the tears trickling down my cheeks. Why am I writing this? It will only make you feel terrible, but at least in a way it should tell you how much I love you.

My fungus infection has spread and is on my whole body. However the part I got first has improved considerably. I go to sick bay daily, and Doc uses some kind of iodine solution on it. He and I have become extra thick the past few weeks and spend a lot of our time together. I am sure you would like him.

We have all been spending as much time as possible trying to get news broadcasts. I still think we will be fortunate if the war terminates in 1945.

January 30, 1944

Dearest Honey:

Since Marky was going to Petaluma for the weekend, we rode with her to visit the Kemmeries at their farm. It was a delightful trip, and the kids were enchanted with the ferry boat ride.

The Kemmeries' place is very interesting, but OH THE WORK! I don't think I could take it. The house was built in the late 1800s and is heated solely by a fireplace and a wood cook stove. It has loads of possibilities but will take a lot of time and money to fix up.

Shortly after we arrived Marge started dinner, and the children went outside to explore. Getting a meal here is a long drawn out process. Marge hasn't yet mastered the science of making the stove get hot at the right time!

After we tucked the children in bed, we ate by the fire and talked until nearly midnight. From about 5:30 a.m. on, each of the kids, one by one, came creeping down the very creaky stairs to the only bathroom.

Because of the desperate need for farms and more farmers, two men from the Department of Agriculture are here to see John about supplying trees and other things he needs. It will be a struggle to put this small farm on a paying basis; nevertheless John loves doing this and thinks it beats being in the service. I suppose we really do need farmers just as much as we need soldiers.

It is rainy, but the kids in their boots and snowsuits are having a marvelous time. I have a cold which started last night, so I have spent very little time outdoors. I want to get out tomorrow and see the rest of the outbuildings and everything else.

SUNDAY. Last night I hated to go to bed in the cold, so I slept on the couch near the fireplace. In the morning, when we went outside, it was marvelous. We walked to their property lines, through barbed wire fences, apple orchards, pastures, eucalyptus groves, cherry orchards, and oak groves, until I was exhausted. What a tremendous thrill for them to know all of that is theirs. However, I was very happy to get back to "city life" on Springhill Road.

We came home via the Benicia ferry, and the children loved that one, too. Chucky just stared and stared at me when I got home, then burst into tears and kept crying. Of course I held him from then on.

In Rae's letter from Harry today he says that in his hut there is a Prudential agent from Chicago, a policeman from N.Y., a lawyer, and a C.P.A., and all eighteen of the fellows have children. To think you were ever naive enough to say, "They'll never draft fathers!"

I received the baby announcement from Anne Pedrick today. It seems so unfair for me to learn the news before Bob possibly can.

I was able to get Special B ration stamps today for fifteen gallons of gas to take Rae and the children to all their doctor appointments. That helps.

February 1, 1944

Well, Honey:

Here I am in Oak Knoll Naval Hospital waiting to be prepped for my wrist operation. Ah, at last she just stuck a thermometer in my mouth, as I sit here on a bench outside the office of 69B. I guess I'm on my way.

It is now about three hours later. I have been luxuriating in bed doing my nails and reading. I had my dinner of hamburger, spaghetti, canned string beans, boiled onions, one slice of bread with real butter, and one half of a canned pear. Since I didn't have breakfast and had practically no lunch, I am still hungry. I'm dying for some milk, but what can I expect for $1.75 a day?

The nurses are all so nice. The WAVE corpsmen (women) are mostly rather sloppy looking. My room is darling with a big maple chair, maple chest, two beds, but so far no roommate, darn it. It would be much more interesting to be in a ward, but unfortunately officers' wives rate double rooms.

I have been reading an amusing and fascinating article in Ladies Home Journal by the mother of three little girls, all under two—twins, who were seventeen months old when the third girl arrived. Imagine my amazement to discover that it was written by the wife of Wede Espy who Catharine went with at Redlands. The author was press agent for Fred Waring.

Ah! I just had a glass of milk. A cute little sailor noticed that I hadn't touched my coffee and asked if I would like some milk. I was finishing it when a WAVE came in with a thermometer, and with raised eyebrows exclaimed, "You're drinking milk?" I told her I was starved, but apparently I shouldn't have had it before having an anesthetic. Good gravy! All this fuss and bother for just a little old thumb that won't work.

I haven't told you yet how I happen to be here. Last Thursday morning it suddenly got so bad that doing the things I have to do became torture. That was the day Rae was gone. Yesterday Mabel and I came here, and I saw Dr. Holcomb again. The X-rays showed he had diagnosed it correctly, and he wanted me to start prepping then and have the surgery this morning. Of course that was impossible without making arrangements at home. Also I wanted to spend more time with Chuck after being away.

WEDNESDAY MORNING 7:30. They moved me to a different room in the middle of the night. I now have a roommate whose husband is in the Pacific and whose nineteen-year-old son is in the Atlantic. I just finished showing off my pictures of you and the children and looking at hers of her husband in his whites, plastered with service ribbons.

LATER. It's all over, and it was so easy. They gave me a pill and a shot at about ten, put me on a stretcher, and brought me here to the surgery building. I was so sleepy I don't remember anything at all until I was in the ambulance going back to my room and sleepily asked how soon it would start. When they told me it was all over, I was flabbergasted.

I have a new roommate, and it is so sad. She came from Philadelphia to meet her husband who had been aboard a carrier for a year. The day he was to arrive, she was rushed to the hospital for strangulated hernia surgery. She has been here a week and still can't keep anything down. Her husband came, and all he can do is to put cold cloths on her head and help her heave. Isn't that cruel? . . .

Lafayette, Calif. Feb. 3rd 1944, 7:50 P.M.

Dear Daddy:

The color of the sweater you gave me is very nice. Blackie is very nice. I like him very much. Chuck is fine. Stevie is sick. Frances is fine.

I got some stripes from Harry. Mother is broke, she said so. Good Luck Daddy. I love you. Donny Fibush

February 3, 1944

Darling honey i think i will skip caps and punctuation because i am doing this entirely with my right hand. i have so much to tell you, but i don't know whether i will get it all said or not. when my roommate's husband saw your picture, he said you looked very familiar to him. he is a warrant officer in communications on a carrier. his name is cutler. she was very sick all night and had to have an emergency injection into her veins. also at midnight they rolled another bed into my room with an emergency appendectomy. she had ether and was so sick. she kept coughing, moaning, vomiting, gasping, calling for water, and calling bill. i could hardly stand it and the tears were streaming down my face. he is a gunner on the uss mississippi, and she hasn't heard from him for five months. I sat up for breakfast and somehow managed to get into my clothes. a wave helped me get my stockings on. i felt so guilty taking up room when there were so many people with really terrible troubles who needed the bed. that is really the only reason i wanted to leave. everybody was so nice. my room had no head so i wandered around in my enormous white hospital p.js. looking for one. i met a corpsman, very cute, who took my temp and pulse. by that time i felt so at home. i slept like a log except for the tragic interruptions. the folks came to pick me up. i was completely exhausted by the trip home, which surprised me. shortly after i arrived, mrs. wood phoned to say they had been feeling very upset since all this news came out about the horrible way our boys have been treated in the jap prisons. i am very disappointed because i am so useless. i'd like to know how long i'll be this way. it is so hard on rae having to do everything. typing with one hand is tiring. i love you honey.

FEBRUARY 4,1944

DARLING:

I JUST REALIZED I CAN DO IT THIS WAY AND IT IS EASIER AND LOOKS LIKE YOUR COMMUNICATIONS TYPEWRITER. RAE AND I ARE BOTH SO CROSS. NOT AT EACH OTHER, JUST AT THE WORLD IN GENERAL. WE FEEL LIKE TAKING OUR FOUNTAIN PENS AND SQUIRTING INK ALL OVER THE RUG OR TAKING THE FIRE TOOLS AND SMASHING ALL THE LAMPS AND MIRRORS. THIS MORNING RAE GOT UP AND HELPED ME GET THE CHILDREN OFF. IT HAS BEEN ONE THING AFTER ANOTHER ALL DAY, AND SHE IS JUST DEAD. I HAVE TO KEEP GOING BACK TO BED EVERY LITTLE WHILE, BECAUSE I GET WEAK. MY HAND WAS SWELLING UP LIKE A BALLOON, SO I PHONED THE DR. HE SAID I COULD UNWRAP THE OUTER WRAPPING BECAUSE IT MUST BE STOPPING MY CIRCULATION. I AM GOING BACK ON MONDAY TO HAVE MY STITCHES OUT. IT IS DISGUSTING TO BE SO USELESS. BUT STILL I HAVE BEEN HAPPY TODAY TO BE BACK IN MY PRETTY HOME WITH EVERYONE AND GETTING BETTER ALL THE TIME. THE CHILDREN WERE ADORABLE TONIGHT. THEY WERE SO BROTHERLY AND SISTERLY AND CUTE. AFTER DINNER WE ALL READ TOGETHER AND PLAYED WITH CHUCKY. THEN THEY ALL DECIDED TO CHANGE ROOMS FOR TONIGHT. DONNY IS SLEEPING IN BEV'S ROOM, AND JUDY IS IN CHUCK'S. THE LAST I HEARD DONNY WAS TRYING TO TEACH BEV HER ARITHMETIC. SORRY THIS IS SUCH A BUM LETTER. I LOVE YOU TO PIECES, HONEY.

FEBRUARY 6, 1944

HONEY:

YESTERDAY YOUR LETTER OF JANUARY 21 ARRIVED WITH THE ENCLOSURES. RAE AND I BOTH GOT A KICK OUT OF AUNT BECKIE'S LETTER WHEN SHE RAVES ABOUT HOW WELL-MANNERED AND RESPECTFUL THE CHILDREN ARE. RAE ASKED ME HOW MUCH I WOULD PAY HER TO KEEP HER MOUTH SHUT AND NOT TELL ANYONE THE REAL TRUTH!

I'M VERY TIRED, SO THIS WILL BE SHORT. I WAS SO LONESOME FOR YOU TODAY I WAS AFRAID I WOULD BURST INTO TEARS.

GOING TO OAK KNOLL THIS MORNING I GOT CARSICK AND WHEN THEY TOOK OUT THE STITCHES, I WAS AFRAID I WOULD PASS OUT, IT LOOKED SO GRUESOME. WALT DINGUS DROVE US. HE WAITED IN THE CAR WHILE ANNE WAS SEEING HER DOCTOR AND WAS VERY EMBARRASSED TO FIND HE HAD PARKED IN THE SPACE RESERVED FOR ADMIRAL NIMITZ' WIFE AND IT HAD TO BE REMOVED BY AN M.P.

I GOT EVEN MORE CARSICK COMING HOME. THE DOCTOR TOLD ME I COULD START USING MY HAND A LITTLE, BUT TO BE CAREFUL. I HAVE BEEN ATTEMPTING A LOT MORE TODAY. IT IS SLOW AND TIRING. GOODNIGHT MY HONEY, PLEASE COME HOME SOON.

February 7, 1944

My Wonderful One:

Bob and I finally had "our" baby! He received a telegram sent by his dad on January 26th. At the same time he received three letters from Ann telling how impatient she was getting.

I asked Doc about your wrist, and he says it sounds to him like either a ganglion tumor or osteosarcoma. He wants me to get information right away on the X-rays as well as the diagnosis. How does one get information "right away" with the kind of mail service we have most of the time?

Yesterday we had visitors, and also over one hundred natives came to put on a Seva Seva for us. Just as I was about to start working, two BIG SHOTS arrived. I was assigned to show them around. It turned out that the biggest big shot had been an insurance broker in S.F. and knew many of the people I do.

The Seva Seva lasted four hours, but I think they would have been happy to go on all night. Their music consisted of clapping and beating on the deck with their hands, plus one ukulele and a snare drum made from a large empty cracker can. The music progressed faster and faster and louder and louder until they would stop very suddenly in perfect unison. Their dances are similar to the Hawaiian dances, starting slowly, gracefully, and increasing in tempo. After the women and the men had each done several numbers, the older women, even the old ones, started to dance, clap, sing, and beat on the floor. The old men sat on the floor on the outside occasionally letting out big whoops. Then the maidens came to each officer, putting strings of shells around our necks and giving grass skirts to some of us.

LATER. Oh Honey, my heart is bursting. Just before supper your letter written at Oak Knoll came. It is such a relief to know that it is all over and that you are ok. I hate to think of your going through that alone. I still don't know what was wrong. PLEASE get the information for me. If you have to get it in medical terms, I will have Doc interpret it for me. . . .

February 9, 1944

Hello, My Honey:

Look! I'm using both hands. It does hurt a little, but I need to do it. I feel so much better. It was a rainy day with a hailstorm at noon. What fun!

Please send me a few native men to do the clearing on our place. If they are such good workers, a week with two men working all day might do the job.

I finally received my birthday gift from Daddy. He had to order the books I asked for, and it took over three months. All of them are books I want for the children—"My Body and How It Works," "Tell Me About God," "Manners by Mr. Do and Mr. Don't," "Flicka, Ricka, and Dicka," and "Snip, Snap and Snur." What a wonderful time we'll have!

My hand is slow in healing. I get very discouraged with my slowness and inefficiency. Just as I was getting Stevie up from his nap and dressing him, Chucky woke up, the children got home from school, the mail came, and an ensign arrived from St Mary's to look at the rumpus room. Why is it everything always happens at once?

He wanted his wife to see it, and by 9:30 they were here and asked if they could start moving in. They have a sixteen-months-old boy named Lee. He is darling. He, Chuck, and Stevie should have a lot of fun together.

NEXT DAY. I had my hair done today and feel really good. Pompadours are going out, and the new flat top "do" is coming in. It is much more becoming to me. When I left for the Springhill Road meeting tonight, I felt as though I was ready for first grade, with my hair all smooth on top, little curls around my face, and my hair ribbon! At the meeting we discussed road signs, investigating about the stuff dumped in our creek, a future possible clubhouse, and your idea about building restrictions.

Marky took Susan to Childrens Hospital in Oakland for X-rays today. Rae went along to take Frances for a checkup. She can go there for twenty five cents a visit because Harry is in the army. She was very well pleased with the set-up there. All the nurses went nuts over Frances, and that didn't hurt Rae's feelings a bit! Susan is to have her eye surgery next Friday.

I forgot to tell you about the Hollingsworths. I hunted through the attic and managed to scrape up a pretty fair assortment of dishes, pans, utensils, etc. for them. Her name is Myrtle. Lee was a year old on Donny's birthday. Holly was a football coach at a college in Minnesota. . . .

February 13, 1944

Honey:

We are taking milk from the Browns now. Their cow had a calf and is giving four gallons a day. They are charging us forty-five cents a gallon.

When I went to Oak Knoll today, the doctor who saw me wrote down the name of what was wrong with my wrist and here it is—seleroseing knosynovitis. I also asked if he knew what anaesthetic I had, as I thought it was so marvelous. He said that of course he knew, because he was the anaesthetist. It is called sodium pentothal. It was injected into my right arm just below the bend (the surgery was on my left). I never heard of an injection which puts you out completely. It certainly is a wonderful thing. He said it isn't completely satisfactory for abdominal surgery because it doesn't give complete relaxation to the abdominal muscles. It is so new that he was extremely interested in learning how pleasant my reaction was to it—no nausea or dopiness, just sleeping and waking periodically, as well as being perfectly comfortable and intelligent in between times. I have gone into this at such length because I thought you might want to discuss it with Doc.

This morning was so much fun. When the girls woke up, they each found a Storybook Doll. When they came to my room, there were more gifts. When we sat down to breakfast, more birthday gifts were discovered. Then "Happy Birthday."

Since I was taking the girls to San Francisco, we went straight to the folks' from Sunday School, and Donny rode home with the Condits. Since the folks were going to the City too, we rode over with them. We got to the Follies just in the nick of time. Our seats were first row in the balcony, perfect for this, much better than seats downstairs.

When the music started I almost cried, thinking about how awful it was to be somewhere exciting like that without you to enjoy it with us. The girls loved every minute of it and hated to leave. We walked out the exit by the stage door, and the girls got a thrill waiting for the performers to come out.

Rae had a beautiful dinner waiting for us with candles, flowers, and Valentine place cards. The cake was a "HAPPY BIRTHDAY BEVERLY" masterpiece, as Rae's cakes always are, with fluffy white frosting and pink candles. You should have seen Chuck and Stevie's faces when it was brought out. Chuck sat in his high chair, guzzling ice cream and beaming from ear to ear. Stevie sat on Rae's lap eating her cake and ice cream faster than she could get it herself.

I forgot to tell you how cute Philip was this morning. He burst through the patio door yelling breathlessly, "Here I am. Happy Birthday Beverly." She seemed more thrilled over that than over the gifts she received. I think she adores him almost as much as she does Chucky.

I just stopped to let Blackie in. He tore down the hall, jumped in bed with Donny, and rolled with delight. He is so devoted to him and somehow knows when it's time for the children to come home from school. He sits out in the orchard waiting, then dashes down the road when he sees them.

Now to your letters. Yes, I think Chuck probably is spoiled. He is so cute, so tiny, so funny, and pitiful I can't resist him. When I come in from somewhere and he grabs me, I sit and hold him. I rock him and sing and let the work go. Sometimes Rae razzes me, but I think he'll turn out all right. Donny might have been better off with a little more of that. Good night Honey.

February 13, 1944

Dearest Mine:

When the Skipper learned of your surgery, he immediately said he would get a thirty-day leave for me. I was given a special plane to take me to another island, leaving on less than an hour's notice. The ride was thrilling. I wish I could tell you about it. I gave the top man the Skipper's letter along with my very best sales pitch. However, even he doesn't have the authority to grant this request but will send a message to someone higher up immediately. While I await the outcome, I am sleeping in the transient officers' fale.

NEXT DAY. I am still here, stewing and waiting. It kills me to think that today is Valentine's Day, again and we are still apart. When I think about the other wonderful ones we have shared in the past fifteen years, I wish I could write poetry, so I could write something beautiful to you.

It makes me sick to think of your running out of Butane again. Won't it be wonderful when the war is over and we get natural gas? No more freezing mornings going out in our robes to pour kettles of hot water over the tank. How do the Condits like oil heating?

Today I had a surprise. Doc arrived unexpectedly. We have spent all day together. Now both of us are sitting here writing to our wives.

I am so consumed with waiting and hoping, I can't concentrate on anything. If by some miracle I do get the leave, won't it be WONDERFUL? OH HONEY!

February 14, 1944

Hello, my Valentine Honey:

Good news today. We got sixteen eggs. After a weekend of few eggs and much egg eating, they produced a lot and ate none.

Myrtle used the Bendix for the first time today and couldn't get over how wonderful it is. It's the first time she has ever seen an automatic washer.

This morning the tractor man phoned and said he would have to charge $22.50 to take out the five pear trees, and he hated to see me waste all that money for such a small job. I talked to Nat Martino again, and he said that in a couple of weeks he and Louie could dig them out for me, and he would guarantee it wouldn't cost that much. He will also bring the horse to plow and will turn the soil over for me.

Just as Rae and I were leaving for a movie tonight, I noticed Chuck's index finger was enormous. It was purple with a huge yellow lump. I started soaking it in hot epsom salts. Try getting a kid his age to happily keep his hand in hot water for a long time! He went to bed very cheerfully, but when we got home Myrtle was holding him in her arms. He awakened, cried for attention, and got it. He sat in my lap giggling and pointing at Myrtle saying "Whozat?" Myrtle asked me not to feel badly about her evening. She enjoyed him. We certainly are lucky in the people to whom we rent our rumpus room, aren't we?

February 16, 1944

Dearest Honey:

Today when it was time to take Chuck to the doctor, I found him with Lee behind the chicken house. Both of them had their noses pressed against the lathes raptly watching the chickens. Both were soaking wet from playing in the chicken's water dish.

When we left for Dr. Beede's office, Chuck was tickled to death to be going "bye bye," but when we got there, he knew immediately where we were and didn't want to go in. There was such a crowd, we had to wait over two hours. Dr Beede said Chuckie's gruesome finger was caused by chewing on it then getting it infected, probably from the boil on his leg. He lanced and bandaged it and wants to see it again tomorrow.

When Holly came home, he brought a package from Rusty containing the Lt. collar bars you have been waiting for ever since your promotion, and A ROLL OF COLOR MOVIE FILM. Isn't that marvelous? Your collar bars are wrapped and ready to go. I wanted to put in other things but didn't dare, since it is going airmail. These darn rules about sending things!

The news surely is encouraging. We were listening to "Little Women" on the radio today, when they broke in with the dispatch from Admiral Nimitz[1].

You should have seen our driveway this afternoon. Chuck, Stevie, Lee, Gary, Philip, Bev, and Judy were engaged in a marvelous cooperative enterprise, tying wagons together like a train and piling on for rides. Love you Honey.

February 21, 1944

My Dearest Donny:

The last letter I received from you was the one in which you told me about your report card. It made me happy to know you are improving. I'm proud of you.

Now don't worry about me. I will take good care of myself. When I was ten years old, my Mother and Daddy took a long trip to China. Uncle Kenny and I had to be nearly a year without either of them. But you have Mother with you, and I will come home as soon as I possibly can.

I haven't shaved for five days because of the impetigo on my face. I look very funny.

Be a good boy and help Mother a lot, won't you? I miss you very much, and I love you very much.

Your Daddy

---

[1]In a surprise attack, seventy-two aircraft downed fifty-six planes and destroyed seventy-two on the ground at Truk, leaving the fleet surface ships to burn and sink thirty-seven ships, including two cruisers.

February 21, 1944

Dearest Honey:

Helen Brown had a little girl on Bev's birthday. Gary came to tell us and to get their puppies who have been here since Friday. Patsy, their red setter, loves it here and spends a lot of time with us. On Friday her five little roly polies staggered down the road after her. I don't see how they ever made it all that distance. She went home without them, so the children fixed them a box in the patio. They adopted Blackie for their Daddy, and he looks so funny with those five fat little puppies following him everywhere he goes.

Because I was tired and sleepy this morning, Donny, bless his heart, changed, dressed, and fed Chucky and then brought him to me.

I can't see why my letter from Oak Knoll upset you so. I tried so hard not to say anything that would make you worry. I am certainly glad you got the next one so soon. I feel better now that I know you know all about it.

Today Rae and Myrtle rode to S.F. and back with Frank Brown. They had a grand day. Rae got a dress, red play shoes, brown street shoes, a white hat, stockings, and a brown purse all for less than $25. She found a darling coat for Chuck. She also got movie film. Isn't that marvelous?

I had fun today with my seven children. When I stuck the three little boys in the bathtub, you should have seen that room a few minutes later! After they had their lunch and naps, the circus atmosphere continued to prevail. Rae had a delightful day, and I enjoyed mine tremendously too.

I don't see how your request can be approved, since my operation was such a trivial thing compared to all the other things that are happening. I refuse to even let myself think about it for fear of disappointment. To me it is all fantasy. I keep thinking of things like: Where would you come in and where would I meet you? If you were to come tomorrow, when the children saw you, they would ask, "Is the war over?" NO, OF COURSE I AM NOT THINKING ABOUT IT, NOT AT ALL. NOR AM I COUNTING ON IT!

The mail lady's youngest son, who is eighteen, just washed out as a flying cadet in the Navy. Something goes wrong with his nose every time he is in a stall, whatever that means. She said he had already soloed and has excellent grades. The one in the Army is nineteen, and the one who is missing is twenty.

Typing is hurting my wrist too much right now. . . .Goodnight, Honey.

February 22, 1944

Hello My Darling:

This morning I visited a supply ship. It's amazing to think that just one ship can contain so many things. To put it in the words of the officer who showed me around, "We have everything here except fresh milk and our families." Since it was Washington's birthday, they gave all officers and crew free ice cold root beer and free ice cream—all we could eat.

After being on a ship again, I am more than ever determined that if I can't have duty at home near you, I want it to be afloat. On a ship almost everyone keeps busy most of the time, no matter what.

Today I met a doctor who has been out here for twenty six months and sees no prospect of getting home any time soon. That's not very encouraging.

Now for questions—Yes, Bob gets very low too, as does almost everybody here. However he is a rather quiet person, so it isn't as noticeable as it is with me. Fungus is practically inescapable here and much more annoying than poison oak. It is almost impossible to get rid of it. However it only itches about 90% of the time. Yes, after the war, I guess we will have to become one of those two-car families. I wonder how soon they will start making cars again. . . .

February 26, 1944

Honey:

I just returned from a very enjoyable evening at St. Mary's. First there was the "sing" which is always fun, then a Tom and Jerry cartoon, the cutest I have ever seen, and an excellent "March of Time" about Sweden. The feature was "The Miracle of Morgan's Creek" with Betty Hutton. It was so funny we all laughed ourselves breathless. I'd love to see it again. Betty Hutton is a riot!

You were asking about Holly. He's an athletic director at St. Mary's. He was captain of his football team in college and also a high school football coach. He was telling me today that they have a Lt. J.G. at St. Mary's who is a full-blooded Indian. He was Officer of the Day when the Admiral visited, and had to do the honors. The Admiral told him he had never seen it done better.

I sold a dozen eggs to the folks this afternoon and another dozen to Myrtle. That makes six dozen in the past nine days. The best part is how thrilled people are to get them.

NEXT DAY. This morning I was awakened at five by rain on my face. It had blown in through the open window. The freshly laundered curtains were drenched.

Donny was in a state when he got home from school. There had been a slight bus accident, which had scared him and also hurt his leg. Then Blackie chased Allen Hoskins' dog, so Allen threw a rock which gave Donny an egg on his forehead. Allen is three years older and at least twice Donny's size. His dog is at least that much larger than Blackie! Finally, when he found the little boys had wrecked his radio, he just wanted to die! Big as he is, I held him and rocked him. Then I gave him some bread and butter and sent him to the Slavens' to see if Tommy could fix his radio.

I have spent the evening paying bills and trying to figure out how to make the money stretch. The Prudential check still hasn't arrived, and the P.G.& E. bill was the worst it has ever been—$63. I guess with so many people using the Bendix and with such a houseful, it is understandable, but GOLLY!

Judy has had a miserable evening. She seemed fine until dinner time when she took a long black look at her food. I'm sure you remember that look. Then she sat not eating a bite. I put her to bed and, for the next two hours, she alternated between saying she felt terrible and being coy and cute. I thought it was just one of her acts, until she gave a yell, walked ACROSS Bev's bed and into the bathroom, vomiting all the way. WHAT A MESS! As I held her head, she stopped long enough to look up at me and say, "I'm trying as hard as I can to get better." Poor little lamb. Then after the next heave, "God isn't laughing at me, is he, Mommy?" Sometimes she just breaks my heart. But I must admit sometimes I could happily strangle her!....

March 2, 1944

My Dearest Precious One:

I'm back on my own island and you know what that means. Luckily, there has been a lot to do since I returned. Today I had to neglect all my regular work to inventory and audit the books of the officers' mess. Doc is treasurer, and he knows very little about bookkeeping. I was reminded of you and your checkbook troubles, as we went through the items which he forgot to enter.

I would hate to have you see me as I look right now. I haven't shaved for several days, and my face is covered with greasy sulfa ointment for my impetigo. However it is getting better, and I hope this will be over soon.

Bob remarked a while ago that I am a changed man since I got the news that you are all right. He says my walk, my posture, my smile, the way I hold my head, my conversation, even the look in my eyes, everything about me is changed. Evidently your operation affected me outwardly more than I realized.

Something surprising just happened. Bob discovered a can on top of the locker. In it was a Christmas package of goodies from you, and several letters. Evidently they came while I was gone, and someone put them up there....

March 2, 1944

Honey:

Yesterday it poured all day. By the time the kids walked up the road from the bus stop, they were soaked. We had a cozy afternoon. Bev made gingerbread. Donny worked on a jigsaw puzzle, and Judy "helped" me sew! In the evening we played records, and Bev taught me some jitterbug steps.

I am making myself a pinafore out of Midge's old dressing table skirt. Since it's almost impossible to get material, I am lucky to have it.

Today when the school bus hadn't arrived by 4:30, I was worried. Just then everyone came walking up the road except Donny. The bus had broken down, and the children had been brought home by the teachers. Donny had decided to walk home, and no one knew where he was. About five Mr. Blackwood dropped him off. Donny's explanation was that everyone had been picking on him, and when the bus broke down, he thought it was a good chance to "escape." He started walking home, and Mr. Blackwood came along as soon as he got the bus running again. He asked Donny what he thought his daddy would think about his behavior and said, "You have the best Daddy that ever walked in shoes". When Donny was telling us about it you could see that tickled him to death. When he told Mr. Blackwood he didn't want him to be mad, he said that he wasn't, then tickled Donny, mussed his hair, and told him to be a good boy from now on. What a nice man!

Myrtle said she hears such nice things about me from so many of the Navy wives. When people learn she is living here, they congratulate her on her good luck. I guess our Bendix is creating a lot of good will. . . .

March 2, 1944

Dear Daddy

I got $1.70 saved up and I get $5.00 a month for renting my room for Stevie to sleep in. What do you think of that?

Tonight I have been making a puppit colt named Frisky. He runs, he bucks, he gallops, he loves me. We are going to do a play at school with him and other puppits. If you come home soon maybe you can see the play.

Love Donny

March 6, 1944

Dearest Honey:

The strangest thing happened last night. I dreamed you were home. Donny also dreamed about your being home. Judy dreamed that "Daddy was safe and coming home on a boat." Rae dreamed that she sat down next to a sailor at the movies, and it was you! She asked you when you got home, and you said at six that morning. When she asked if you had phoned me yet, you told her that you hadn't because you decided to see a movie first. Isn't that weird, all of us dreaming about you the same night? . . .

This morning when I went out to hang up the washing, I took all the little ones outside with me. The next thing I knew, the little boys were climbing the pruning ladders. Remember how high they are? Lee went straight up to the ninth step. Chuckie followed, but laboriously. Stevie, despite his cast, made it up three steps and looked triumphant. It is obvious that Lee climbs for the pure joy of climbing. Chuck took each step as a big accomplishment, calling to me to admire it each time he went higher. Stevie just grinned from ear to ear and enjoyed himself.

Markie brought us some lovely flowering peach branches from their prunings. Rae fixed them in the white bowl and put them in the recessed window. What a picture they make, framed by the window and the white ruffled curtains. Myrtle brought us a dozen lovely yellow daffodils yesterday, and they look spectacular in the front hall. Rae arranges flowers so beautifully.

Betty Imrie has just heard something more about her parents. A man from their prisoner-of-war camp came back on the Gripsholm. He said he had twenty-four hours notice, and in that time he memorized the names and addresses of the next of kin of all five hundred people in the camp, so he could get in touch with them. He talked to Betty's sister in L.A. and told her that conditions are better than they were. No husbands and wives are allowed to live together, but now they can see each other at stated times of the day. When they were first there, Betty's father was knocked out for speaking to his wife at the wrong time. There were 52 babies born during the first few months, but of course no more now. There are about 150 children there. Of course Betty worries about what will happen to the prisoners as things get more and more tough for Japan.

After everyone was in bed tonight, I took a walk up the road. It was a beautiful night, and the further up the road I went, the more beautiful it became. The blossoming trees are so lovely now. I felt that I couldn't stand it for you not to be here enjoying it. I stood at the top of the rise and looked back over our valley and the lights in the few scattered houses. I listened to the owls and the frogs, realizing how beautiful and peaceful our valley is. I thought about how far away and how uncomfortable you are. By the time I got back, the moon was so bright it threw my shadow. Now my time with you must end.

March 7, 1944

Honey:

The weather was simply superb today. On the other hand, the day started with a big frustration. I wanted to start painting the girls' room right after breakfast, but they had sent the wrong color paint, and I had to take it back. That expedition was one disaster after another. The car started to smoke. It turned out the fan belt was broken. The first two service stations didn't have one. The third one did, but when I walked back to the car, which I had left at the Associated Station, they said it was the wrong size, so I had to return it.

Since I had Chuck and Judy with me, all this walking was not accomplished very quickly. I had to try two more service stations in order to get the right size. While they were fixing the fan belt, we walked clear to the other end of Main St. carrying this huge can of paint. I learned later that it weighed over nineteen lbs. They weren't able to exchange it for the right color, so I had to take a refund. I couldn't get that until the manager came in. He finally did, and back we went to the car. Then I was told they couldn't fix it, because the belt was jammed and I should take it to a garage. Next I had to find a garage that could work on it. The third one I went to said they could do it right away. Then, can you believe this? It turned out that fan belt was also the wrong size! I should have had the size I got originally! The manager got his car and went back to the other service station, got it for me and, in no time, it was fixed. They only charged me fifty cents. I think the reason they were so nice was because I had Chuck and Judy with me. And THAT, my darling absent husband, is a fair example of the trials and tribulations of the struggling wives and children of our men in the service of their country!

It is taking my wrist a long time to heal. It ached so badly today from wielding that huge paint brush. Then I whacked it, right on the incision, on the corner of the chest of drawers. In an instant it turned black and blue.

Donny wants to go uptown tomorrow during lunch hour to buy some "perfume" for a girl he likes. He whispered in my ear, "It's funny. Caroline loves George Brown, and he doesn't love her, and I love Caroline, but she doesn't love me. How come?" I told him that's the way it goes until you meet the right one. He said, "Well, I've met the right one and Oh Boy! I'm never going to change!". . . .

March 9, 1944

Honey:

Today we went to our first Child Psychology class. It was good to see Dr. Bryan again after all this time. We meet in the auditorium of the Community Church in Lafayette. We had a good turn out—forty-two mothers.

Helen told me with great distress and in all seriousness about the TERRIBLE TRAGEDY at her in-laws'. In this world of war and other disasters I thought you should know that "Frank and Dorothy are FRANTIC because the Hoskins' dog broke into their garage and ASSAULTED, I mean CRIMINALLY assaulted, their little cocker. They rushed her to the vet and wanted him to give her a douche or an abortion or something. He told them there was nothing he could do. She would just have to have the Hoskins puppies! Isn't that TERRIBLE?" I really had a hard time being properly sympathetic. It's too bad, but after all—

Holly just scared me to death. He opened the patio door and stuck his head in to ask if I had heard from you this week and when. I was afraid he had some terrible news, and I got weak and shaky. He had heard about your promotion. I am thrilled for you that you got it. But in a way I don't like it because people may think of you as older, maybe thirty seven or so from now on.

NEXT DAY. I wish you could have heard Judy this morning talking about you while we were making her bed. She was wishing you would come home because she likes you so much, and wondering if you would come home soon. Her voice was just dripping with tears. Do you realize how little she has known you? Just a little over eight months before you left, and then the nine weeks at the beach. That's not long to have known a father.

I took Beverly for a walk up the road to see how beautiful the blossoms were and to have some time for just the two of us. When we got back, I put on records, and we danced—Beverly with me and Donny with Judy. They loved that.

I'm like Judy, I wish you would come home because I like you SO MUCH.

March 11, 1944

Good evening, Lovely Lady:

Yesterday one of the enlisted men's barracks challenged the officers to a baseball game. Against my better judgment, I finally agreed to play. It was a lot of fun but awfully hard on an old man of thirty-four! During the game I figured out that I hadn't played a ball game since before some of these enlisted men were even born—1926! I never knew that seven innings could be so long, and I have certainly been stiff today. Of course they swamped us, 17 to 4.

Your letter of February 17th failed to mention what a famous day that was, so I am one up on you, Honey. Have you forgotten that was our first date, fourteen years ago?

I've been making arrangements for us to put out a daily newspaper. Our first effort came out today and received some very favorable comments. This is a new experience for me and should prove to be interesting. I'm sending you a copy and will be eager to hear what you think of it.

Another thing I am inaugurating is a week in the coding room for every officer who is eager to become familiar with the different codes. . . .

March 12, 1944

Dearest Sweet Honey:

Rae went to the officers' club with Myrtle and Holly last night. She met a flier just back from Alaska who didn't waste any time. When he asked, "You say your husband is in Mississippi? My wife is in Kansas, what's your phone number?" Rae told him she didn't have a phone!

When I woke up this morning, I lay watching the bare branches of the Martinos' walnut trees being blown back and forth against a sky that was dusty pink at the horizon and black with clouds above. It looked so threatening, but gradually as the wind grew stronger it blew all the clouds away. It also blew out the pilot light for the furnace. Bernice and I worked fruitlessly for ages. Finally when Dan got home he got it going. I am getting to be a terrible nuisance to my neighbors but it's good to be warm again.

Donny brought Duane home from school to stay for dinner, a bath, and overnight. We had discussed this previously, and I had conceded he could come for dinner and could take a bath, too, but that there were just no more beds in our house. I could really feel for Duane and how he must long for a bath. But Donny had gone ahead and invited him for the whole works without consulting me. When I said "No," Donny was embarrassed, and Duane's feelings were hurt. I felt awful. I invited him to stay for dinner and bath, but he went off in a huff.

It had been a very bad day for Donny. He wanted to get Caroline some perfume but couldn't find any for the fifty cents he had to spend. So instead he spent forty-five cents on a cap gun for Duane, who wanted one so badly. All he could buy Caroline was a five cent pencil. Then he felt terrible. He was so crestfallen about the whole thing. I persuaded Beverly to sell him the tiny bottle of "perfume" she got in her stocking, for ten cents out of his next week's allowance. I found a pretty little hanky I had never used, and we wrapped those two things and the pencil in pretty paper. Donny said, "Oh Mother, I'll never forget this. I will never forget your helping me out like this." He told me tonight that when he gave it to her, "She liked it real well because later on I could smell it all over the whole school room."

"Everybody" is going to the dance at school tomorrow night, so I'll take Donny and sit and watch. Wish you could be there too, then it would be fun.

We have now been cut to two gallons of gas a week. I must apply again for extra gas for our trips to Dr. Hartman. That alone takes two gallons a trip.

Here I sit nodding again. I think I'll write a song that goes, "Here I am a noddin' and a ploddin' along, writin' to my Honey and singin' him a song. How I miss my Honey, My love for him is strong, so here I am a" —etc.

NEXT DAY. Today on our way to Dr. Hartman we picked up an English lady who was also headed for Berkeley. Three buses crowded with soldiers had passed her by. She has one son in the Pacific, one in a Jap prison, and has lost three nephews in the R.A.F. Her son-in-law is a Wing Commander in the R.A.F.

Dr Hartman, the orthodontist, finally got down to brass tacks. The down payment will be $75, which I will pay next week. Then it will be $25 a month for the next twenty months. This doesn't cover anything that arises later. That will be extra. For starters he had to pull a lower incisor. Donny gave only a couple of "ows" when it was pulled and is very proud of his tooth.

FRIDAY NIGHT. I have just come from a most entertaining evening. I took Donny to the dance at school. When we arrived the place was filled with kids, but I didn't see any parents I know until I caught sight of George Brown. Every other dance was either a girls' tag or a boys' tag. When it was a girls' tag, Donny was besieged by Nancy, Ann Seulberger, Gretchen Glover (Navy), and Joan, who is a head taller than he is. George and I had great fun egging our boys on.

I was dying to dance but could see George didn't feel like it. He's on edge waiting for his Commission to come. The lights were out for a couple of dances, but Mr. Ellis didn't do anything about it, which surprised me. Donny told us, "Boy! When they say they turn the lights out so they can hold the girls closer, they weren't kidding. Gretchen sure did it to me."

SUNDAY NIGHT. Yesterday I mounted the Storybook Dolls on the walls in the girls' room, and they look too cute for words. I think their room looks good enough to be in "The American Home" magazine. It's a dream.

Our lawn and the flowers around it are a real haven on a hot day. We invited Myrtle, Holly, and Lee to join us there for a picnic supper. Afterwards we sat watching the children play. It was a kick watching Chuck try to do everything the older ones did. They were playing "red light, green light" at first. Then they turned somersaults, stood on their heads, tried to do handsprings, and played ring-around-a-rosie with the little ones.

This morning dawned bright and beautiful. The girls looked adorable in last year's Easter dresses, the yellow flowered dimities with the big sashes. Donny was unhappy because I wouldn't let him wear jeans to Sunday School. A few little boys do that now, but I don't think it's right. . . .

March 20, 1944

Darn it, Honey!

I awakened this morning absolutely limp from horrible dreams. Donny was a lamb. He told me to stay in bed, and he would take care of breakfast. He separated the cream, heated the milk, and set three places with shredded wheat, canned pears, and glasses of milk. He wanted to fix the eggs, too, but I took over so he would have time to feed the chickens as well as himself before the bus came.

Tonight, while Donny and I did the dishes, he launched into a deep discussion. He said Duane was afraid we were Catholics. Duane thinks "They are terrible because they teach you all the wrong things." That led us into a discussion of prayer. It seems that Duane prayed he and Donny wouldn't meet any bobcats on the trail back from the army camp, and his prayer was answered. But when he prayed that he could stay here all night, God didn't answer that one. That led into a discussion of miracles, which in turn led us to the subject of Easter. Next he wanted to know, "Why doesn't God make the war stop?" He was very bitter about it. I'm afraid I wasn't much help. We talked about the fact that people have to want to do the right thing with God's help. Of course each side is convinced it is in the right and that God should be on their side, but how can God take sides?

The Junior Commandos collect needed items. The cleaners are desperate for coat hangers because none are being made now. They pay a cent apiece for them. The coffee jar drive brought in over $400. The next "raid" will be for newspapers and magazines.

March 20, 1944 11:45 P.M

My Dear Young Man:

I guess you are wondering why I am writing to you so late at night. Well, the reason is, I haven't had any mail for over ten days. I have felt so lonesome and blue all day long that I haven't felt as though I could write a letter. I was all ready to go to bed when I said to myself, "Tonight is Monday night, and that is when Donny asked you to write to him. You have been thinking of him all day, so you simply must do your best to write a letter."

How is Blackie, and does he follow you all the time? Are you good to the girls—I mean your sisters? Do you have time to play with Chuck and Stevie?

I am all over the skin disease that bothered me for so long. You should have seen me when I had that beard. I'll bet you wouldn't have known me.

I am so homesick for all of you, and I love you, Donny, very very much. . . .

March 21, 1944

Hello, Honey Bunch:

I dreamed about you and the children last night. It started at Carpinteria and ended in San Francisco. I can't remember any of the details except that I kept saying to myself, "Just think, I am dreaming about Dot and the children!" Do you ever do that? I mean realize while you are dreaming that it is a dream?

Yesterday we had ball practice. After being beaten as badly as we were, we thought we had better brush up. We had the game today and did better this time. We were only beaten by a score of 5 to 6. I played right field.

In the evening I spent some time with Doc. We enjoy being together because we can each talk nonstop about our families and know the other one is really interested. He and his wife are as crazy about kids as we are. . . .

March 21, 1944

Darlingest Honey:

Today Rae learned that Schick heads are obtainable at a shop in the Monadnock Building. Harry's sister will get one there and have it sent directly to you. I know what a relief that will be.

Today our Sears order came with the white flats I ordered. They have regular soles! No more ugly black marks on our floors, at least not by me.

The Hench twins came home with Donny yesterday. They went up to the Army camp and on the way home stopped at the Schneiders and frightened the cow.Marky called Donny over after dinner and told him they got a gallon less milk tonight. Isn't that awful? Donny said she didn't scold him but just asked him to explain to his friends what happens when they frighten a cow. Don't we have the kindest neighbors?

Jack stayed home from work today to disk their place and ours. He no sooner got started than suddenly he was hit with stomach flu. By noon Marky was in the same boat. I went over after supper to see if there was anything I could do for them, but they just wanted to be left alone in their misery. I fed the chickens and brought Susan home with me.

NEXT DAY. After we left Dr. Hartman's today we stopped on Shattuck. I had heard there were typewriter ribbons available. Sure enough, I was able to get one. What a treat! I hope you are enjoying it. . . . Goodnight, Honey.

March 23, 1944

Dearest Honey:

Gary Brown had Mr. Serby clean up after the pruning and do the disking. He is as hopeless as ever. He burned the prunings, so last night I had to go out with the hose at 11:30 to put out little fires all over the place. While I was gone today, HE BURNED UP MY PRECIOUS COMPOST HEAP! It was the loveliest collection of leaves and chicken manure. It breaks my heart.

While the children were playing in front today, Mrs. Guild drove by and was so interested in looking at them, she went in the ditch. We went to work with shovels and boards. A girl in a Cadillac came by and stopped to help. We talked to her while all this was going on, and who do you think she is? Mrs. Tom Coakley! I mentioned you were in law school with him and what you are doing now. She was so impressed with our family, the fact that there was no Daddy around and that somehow we manage. Oh Honey, when can we be a family again? . . .

March 24, 1944

Hello my Beautiful:

You are getting to be an expert at handling things. But it makes me so mad when I hear about the way garage people take advantage of a woman's lack of knowledge about cars. I'm glad you finally found someone with consideration.

Right after breakfast this morning the "Quiz Kids" went into session and kept at it all day. We examined seventeen men. I enjoy it because I feel we are teaching them as well as examining them.

We learned in mid-afternoon that there was to be a ball game. Bob and I dashed over, and it was my turn at bat the instant I got there. I hit the ball and got on base. To make a long story short, we finally won a game—14–11. I played right field and got two hits out of three times at bat.

Yesterday and today I have been wading through official mail. It is up to me to read everything that comes in and route it where it should go. As a consequence my knowledge about things military enables me to answer almost any question without having to look it up. . . .

The sunset was exceptionally beautiful tonight, but I needed to have you beside me. I hate to quit now but must. Goodnight, Dearest

March 27, 1944

Dear Baby:

Just an individual note to tell you how much I enjoyed your letter. I hope you keep them coming every week. The news about Harry's medal for sharpshooting is great. Will he get an extra $5 a month for that, the same as in the Navy?

Dot writes a lot about Stevie and Frances. That, plus what you write, really gives me a good picture of both of them. Give them each a hug and kiss for me. Of course I will be thinking of Stevie on his birthday Saturday. I wish I could be there to help celebrate. Love to all three of you.

March 31, 1944

My Darling Honey:

We invited Marky and Susan to join us for dinner tonight because Jack was away. It was Donny's turn to help with the dishes, but he was out of earshot on his bike when the time came, so Marky helped me. When he came in, I told him he could help Marky with hers tomorrow night, and he was delighted with the idea.

You'll love this. Susan has a reputation for being a cry baby. Perhaps having to hold her own constantly against six little boys has something to do with it! Marky told us that today she got into a knock-down-drag-out with Gary Pickins who wanted her tricycle while she was on it. They tussled over it. He socked her. She socked him. This went on and on. Finally she noticed that his overall strap was unbuttoned so she said, "Wait a minute, I have to button you." Having done that, she continued socking him until he gave up.

You should see this kitchen. There are clothes hanging everywhere. It takes ten to twelve dresses a week for the girls, plus their overalls, slips, and sunsuits. Then, at least six shirts for Donny, as well as all his play clothes. For Chuck I usually have only a few overalls and one or two little suits a week. Of course, sheets for seven beds and two cribs take a lot of time, too. I wish someone would invent sheets that don't have to be ironed.

Dr. Hartman got Donny's first band on yesterday, and he has been terribly uncomfortable. Last night he just could not eat. He made a determined effort tonight and managed to get all his dinner down. I phoned Verna and learned that Mardi also was acutely uncomfortable when she first had her bands.

I have finally learned to sleep without you. Nevertheless, I would welcome some sleepless nights if you were home. I love you to pieces, my Honey. . . .

April 1, 1944

Oh Honey!

When we gave Stevie his cards and gifts first thing this morning Chucky was so excited you would have thought it was his birthday.

After breakfast Louie Martino arrived with the plow. The next hour or so was spent keeping the multiple little ones out from under the horse's hoofs.

Yesterday, a darling girl named Mary came to look at the rumpus room. She was crazy about the place. She is to be lifeguard when the swimming pool opens at the high school next month. She wanted to know if we would object to a small Boston bull they keep in the house. I was amused. Dogs were fine, I told her, but we had already made a rule that the next tenants had to have a child the age of Lee, and we had also decided not to rent to anyone named Mary, Marge or Mildred, after having had a Myrna, a Mabel, and a Myrtle! But we said that we would make an exception in her case!

Stevie's party was at two. Chucky looked adorable in a little white knit suit Stevie had outgrown. Since the party was strictly for two and three year olds, the girls weren't expected to be a part of it. However, Nancy, Lois, and Betty Jean were here all day, and all five girls had been dressing up. They arrived on the scene in long trailing dresses, picture hats, and high heels.

The kids played ring-around-a-rosie, and I took lots of movies. The cake Rae made was simply gorgeous. She was all in when it was over and terribly low because of it being Stevie's birthday without Harry here.

Holly came to tell me that a Marine captain had spoken to him about our place and wants to come see it. Just as he was telling me, they rolled up with their TWO little boys. I asked them how they could possibly live in one room with two children. They said that was better than being separated again. The wife said plaintively, "We've only been together three months in the past two years, and look what happened," pointing to the two children. "I don't know what will happen this time." "A girl, I hope," I answered. Their boys are Lance, aged ten months, and Michael, aged two years. Since I hadn't heard definitely from Mary, I took the deposit they handed me.

Tonight was the last chance for Myrtle and Holly to go to the club, so they invited me to go along. Mabel and Rusty were there (really cutting a rug[1]). They are magnificent dancers. It killed me to be there without you, and finally, when they played "Who?" for the third time, I wailed, "Take me home!" Oh Honey, how long is this going to go on? . . .

April 2, 1944

Dearest Honey:

When we got home from Sunday School, it was time to get ready for Johnny Gregg's birthday party at Tilden Park. Our trip to Berkeley was rather hair-raising because we couldn't find gas anywhere and were driving on "empty".

---

[1] Doing fancy dancing.

There were twenty four boys, six adults, and five little girls. Before Barbara had even unpacked the other food, seventy two hot dogs had been devoured. Altogether we got rid of eight dozen wieners, two loaves of bread, six dozen rolls, a huge bowl of fruit salad, seven gallons of punch, and three huge cakes. It was bitterly cold and windy. Keeping warm was a full time job. The boys played ball, went on hikes, and everyone had a wonderful time.

NEXT DAY. Donny was eager to get to David's this morning, so he flew through his work with no delays. I decided that if he was determined to spend every waking moment there, I had better get acquainted. I put Chuck and the girls in the car and drove down as he led the way on his bike. We turned down the first road past the high school and drove way down into a beautiful grove of trees surrounding some dilapidated old barns beside a stream. Finally, as we went around a bend and crossed a bridge I saw an almost completed house.

When Donny called to David, his mother came out and introduced herself. To make a long story short, David is the grandson of David Prescott Barrows! The General bought this farm many years ago so the grandchildren would have a place where they could run free and also learn about farm life. David's parents were in the Class of '24 at Cal. He was Dean at Lawrence College in Wisconsin.

They are eager for Donny to come over often and said he should bring his trunks on hot days, since their creek is waist deep. It is an ideal spot, so secluded and yet so near to the highway. Goodnight, my very darling Dear.

April 5, 1944

Hello, Honey:

Today we had a lovely time in Berkeley. First we headed for our old neighborhood at Vine and Berryman. Our friends gathered at Joyce's for lunch. The children enjoyed each other so much, and so did the mothers.

Donny's session with Dr. Hartman was a lot easier, and he is much less uncomfortable. However, he has a new crisis in his life. His one good tire has a leak which Dan is unable to fix, and his solid rubber tire came off.

Frances is here with me. She is talking and cooing in her bassinet, peeking over the edge to smile at me. What a joy she is to all of us.

This evening after the children were in bed I took a bath, put on my fancy slacks and silver sandals, a big white velvet bow in my hair, and perfume. Then I pretended that the doorbell would ring, and there you would be. However, it is after ll:30, and you aren't here yet!

NEXT DAY. I accomplished a lot in the garden today. Judy rode herd on Chuck and Lee. Somehow they got away from her and walked up the road to see the Wooleys' chickens. I had a fit when Mrs. Wooley phoned to say they were there. Oh dear! Obviously their previous punishment didn't sink in!

Duane (the Okie boy without a bathroom) arrived right after breakfast this morning, and Donny welcomed him with a whoop of delight. As soon as his jobs were done, they worked on the bike most of the morning. They fixed it temporarily and went to Lafayette. Donny had fifty cents to spend on the bike, and he bought five rolls of tape with it. When they got back, he painted the bike red, white and blue, wound the whole tire with the tape to keep it on, and patched the other tire. They took off the handle bars, put on the ones from my bike and put my bike rack on his bike. Then he took off his stand to sell to Sonny, who needs it for his paper route. No comment!

I wish you could see the pear blossoms. They are superb this year, thick and white like popcorn. . . .

April 9, 1944

Good evening, my lovely Lady:

I finally received the second class mail—three Tribunes, a Reader's Digest, two Weekly Records, and the box of Christmas cards from all our friends. Sending those cards was a real inspiration. The old newspapers are being devoured voraciously by one and all.

Today I conducted a new class for my radiomen. I am beginning it with lots of math so they'll be able to understand the rest of the course. There are nine in the class, and only three have had anything beyond basic arithmetic. I'll give them algebra, geometry and trigonometry.

It was unbearably hot as I was driving to the other island. Suddenly there was a long refreshing downpour. Because our jeeps, with the tops down, accumulate such a huge amount of rain water, we have drilled several good sized holes in the floor so the water can drain. If the holes become stopped up with leaves, the water in the jeep can be several inches deep in no time at all. As far as I am concerned this is great because the more water, the more I can keep cool.

Your last letter was one in which you did so much griping. I'm glad you don't hesitate to get things off your chest when you write. The best way for us to stay close is to share all our feelings, no matter how depressing they are.

Today had one bright spot. A plane surprised us with mail, your letter of April l, telling all about Stevie's birthday and your evening at St. Mary's. I am so happy that Myrtle and Holly took you out.

I had no idea a cow could be affected that way, so I suppose the boys can't be blamed for not knowing. Why do boys like to frighten animals! Why should I be asking you, when you have never been a boy?

Tonight, since we appear to be leaving soon, we decided to use up our store of treats. Our spread consisted of cokes, olives, peanuts, pretzels and crackers, along with prawns, catsup, A-1 sauce and tabasco sauce!

The latest news here is very disappointing. We won't be paid before late May, if then. That means I can't possibly send you any extra money. Also, the ship which was coming for us, isn't! We have no idea when transportation will arrive. That is the biggest disappointment. I had hoped to be able to phone you on our anniversary. We are packed and ready, so you can imagine how we feel.

I was interrupted last night when a number of the radiomen from the other island came to ask if I would resume the course, which we had to stop because of our preparations to leave. They are eager to start again. . . .

April 10, 1944

Dearest Honey Presh:

This has been the nicest day. I have been spending money! Not a whole lot of money, but I certainly had fun. Chuck was so happy to stay with "Myrno." We planned to take Stevie to the Hotel Oakland, which is now an Army hospital. Rae had already been there twice to find out the regulations and each time had been told something different. Today we were told they took no one under twelve, that the place was full of communicable diseases, and it wasn't safe.

So we went shopping, with Stevie in his Taylor Tot. Rae and I each bought Dutch bonnets. They are very "in" now. Hers is brown, and mine is white. I LOVE IT! Next we saw a sale of pinafores for $1.98. We each got one. Then I got red and white polo shirts for the girls and white ones for Donny and for myself. Next Rae got a doll of a bathing suit, blue and white checked bra top with a full skirt bordered in red flowers. She wants to have her picture taken in it to send to Harry for his "pin up girl."

I got a cute little red wooden wheelbarrow for Chuck for $1. It is so unusual to find well made toys, I couldn't resist. I found a beautifully illustrated copy of "Hansel and Gretel" for the girls and a twenty-five cent copy of "Claudia" over which I chuckled and chortled the rest of the day whenever I had a chance to dip into it. Tonight I totaled up my expenditures. Counting all that, plus three combs, six birthday cards, cookies, shoe cream, stamps, and toothpaste, I had spent $12.58. Not bad in these days of inflation! So at last a weary, goodnight to my very dearest Honey.

April 14, 1944

Honey:

The first event of the day was the departure of the Hollingsworths. The children went out to tell them good-bye before leaving for school. I heard Donny say, "I hope I see you again some day." It made me want to cry. They have a horror of saying good-bye and sneaked off while I was feeding the chickens. I felt so sad about their leaving.

Talk about timing. At that moment the Lembecks arrived. They didn't wait to decide if she liked it, just paid me and started moving in.

There has been a changing of the guard at St. Mary's. Scads of new officers are coming in. Rusty got his orders and right after lunch Mabel came to tell us goodbye. They leave tomorrow at 5 a.m., heading for South Carolina, where he is to be stationed.

The Pickens will be leaving. He is being sent to Corpus Christi. With the baby due any minute, Catherine is in a quandary. She doesn't dare go that far with him by car, or take Gary and go by train to her mother's. Whichever she does, she might have the baby on the way.

While the Lembecks were unpacking, I happened to be doing some planting and cultivating right outside their window. After about half an hour, he yelled out the window, "All right. You can quit now. We're impressed!" However, I continued until I finished and then gave everything a good watering. . . .

April 14, 1944

Lovely Lady Mine:

I have a confession to make, but I don't want anyone to know about it except you. Please don't let it slip, whatever you do. I must finally admit that I share some of Leta and Charlie's feelings about this whole thing[1]. The reason I am telling you this is to help you understand my letters a little better. Also it is impossible to be as close to you as I want to be if I am holding back some of my feelings. Despite all this, I can't say that I'm sorry I took the step. I do know one thing, and that is, after what I have been through and will continue to go through until this mess is over, I will enjoy the years to come so much more fully than I would have had I remained at home.

I see we have traffic signals at Orinda Crossroads now. How come you haven't told me about them? How do I know this? Well, today I saw pictures of them and also of our new four-lane highway. Pete's November-December issue of the California Highway and Public Works magazine has two pages devoted to it.

You were asking about Bob. In civilian life he was a college instructor. His field is Botany. He is certainly a fine person. It is wonderful to have found such a good friend over here so far from everyone I love.

Last night Doc and I talked about everything from whether Woodrow Wilson was a good president to the landscaping of the cemetery here! Several other officers dropped by, and Howard, who is in charge of the commissary, brought some ice cold orange juice. It was a real treat, even though it was made from Florida oranges. We kid each other a lot because he is from Florida and we are always arguing that "our" fruit is better. . . .

After seeing the enclosed picture, I'm sure you are wondering about my "Harem!" You can see how good natured the women look and how very

---

[1] Disillusionment with the waste of personnel and material, with the attitude of the infallibility of Naval Academy graduates, and the treatment of the Stewards Mates (the negro sailors) by many of the officers.

unattractive they are. These are supposed to be the beauties of the island! The men here like their women well padded!

Goodnight my Precious.

April 16, 1944

Dearest Honey:

As I look out the kitchen window I see Betty Lembeck, Lance, Mike, Bernice, Philip, Chuck, and Stevie. It's like watching a three ring circus, trying to keep track of everything that is going on. Betty is the prettiest thing and not at all artificial as we thought at first. You would like her.

I used Jack's heavy hoe to chop weeds most of the day. The more I chopped, the more hopeless it looked because there was still such a huge area left. Wouldn't it be wonderful if some day someone would discover a way to get rid of weeds painlessly and permanently?

Captain Lembeck's father came from L.A. for the weekend. In no time he and Captain Lembeck had built a framework for the bunks, so they can hang drapes to keep it dark for the boys when they go to bed.

Betty was afraid we would be bothered by their dog, Gretchen. She is really a lovely dog, spayed, very intelligent and well behaved. She and Blackie are good friends already.

As soon as we got home from Sunday School today, Donny was off with his gun. Oh, I forgot to tell you. When they arrived, Captain Lembeck brought Donny a practice rifle. I had suggested that he talk to Donny about not teasing Gretchen, and he figured giving him the gun at the same time might be a good idea. You never saw anyone so thrilled as Donny was. It is nothing to worry about. It's all wood, just a dummy gun.

When he got back just before dinner, he arrived with a BB gun, a helmet, and a bicycle flashlight. Sunny had persuaded him to trade. He knows we won't let him have a BB gun, and I was furious. He said he couldn't possibly trade back because he had "crossed my heart and hope to die." I'll have to go to Sunny's tomorrow and get that straightened out. I love you, love you, love you.

April 17, 1944

Dear, Dear Honey:

We like the Lembecks better all the time. Tonight I looked out and saw him mending the back fence. He has made a swing for the little ones and asked if he could take Donny's and Stevie's wagons to St. Mary's and get them fixed.

Today Rae and Betty shopped together, so Rae came home with lots of information. Betty is twenty-three. They were married just six weeks before Rae and Harry. Betty, like Rae, had just a year of college, and a try at Hollywood before marrying. He graduated from U.C.L.A. and was San Diego manager for Commercial Credit Corporation for ten years.

Betty loves to sew and has the most gorgeous outfits for which we assumed she had paid a small fortune. She is enjoying our rumpus room thoroughly because of the minimum housework involved.

NEXT DAY. Just in case you may have forgotten, today is the 169th anniversary of Paul Revere's Ride! Also thirty-eight years ago was the S.F. earthquake and fire! I wonder what historic event happened in our world today.

Bert brought Donny two huge colored charts about service insignia. He also brought film and the wagons he had fixed. Tonight he repaired the electric heater and asked what else he could do, so I handed him the broken vacuum cleaner cord.

Donny was going to leave home tonight, but I told him I would like him to have a good night's sleep first so he would be well rested before he started. He wrote a memo to himself and put it on the end of his bed with his clothes so he wouldn't forget to leave home. Then he asked me to be sure not to destroy it, or he might forget to go. The reason he is leaving is because he isn't treated right around here! He had to stop playing tonight and dry the dishes! Beverly and Judy were in tears over his departure. Beverly sobbed, "If he goes, I won't have any brothers left except Chucky and Stevie."

Rae brought hula skirts home for the girls from Babe. You can imagine the joy around here this evening. You know how long the girls have been dying to have them. One is orange and quite long. It looks superb on Bev. The other is cerise and purple, and does Judy ever look seductive in it!!! They had a great time in their room after dinner, putting on a show, with bandannas tied around them for "bras". Good night, My Beloved. . . .

April 18, 1944

My Love:

A very sad thing happened this afternoon. The colored boy who takes care of our fale drowned. He was young, single, and such a nice kid. It is a shock to all of us. Two other men almost drowned and are in sick bay suffering from shock and water in their lungs. They were on liberty and had gone to the island where the natives live now. They couldn't swim in the strong tide as they waded back to the boat.

This meant I had a lot of details to take care of this evening. I had to send dispatches to Washington and to the chain of command. There will also be a lot of reports to complete within the next few days. The funeral will be tomorrow, and I had to make the arrangements. Doesn't it seem strange that in an outfit as small as ours, we have had two such similar tragedies? We are all pretty low tonight.

This afternoon, when I finished teaching my class, I discovered the rain had flooded the jeep, the plugs were wet, and I had to be pushed nearly a mile to get it started.

The picture I am enclosing shows our ship being loaded. In the background you can see the church and the missionaries' house. You can also see how steep the mountain is on which we lived. The light spot near the top is the edge of the cliff from which that seaman fell. . . .

April 22, 1944

My Honey:

Taking the children and Betty Jean to see "Lassie come Home" last night was quite an experience. It turned out to be an emotional orgy for the children, and it's lucky I took four hankies along. The dog is just wonderful. She made us all love Blackie that much more. The story is about a poor Yorkshire family who, not having enough food for the family, had given their dog to a Duke. Even when she was taken to Scotland, she kept running away and coming back to them through all sorts of narrow escapes.

Judy was the first one to break down. Soon Donny was sobbing and reaching for a hanky, then Beverly. Finally Betty Jean gave in and reached for one too. If you could have heard Judy's dear vibrant little voice ringing through the theater, "Oh Mother! Is she going to get away? I can't bear it. Oh Mother, is she going to drown? Oh Mother, is she going to get shot? I can't bear it." Finally I took her in my arms and held her. Then Beverly leaned over to cry on my shoulder. Eventually Betty Jean and Bev sat together in one seat with their arms around each other, sobbing into each other's tangled red curls.

As we prepared to leave, a Hollywood Preview started. Even though it had the trivial title of "Four Jills And A Jeep", we couldn't resist it. It was the story of Command Performance tours put on by stars to entertain the boys overseas, and we loved it! Betty Grable sang "Cuddle Up A Little Closer", and I never in my life heard anything sung so cuddly. Of course I was crying over that one, but lo and behold, so was Judy.

Bert is off on Fridays at noon, so they have a standing date to go out on the town. A nice elderly lady named Mrs. Powell comes to stay with the boys. I asked if they would leave them with me, but they wouldn't consider it for that length of time. However when I suggested they go over to the base tonight, they agreed to let me "baby sit". That is a new expression and seems to include all ages, not just babies. I wish you could have seen Betty when they left. I doubt if there's a Powers model who could outshine her. I never dreamed anyone could look like Betty and still be as sweet, genuine, and down to earth as she is.

I forgot to tell you the sad news. Marky's turkey died on the nest which, in case you didn't know it (I didn't), is, in Turkeyland the same as dying in childbirth. There were seventeen eggs, and they are trying to keep several hens on them to keep them warm until they hatch. Tomorrow will tell the tale. They need those seventeen little turkeys to fulfill their War Production Board farming quota. . . ."Time to retire," as the billboards for Fisk tires proclaim.

April 23, 1944

Darling Honey!

Betty came in just as Marky and I were leaving for our class. Mike had stuffed toilet paper way up his nose, and she hadn't been able to get it out. Marky and I both tried and failed, so I told Betty to use my car and take him to the clinic at St. Mary's. As a result we were pretty late to class.

Afterwards Dr. Bryan asked all about you and bawled me out for taking on too much. She said I should think of myself more, and I shouldn't have so many people in the house. I explained how good it is for all of us, especially for Donny, to have a man around. As she got into the car, she added, "I'm sure you know I wouldn't dare talk this way to you if I didn't love you so much." I certainly hope she knows how grateful I am for her help when I was in that deep depression two years ago. I really owe what emotional strength I have to her finding the magic words to say to me. Remember what she said? "The trouble is, you are trying to make life Heaven on earth for every member of your family, and life just is NOT Heaven on earth."

When I got home, Betty had done the dishes and was hanging out my wash. She thanked me again and again for letting her use my car. At the clinic, with the doctor and two corpsmen holding Mike, they took a wad of paper the size of a marble out of his nose. It was way up near the eyes.

Rae received a record from Harry telling all about his leave in New Orleans over Easter. We all enjoyed it so much, but the needle got stuck on "Say hello to Dot," and kept saying that over and over. Too bad it didn't get stuck when he was saying "I love you" to Rae. Goodnight Honey. I love you to pieces.

April 24, 1944

Dearest Honey:

After Sunday school Bert and Donny started working on the play-house. They are screening the latticed window and putting hinges on the door. It's getting to be quite an edifice. Bert is going to bring 2x4s, which they are "surveying" (throwing out) at St. Mary's, to build a fence around the vegetable garden. I have chicken wire around it now to keep the dogs and chickens out.

Gretchen got herself in bad today. She followed the girls up to the Browns' and came home with a young chicken in her mouth. I quickly got Betty. She and Bert talked to Gretchen, whipped her with a newspaper, tied the chicken around her neck, tied her to a tree, and kept her there for several hours. I hope she knows better now.

The turkeys started hatching today. We all went over there, and Marky held eggs to our ears. We could hear the pick pick and chip chip inside, and one had a series of tiny holes picked clear around one end. After supper we all went back again. One little turkey was out, and several others were making headway.

Betty and Bert have such good times together. I used to envy Myrtle and Holly, and likewise Mabel and Rusty, when they lived here. I think I envy Bert and Betty most of all. No, I think the couple who used to live here a long time ago—it feels to me like a VERY long time ago—Don and Dot. I think they are the ones I envy most of all.

I often get scared when I think of how it will be when the war is over. I'm so afraid life won't be up to our expectations. Will it be the same rush, rush, rush? I want it to be different. I think you too have an idyllic picture of it. If it could only be the way it was at Carpinteria, those wonderful, terrible months, but without the pain of the impending separation hanging over us. It was so heavenly there when we could forget why we were there, just the six of us with no outside demands coming at us from all directions.

Yes, Blackie is the nicest dog we have ever had. Bert and Betty are so pleased at the way he and Gretchen get along and also especially pleased at the way Gretchen and Donny get along. She has never tolerated boys before, always barked and growled at them. She and Donny adore each other. ILOVEYOUILOVEYOU.

April 27, 1944

Dearest Darling Honey:

This morning Bev and I went to Dr. Beede. We each had our shot. Then he gave her a thorough examination. He said she is fine physically, and her posture has improved. He was very nice and leisurely with us. Out of her presence, he said he could find no physical reason for her actions lately. He suggested I find out if she gets teased about her red hair and freckles or anything else. He too thinks it might be your absence that causes her unhappiness.

I took everyone along today when we went to the orthodontist. We had to look for shoes, try to get the bikes fixed, leave some stuff off at the folks for the various scrap drives, and try again to find some satisfactory panties for the girls. We had no luck with shoes, panties, or bikes, but we did have a delicious dinner at the folks' afterwards. The children ate as though they hadn't had a square meal in months. Of course that made Mama happy.

They all had a good time with Daddy, and I read fifteen of John's letters. Like you, he can't say much. He can't see why, because the German planes fly overhead and see everything that's going on. He says he is in a historical spot, does back-breaking physical labor, and has to travel fifteen miles to get a shower!

You asked about the Junior Commandos—Jean Hall came up with this idea for the Walnut Branch of Children's Hospital. It helps the war effort, makes money for the hospital, and fosters patriotism on the part of the kids.

Billy Woo is missing in action over Austria. Daddy is terribly worried about him. . . .

Goodnight, my Honey.

April 28, 1944

My Dearest:

I have never been busier than for the past thirty six hours. Right now I am in the back seat of the Command car, having just awakened from an hour's sleep, the first I've had since 6 a.m. yesterday.

LATER by one day! I was interrupted at that point. BE SURE TO REMEMBER TO ASK ABOUT THIS INTERRUPTION WHEN I GET HOME AFTER THE WAR.

I'm enjoying the breeze in the very same spot where I sat to write you as I waited to get leave. This is our stopover on the way to our destination. We're waiting for the unit which came with us when we left the States.

Today I sent a box to you containing two grass skirts for the girls and a large boat for Chuck and Donny. It's an exact replica of the native pow pows on our island. There is also a native fish hook for Harry, shell necklaces for you, Rae, Midge, and Mother, and some rather special sea shells. It only cost forty-five cents to send all that because the Navy ships it from here to S.F. free. The postage is only from S.F. to Lafayette. . . . Your Honey.

April 30, 1944

My Honey:

The Bendix man came this morning and took the motor to the shop for a new clutch. That will cost $1. The labor could run as high as $4.50. Something to wreck the budget always happens. This month it's cold shots for all of us, too.

Last night was Open House. Donny was so proud to show us his array of spelling papers on the board, all marked 100%. Beverly had fun showing Judy everything in her room. Judy is anxious for the time to come when she can start to "real school." I hope we'll have a kindergarten by the time Chuck is five. It's too bad everybody can't have a teacher as fine as Donny's. Mrs. Christian, in her gentle, no nonsense way, brings out the best in everyone. NEXT DAY. I had to get up at 4:30 to start our car because Babe wasn't able to when she and Rae left for Oakland to meet Harry at the train. Harry looks so nice and tan. He couldn't get over how much Frances had changed since he left.

Donny came home with the news that Miss Muir came back and is now Mrs. Peterson. Her fiancee had three weeks leave before going overseas, so they decided to get married. There is so much of that going on, and we are losing teachers right and left. Either they leave to join their husbands who have been transferred, or to marry before they go overseas, or to have a baby. The war is tough on us, but even tougher on the younger ones whose lives are getting messed up right from the start.

Do you realize that seven years ago today we brought home that precious little pink-cheeked, blue-eyed, red-headed Beverly of ours? What a joyous day for us all, and what a joy she has been! Can you possibly imagine life without her? Actually it is beyond me to be able to imagine life without any of them.

Bert bought a '31 Ford and was having it worked on, so he invited Donny to go with him to pick it up. Donny was in seventh heaven. When they got back, Donny washed the car, cleaned off the tires, and really did a swell job. He was so pleased with himself. Having Bert to work with is so good for him.

Rae and Harry went fishing today and brought home three gorgeous bass, 4 lbs., 9 lbs., and 15 lbs. They are here in the kitchen cutting them up. The whole neighborhood is going to be eating fish!

The Stocktons are buying a farm and moving to Washington. Since they both come from a farming background, they expect to do well. He worked everything out with his draft board. Their plans are acceptable, and his worries about being drafted are over. I was stunned when she phoned to tell me. They sold their house in one day and got $5600 for it. Isn't that amazing? That $1000 profit will come in handy. The farmhouse is far too small for their family of six, but they expect to add to it right away. Since farmers are needed so desperately Milburn should have little or no trouble with the War Production Board in getting materials. . . . Love you to pieces!

May 1, 1944

Dear Daddy:

How are you? Bob Keeney said he is going to sell a pony. Mother said if you were home, I'd have the pony right now. Today I'm going to find out how much it is. Then I'm going to save my money. I asked Mother if I could have $5 out of the money I get for my room. But she said NO!! Love, Donny Fibush.

P.S. Because $4.50 of it has to go for war stamps! I spanked Chuckie because he pulled my radio down and broke it, and I lied about it.

May 1, 1944. AT SEA

My Precious One:

This trip may last quite a while. So far two major events have occurred. I just had a wonderful fried chicken dinner, my first since we left California. Secondly there are white women aboard—nurses. Yesterday Bob and I talked to a couple of them. They were standing next to us on deck, so it was very opportune. One of them is from Jeb's home town and knows his wife. She is on her way home after being out here over a year. Her husband is in the army.

My bunk is just three feet from the fan. What a break! This ship will be going back to the U.S. eventually. If only it would forget to make any other stops before doing that!

It is nice getting reacquainted with some of the fellows we haven't seen for so long. The main topic of conversation is where we might be going. Our unit looks like a bunch of tramps compared to the other officers. Our clothes are so worn out and so faded, we are ashamed to be seen in them.

I am so glad that Donny has David Barrows to play with. When David Prescott Barrows was president of Cal, we never dreamed that some day our son would be the playmate of his grandson. I'm so glad you are finding more ways for Donny to be with other boys. I know it must have been a hard decision for you to let him ride his bicycle on the highway.

I just counted noses and realized that right now, with Harry there, you have five adults, eight children, and two dogs. I would call that a "full house!" I didn't even count the chickens—how many?

I know where the food of which you civilians are being deprived is going. It's coming right here. The meals continue to be superb. It's hard to believe we can continue to have real eggs and all sorts of fresh foods. No SPAM! No beans! No powdered eggs! One thing we still long for is fresh milk.

There are seven of us in our stateroom, and we have a FRESH WATER shower. It is only turned on for a few hours a day, but what a treat it is. The ocean has marvelous swells which most of us enjoy but which cause some to get seasick. Our watches help break the monotony. . . .

May 5, 1944

Dearest Honey:

Yesterday Rae and Harry were gone most of the day, then changed and met Babe and Mitch at the Claremont Hotel. Incidentally the Claremont is charging $7.72 a couple for dinner dancing now, even on a week night. Isn't that atrocious? Sounds more like Big Game night or New Year's Eve.

Before they left Harry showed me how to use his paint spray equipment to paint the playhouse. I got the job done by noon. It really looks good.

After I fed the little ones and put them down for their naps, I sprayed the chicken house. It certainly looks improved, and it's surprising how attractive pale green chickens are! About the time I finished, Bert got home from the base, and he had no criticism for my paint job. However he did have a few cracks to make about my appearance. I far outdid the chickens.

By four I had finished the gates, two saw horses, the clothes line posts, and a ladder. It took over half an hour to clean the spray gun. You should have seen me. Talk about a MESS! By this time I was shaking with fatigue.

Mrs. Powell was taking care of Mike and Lance and having a hard time coping. Lance was burning up, but believe it or not, she didn't know how to take a temperature rectally. She explained she'd always had a nursemaid for her children and knew very little about how to care for them! When I took his temp, it was 103.4. I showed her how to cool him down with wet towels.

NEXT DAY. This has been quite a day. Briefly the kids cooked their breakfast over an open fire, your friend Dave from Argus 9 Unit phoned, I went to pieces, and we made ice cream in an old-fashioned ice cream freezer.

I was quite impressed with Donny's prowess over the fire he built. He not only fried eggs but made hot cakes which they all enjoyed. Then he helped me saw 2x4s until time for us to get dressed for Sunday school.

Dave said he was arranging his transportation home, so would phone later to let me know what time he would be out to see us.

Rae and Harry were just getting up when we got home from S.S. I was trying to fix lunch for the kids. Rae and Harry were fixing their breakfast. I was on pins and needles waiting for Dave's call. Uncle George and Aunt Gertie were due shortly, and the place was getting messier by the minute. Suddenly it was all just too much for me. I flew to my room and burst into tears.

Donny was scared and went to get Bert. Bert called through my window to ask what was wrong. I was crying too hard to answer. In a minute Betty came in. She stroked my back and talked to me very softly, telling me that I had to stop doing so much and take more time out for myself. It felt so good to have someone taking care of ME for a change. She asked me to lay there and relax for half an hour. I tried, but I just couldn't.

Chuckie started crying, and when I went to him, the tears were rolling down his cheeks. He kept saying something over and over which I couldn't understand. This left us both frustrated. Just then Rae came in. She hadn't been aware of what had happened. "What's going on?" she asked."Betty told me she had just put you to bed and to please be quiet," she said. "I told her I wasn't making any noise, but she looked as though she meant business, so I didn't argue."

I tried to calm my face down with cold water and got into my white shorts and blouse. Then just as Betty and I were getting the mess in the kitchen cleaned up, Uncle George and Aunt Gertie arrived—in the kitchen. They left immediately with Rae and Harry, taking Stevie with them.

In the meantime, Bert and the kids were having a marvelous time turning the handle of the Condits' old-fashioned ice cream freezer. When they finished, the nine of us demolished the whole two quarts in a flash.

Dan came to measure for a pipe to run through my vegetable garden to make the watering easier for me. Jack came by to see if I wanted them to spray our poison oak along the creek when the Underhills' rig comes to spray theirs. Was I thrilled! I have been dreading doing that two hundred foot stretch of it myself. Aren't people nice to me? How lucky I am to have such wonderful neighbors.

Just as I was about to start dinner, Dave Gould called back to say he couldn't come. His transportation was arranged, and he was leaving immediately. I was TERRIBLY disappointed. There were so many questions I wanted to ask.

Just as I hung up, the Woods arrived unexpectedly. I showed them all the pictures you sent, and they were fascinated. He said Glassburg and Clotier have both been drafted. They appealed to the draft board, because Glassburg has five children and Clotier has six, but it didn't do any good.

The kids had a great time cooking hamburgers and potatoes outdoors and consumed large quantities of raw carrots, celery and lettuce while they were doing it. After that they came in and had more home made ice cream along with crushed strawberries from our garden. Is your mouth watering?

May 9, 1944

Honey:

No school yesterday—teacher's institute. The kids had a great time playing in and around the playhouse all day. Chuckie huddled inside with them just like one of the gang. I love it when they play so beautifully together.

After all six of them were tucked in bed, Marky came over to give me last minute instructions about feeding the dog, cats, chickens, and turkeys. Susan is having her eye operation, and Marky will stay at the hospital overnight.

Today I gave the kids a big thrill—notes to their teachers so they could eat lunch uptown. They had acquired quite a bit of money for defense stamps and had also been wanting to go uptown to buy my Mother's Day present. They had $10 to spend on stamps. Also they each had their twenty five cent allowance and a quarter apiece for lunch. They shared toasted sandwiches and a milk shake. Donny bought nail polish remover, stationery, and air mail envelopes, and Beverly bought nail polish. All were things they knew I needed.

Bert brought your uniform back today. The new stripes are very impressive. The charge was $2, including having it cleaned. He is also trying to get the wristwatch band you want. I love you to pieces, Honey. Goodnight.

May 9, 1944

Dearest Mine:

So much has happened since I wrote that it would take weeks to tell you about it, even if I were allowed to. Sunday was one of the most interesting days I have ever experienced. I will NEVER forget the things I saw[1]. Our quarters are excellent. The food is marvelous but expensive ($1.50 a day). Everything is spread out, but luckily I have government transportation.

We were anxious to see our surroundings. Bill and I took a bus to Honolulu, walked for hours, then had the best steaks west of California, wonderful tenderloins an inch-and-a-half thick.

This morning I bumped into Al Hargrave. He says never a day goes by here that he doesn't run across someone he has known either at Cal or in the Navy.

At Ship's Service I bought the clothes I have needed so badly. I got the grays—

---

[1]The devastation at Pearl Harbor.

two trousers, six shirts, also a tie, a belt, a pair of shoes, three skivvies, and three shorts. I still need a grey jacket.

I'm hoping to phone you while I'm here, but I might not be allowed to.

MAY TENTH! I have been perishing to write ever since we talked in the wee hours this morning. I intended to get transportation back to quarters and then write to my heart's content. Instead, I found everything had stopped by that hour because no one is allowed on the streets. In desperation I thought of the Army-Navy Y.M.C.A. The sign on the desk said NO ROOMS OR COTS. When I explained my predicament, the man at the desk said he would see what he could do. As soon as there was no one around, he motioned to me and took me to a room all to myself with a REAL BED.

I was so excited by the phone call. It was marvelous, wasn't it? I couldn't sleep, so I re-read the twelve letters I received yesterday. Then I kept thinking of you for over three hours before I finally fell asleep. I thought our phone conversation was so satisfactory and enjoyed every second of it. That is the best value I have ever in my life received for money spent. Almost two-thirds of the time your voice was quite clear.

I have been on the go every minute today and finally succeeded in getting the kind of duty I want. Everyone thinks I have gotten a marvelous break, and so do I. If all goes well, I should have good duty for the balance of the war.

Bob will be calling you before long. No matter what you're doing, arrange to see him. It will probably be some time before you hear from me again. Use the address on this envelope until I can send my new one.

I am even more restricted here as to what I can write, but I think it's all right to tell you I will be on an Admiral's staff and will be doing what I was trained to do. I wanted to send you flowers or a plant for our anniversary, but it's verboten. I was lucky to be able to phone. It took a bit of doing!

Midge will probably be thrilled to know Henry Fonda has the bunk right next to me. Today we rode together on a boat and also the officers' auto transportation and had an interesting conversation. He is a j.g. Nice fellow.

I am wearing my grays today for the first time, and I feel like a Greyhound bus driver! I'll have to get used to them. Goodnight for now . . .

May 10, 1944

My Darling Honey:

I've been having a lovely time thinking about our phone call, enjoying it even more in retrospect than I did at the time it happened. I was so excited all day I wanted to stop strangers on the street and tell them.

At two minutes past midnight the phone rang. As I bounded to the phone (after the war let's get a phone beside our bed), I wondered if it could be you. After the operator ascertained who I was and told me the long list of things we couldn't mention, she said it would take a while for the connection. I put on a robe, closed the windows so I wouldn't freeze (can you vaguely imagine freezing?) and got the paper to read while I waited. I was so calm. I wasn't shaking at all. She called back sooner than I expected. It was good I had a little wait so I wasn't all fuzzed up with sleepiness.

You mentioned that a lot more of the fellows are coming home on leave. Have they all been out eighteen months or more? I got a kick out of your saying you were more nervous and excited than you were twelve years ago at our wedding. I felt the same way. No wonder. We love each other so infinitely more than we did then.

For a long time I was too excited to sleep. When I woke up it was so light I thought I had overslept, that Harry had missed the bus and would be AOL! I went into the living room to look at the clock. It was 4:15 a.m. The full moon had made it look like daylight.

Unfortunately, when we started the day at 5:30, all the children woke up, too. It was lucky we left a little early, as Harry's bus arrived just as we did. During the afternoon Rae was lying in bed crying and saying she guessed life must go on, but she didn't see how it could. I went downstairs just in time to see Steve kicking off an extremely messy diaper. I picked him up gingerly, dashed back upstairs with him, and handed him to her to clean up, saying, "Yep, you were darn right when you said life must go on," as I dashed back down the stairs to clean up his mess on the kitchen floor!

When Susan got home from the hospital, Judy, Chuckie, and I took some records and the toy piano over for her to use while she is recuperating. Her whole face is bandaged, and she has to grope for things and people. She wants to hold on to people when she talks to them. It is a relief to have it over.

NEXT DAY. This morning Judy and Chuck were playing at Bernice's. Bernice came in to see if I had any two-inch adhesive because they had discovered Susan could see out of her bandage. A minute later Judy and Philip came in with a very black Chuckie. While Bernice had dashed over to the Schneiders', leaving them for a minute, he had gotten into her bottle of jet black ink and spilled it on their bedroom rug. I spent hours trying to get it out with lemon juice and vinegar. I feel terrible!

When the mail came, there were your letters from May 1-6. What a thrill. I lay down to read them and fell asleep. When I woke up, it was 3:30, and Frances was screaming hard. I called upstairs to Rae and asked her if Frances needed anything. Then she remembered she hadn't given her any lunch. I am getting so discouraged. She spent yesterday talking about taking poison and then dreamed all night that she had. I'm frightened. I don't know what to do.

We had a 4 o'clock appointment with Dr. Beede. What a mob! His three waiting rooms were full, with a child on almost every mother's lap. I wonder when we will ever have more than one doctor in the entire area again.

I hope I can send the movies to you before you move on. There is one shot of me in the ocean at Carpenteria, holding Chuckie, that you would love. Bert asked, "Who's the babe?," and he didn't mean Chuckie. In our last roll there is a shot that just slays me every time I see it. I'm herding the children from the house to the car, with a top sergeant look on my face, saying, "Come on! Hurry up!" I'm afraid those four words are the main thing my children will remember about me when they grow up! . . . I miss you so Honey.

NEXT DAY. I must tell you about the meeting tonight. It was at the Senior Browns'. The main subject was the proposed leasing of all our properties to Shell Oil. Now don't panic. They no longer use derricks, and the restrictions would make it impossible for them to drill on any of the property in our part of the valley. As far as the money is concerned, it would be practically nothing for us. Everyone who signs will get $1 a year per acre and then a pro rata share if there is any production. The most interesting part of it for me was, when they introduced the speaker from Shell Oil, he said, "Oh yes. I've known Dot since high school and college." It was Bub Hugill! . . .

Saturday, May 13, 1944

Hi Beautiful and Wonderful!

I have been on the go constantly since I last wrote. In fact I'd had only thirteen hours sleep in the previous eighty four, when I finally got to bed. There is so much to tell you and at least four times as much that I can't.

The fellows gave me a grand farewell; then I learned I would be detained another day. I ran into Warren Olney, who graduated from Boalt in '27. I hadn't seen him in years. Since we were "both in the same boat" LITERALLY, we spent the intervening time together. We were able to get a room at the "Y" and spent our time at Waikiki Beach. The swimming was good but no better than the California beaches, and the breakers didn't compare to those at Carpinteria.

After I wrote my last letter to you I received a lot more mail including the Schick head and the copy of "Claudia" you sent. I have read over half of it and am enjoying it even more than I did the first time.

I am thrilled about my new duty and wish I could tell you more. The fellows are all envious and gasped when I told them about it. Also, I learned that my time at Port Hueneme definitely counts as sea duty. That will make me eligible for shore duty three months sooner. Wouldn't it be wonderful if I could be home for Christmas?

I have your picture and the snaps of the children in front of me as I write. Oh how I enjoy them. I had fun asking people how old you look. Everyone guesses between twenty-five and twenty-seven. I must say "Goodnight" now.

May 13, 1944

Dearest Honey:

Now for the pleasure of answering your letters. No, David never comes here. He is too fond of his horses to leave them. Sonny is Sonny Cole. The

Coles are the Okie family who live in the Jap shack on the Hink place and work the land for him since the Japs were taken away. Yes, we did get the dummy rifle back from him. Your trip sounds swell. It must be wonderful to have such "deluxe" surroundings after the way you have been living.

Now it's 8:30. It just about killed the children when I called them in. They wanted to stay out till dark and play hide and seek with Bert and Betty. Sometimes I think I'll never live through daylight saving, or "War Time" as it is called now. It's hard for them to go to bed when the sun is still so bright. Tomorrow is the big day. Lance will be one year old. Chuckie and Mike are both excited about the party, but the one who is most excited is Bert!

SUNDAY NIGHT. Today was rather disappointing because it clouded over, turned dark and cold, and then started to rain. It was coming down in torrents as we drove home from Sunday School.

After lunch Bert and the children made ice cream for the party. Chuckie woke up from his nap yelling, "Party, party, party." It was disappointing having to eat indoors. Betty set a darling party table, and the angel food cake she made, covered with strawberries and ice cream, was superb.

Rae talked with me tonight about how dissatisfied she is with everything, including herself. She says she is not only lonesome for Harry, but she can't stand anything or anybody, and she doesn't want to do anything at all. She says she wishes she would help me in the garden, but she doesn't feel like it. It bores her. She would love to get a job. She is going to try to get her house back. I'm sure Uncle George would help support her if she did. She says it isn't my fault she isn't happy here. She realizes it's all within herself. My heart aches for her, but I don't know what to do. Having to be away from her own home is tough on top of having Harry gone. Oh Honey, I need you so badly.

May 14, 1944

Hello, my Lovely Lady:

Yesterday we had fresh fruit! We have plenty of it here. There are apples and oranges available in the wardroom every afternoon. Also did I tell you, while we were at Pearl Harbor, I had FRESH MILK!

Last night I had a wonderful sleep. My bed is SO comfortable. I have finally learned to sleep without you, but I'll NEVER learn to enjoy it.

This is an enormous place. I'm gradually getting acquainted and last night met two officers from San Francisco. We had some interesting conversation.

I must get appointments shortly for dental work and a haircut. Officers here have haircuts by appointment only, instead of having to stand in line.

I enjoy the letters from Leta and Charlie as well as the others you send. It is hard to answer your questions about how I feel as compared to them. It is against censorship rules to say anything derogatory about the war effort, so I will have to wait until I see you. Perhaps Bob can supply you with answers. He knows me so well. By the time I see you I might have a different attitude.

It's going to be even more difficult to write interesting letters than it has been in the past. There is even less that I can tell you about here. For example— "My Day"—I got an excellent haircut without having to wait. I moved to a different room which I think will be more convenient and comfortable. We had ice cream again for lunch. We can always have cake or a cookie with it and as many helpings as we like. Had another orange in the middle of the morning. I had a meeting this morning and will be going on duty as soon as I finish this letter. Exciting, huh?

I'm glad to know Beverly is ok physically, but what do you think is causing her to be so droopy and unhappy? Do you really think it could have anything to do with my being gone? In what ways does she show her unhappiness? I can't bear to think of our precious Poochy being that way. . . .

May 16, 1944

My Own Sweet Poochy:

I love you so much and miss you terribly. Please write me another nice letter so I can answer it.

I hope you are fine and that you help mother a lot. How is school? Are you enjoying it? Are you having fun with Betty Jean? I'll bet you have a lot of fun with Frances and with Chuck and Stevie. Here is a big kiss and a big hug. O X

Daddy

May 17, 1944

Honey Darling:

I don't know whether I like your new duty. Will you be on a carrier? Is there any way that you can tell me the name of the Admiral? Is it Nimitz?

I'm excited about the prospect of meeting Bob, but so envious. How come he gets to come back, and you don't? I'm happy for him and for Ann but—

Beverly is simply palpitating over your proximity to Henry Fonda! Me, too! But you're the one I LOVE!

This morning Marky and Rae took Susan to have her bandage taken off. Afterwards they went to the Army commissary and came home with six dozen bananas!!!!! On the way home they gave rides to two soldiers and a sailor who is crazy about children and would LOVE to come out some Sunday and play with all of ours. Apparently he took quite a shine to Rae!

Since it was orthodontia day, we looked for coats for the girls while we were in Berkeley. Then came the exciting part. We stopped at the bike shop, and I paid a $25 deposit on a bike for Donny. If I know he has a good dependable bike, I can let him visit his friends in Lafayette and Happy Valley this summer. It will be good for him to have a chance to be a little independent.

The bike will have balloon tires, good brakes, almost all new parts, and will be the right size for him. Fortunately he didn't go into the shop with me, so it will be a surprise. He is resigned to waiting three more weeks to get his old bike back with new tires and brakes. He is so thrilled about that. Imagine how he'll feel when he sees what he does get!

We went to the folks' for Mama's usual outstanding dinner, after which Daddy played games with the children. Then Donny read the paper to him. He was floored at how well Donny reads without faltering over foreign names.

Rae and I had lots to talk about when we got home. She is hoping she and Gram can find a place at Santa Cruz for three months this summer. She can't face the thought of summer here with all the children home from school. I'm looking forward to summer. No pressure of bus catching, less ironing, and the swimming pool at the high school. If only you could be with us. . . .

May 17, 1944

My Precious:

For a while we won't be able to mail letters very often. Don't worry if letters don't come regularly. I am still being sustained by our telephone conversation a week ago. It seems so much longer ago than that.

The last twenty-four hours have been plenty busy. Everything is so different and so interesting. I am enjoying my new experiences to the fullest.

Yesterday I was in the dentist's chair for over an hour and a half. He worked very fast but is nowhere near finished. I have another appointment tomorrow morning.

I don't think I've ever told you about our daily newspaper. It's about seven by nine inches and has four pages. The first page deals with world news, and the last has funnies. One of them is "Li'l Abner". You can imagine how much we all enjoy it. At breakfast a copy of it is at each place.

I certainly do miss Bob, Doc, and the others. So far I have found no one else I really enjoy. They are a fine bunch of fellows but don't seem to create close friendships. I wonder if that could be because of the nature of our duty and circumstances. I'm thankful I am busy and will be kept even busier.

I am enclosing a check which includes all the pay I have coming, up to now. I think it should be put into a separate account. We will have to buy a car when they start making them again. Of course we will want to pay cash for it as always. I have changed the allotment to you, and you will be receiving $250 a month starting August 1st. That will leave me just enough to get by. There is really no way to spend money where I am now.

I have set my heart on being home for Christmas, either on leave or for a new assignment. If I'm not I'll be very, very disappointed. I know I'm foolish to count on it, but that's what I'm doing.

MAY 18th. I just finished another hour in the dentist chair after being on watch all night. The entire hour was spent on cleaning, and it was rugged, much worse than a filling. My teeth were so black, but now they look as good as new. I didn't think it was possible. I wonder if it's caused by the climate, or the food we had the past nine months.

Your garden sounds wonderful. Lucky Bob will probably be able to have all kinds of delicious things from it. Lucky Bob will probably sit at our table and be with you and our wonderful children. I really miss Bob. So far I have found no one with whom I share so many ideas and interests.

The enlisted men here have a dance orchestra, and they play every day through the noon hour. I can hear them now in the distance, and it sounds really good. If only we could be dancing to it together. . . .

May 20, 1944

Honey:

We all overslept this morning, so I drove the kids to school. I talked to Mrs. Berta a minute, and she said Beverly's arithmetic is improving. Then I dropped by Donny's class to tell Miss Muir how happy I am about her marriage. She volunteered that Donny is doing just fine now, nothing out of the ordinary, just little boyish pranks that are to be expected.

After we went to the P.O., Chuckie for the first time announced, "Go. Go!" I tore home forty five miles an hour, hoping no cops were around to catch me. I sat him on the "duck" for a fruitless twenty minutes. One minute later, he was drenched! Oh the vicissitudes of toilet training! Why can't they all be the way Beverly was? Remember how she trained us? After she patted the toilet seat a few times, saying "Go, go," we finally caught on!

Bob Pedrick just phoned! He is at Alameda and will spend this evening trying to put through a call to Ann. He'll call me tomorrow to arrange what time to meet. I am SO EXCITED! When he phoned and said, "This is Bob Pedrick" I said, "OH! WHEN can I see you?" and then, "Oh my, wasn't that forward of me?" He said, "What a way to talk to a man you've never even met." He sounds so nice. I can't wait.

MAY 22. After I took Bob home, I was bubbling over with things to tell you, but yesterday I was so low and lonesome that I just couldn't write.

Rae and Stevie left for S.F. Friday morning with Frank Brown, which was a break for me. I needed the gas to go pick Bob up in Oakland. Also it gave me more time for cleaning, cooking, and getting organized so it wouldn't be too hectic while Bob is here.

We arranged to meet at 14th and Broadway a little before six. I slid up to the corner at exactly 6 o'clock as the light turned red. I looked wildly around all four crowded corners and saw a j.g. in blues across Broadway. I yelled "Bob!" at the top of my voice. He turned. I yelled, "Pedrick." He ran across Broadway, slid into the car, the light turned green, and away we went! Did you ever hear of anything so neat?

After we got away from the thick of things, I asked him if he would like to drive, and he did. I don't know when I have met someone I liked so much or felt so at ease with immediately. Chuckie made up to him right away, and when we got home, the rest of them practically took him apart! With Rae cooking the dinners for the past six months, I was afraid I had forgotten how to get a nice meal, but it all went off perfectly. I had the children take Bob on a tour of the place while I did the last minute things.

It was such fun feeding him because he enjoyed everything so much. He just couldn't get over having things so fresh from the garden and thoroughly enjoyed the veal cutlets, baked potatoes, and finally the homemade chocolate ice cream. He topped it off with a big dish of strawberries. We took nearly an hour and a half for dinner, with loads of conversation.

I took Bob upstairs to see the room you built for Donny. He had asked to see it because he knows how much you dislike doing that sort of work. He was very impressed and thought you had done a beautiful job. Then we got down to the real business of the evening with the maps he brought and the pictures you had sent. It was fascinating to hear so many things you couldn't tell me and to put names with faces in the pictures.

I had hoped he could spend the whole weekend. It would have been a perfect time because he could have had Stevie's room. He had a lot of work to do decommissioning the unit and said he would have to catch the 11:30 bus back. I told him it would take him forever that way. Actually, I wanted to hang on to him as long as I could. When we got to Oakland I insisted on driving him until we found transportation from Oakland to Alameda. I told him I couldn't bear to part with him any sooner. He said I couldn't flatter him that way because he knew it was just that I wanted to hear more about you. I told him he was absolutely right.

When we finally saw a streetcar headed for Alameda, and he hopped out and caught it, I felt like crying. I felt as though I couldn't bear it. He told me so much, and yet there was so much more I wanted to know.

He was so cute when we talked about Ann. I told him that, although I had only seen her for a few minutes, I just loved her. He said, "Well, so do I." When I said I just love little people, and she is so little, he said, "Well I certainly do love THAT little person." He said she hadn't the slightest idea he was coming, and when he phoned, she was in a daze. He will be with her and the baby in two more days.

Yesterday morning I was higher than a kite. By noon my mood had changed. I began to realize that it was all very well for Bob and the others to be home, but where were you? When would you be home? I got lower and lower as the day went on. I finally came in and tried to eat while Rae gave me a lecture on how I should take it easier. I couldn't take any more of that, so I went back to the garden and worked while I cried, until I finished planting by flashlight.

This morning Ted Rodgers phoned to say he and his wife would be out to bring your things. He seemed quite shy, and so did his wife, but both very nice. They couldn't stay long, which was fine with us. We were dying to explore the sea chest. I put the towels, linens, sweatshirts, etc. into the wash right away. You don't know how thrilled I was to see that sheet. If you have a chance to "survey" any more, I'd be delighted. It is nearly three years since we've been able to buy any. The children had a great time today with the helmet. Donny let the girls join his army! I can see them out the window right now, on top of the playhouse. Beverly is wearing the inner helmet and Judy the outer one, with Donny's rifle beside them.

Donny did another "commando raid" yesterday. He piled the clothes he had collected into his wagon and took Chuckie and the girls with him to the fruit stand to have it picked up. He got 279 points, which makes him a 1st. Lt. He will get his award tomorrow. In the meantime Bert has given him a set of Lt. shirt collar bars and a dummy bayonet which he now has on his dummy rifle. He was delighted with the calendar in the sea chest and hung it in his playhouse.

Bob answered so many of the questions I have asked you. I take it the quarters you described are on the Lexington. Wasn't it sunk originally? Isn't this a new one? Bob stressed the fact that carriers are so much safer now than they were earlier in the war. I realize now that all those worries I had last fall were because the Commissary Chief told me you were on Funafuti instead of Nukufetau. It is much easier to understand everything you have told me, since Bob drew a map showing how everything is situated—I mean the group of islands that make up the atoll.

Bob explained yours and his dislike for two members of your Unit and the reasons for it[1]. I certainly had no idea. It must have been hard for you to remain tactful. Bob said he is the only one who has a job to do here. The others are just sitting around on pins and needles waiting for their orders. Ted Rodgers is the only one close enough to go home.

The picture of you which was doctored up is really a prize! I carry it with me at all times so I can whip it out and ask people to guess who it is. No one can decide whether it is a criminal, a dope fiend, or a zombie! I wish I had a good one of you by yourself. The one with the natives was excellent.

Monday, May 22, 1944

Dearest Sweet Honey:

I am so excited. I am going away! I'm meeting Fred Banducci at his office tomorrow and will spend two days with them. It was all planned very suddenly.

Everybody has been saying I needed some time off. This afternoon Rae learned that there is a place available near Santa Cruz. She phoned Gram and Uncle George. He will come over with a trailer on Tuesday and move them. She has already gone to the ration board for gas.

---

[1]They were extremely intolerant and racist.

It suddenly dawned on me that if I was going to get any time off, I had to do it before Rae leaves. Fred and Elva have been after me for ages to come over and are delighted that I finally can. I dread leaving Chuckie, but I simply must do this while I can.

"Rae's sailor" phoned to see if he could come over. I drove over to the highway to pick him up. He had hitchhiked from Camp Shoemaker, which is the Navy camp adjacent to the Seabee camp at Pleasanton.

His name is Cliff. He is twenty-nine, seems extremely young, but looks older because of loss of hair. He really has a case on Rae. She was able to get him to understand that she doesn't date before he actually asked her out. He brought her artificial flowers he had made and a bracelet he carved with her name on it. After dinner he helped her get Steve and Frances settled for the night. Then she came out to the kitchen and whispered, "What shall I DO? We've talked and talked, and there's nothing left to say. Never again!"

At that point Betty, knowing what a time Rae was having, asked her how soon she was going to start developing and printing. That took care of the situation nicely for several hours. What an inspiration! Cliff had never done any photography and was fascinated. When they finished, he insisted he could easily hitchhike back to camp, so I didn't have to take him to the bus.

Dear Daddy,

I hope you come home soon because I like you so much. And then when you come home I am going to love you so much. That's a good idea because you were away a long time. I liked the letter you sent me. I've been playing with Philip and Susan and Betty Jean, and lots of times Bucky Hall and sometimes I walk home by myself. I have been at Grandma's and I have been at Sunday School dressed up in my black shoes, my pretty red dress and my pretty Dutch hat.

I love you. Some day when I am bigger I can write to you myself.

Judy

Larkspur, May 25, 1944

Dearest Honey:

I am having a marvelous time. Right now I'm sitting in the Banduccis' breakfast nook, typing on their antiquated Underwood, and enjoying their magnificent view. There is a grand program on the radio of pieces from way back in our day. The weather is absolutely gorgeous, and GOLLY it's fun to be free!

I left home as soon as the children left for school and enjoyed browsing in San Francisco before meeting Fred at his office. What a wild ride we had on the Greyhound bus! The driver swooped around curves and over bumps at high speed, and we really had to hang on.

Fred and Elva have a little family living in their basement room. They had been staying in a one room auto cabin near Camp Roberts for the past ten months. When he was transferred here, they couldn't find even a room. When he went into the S.F. branch of the insurance company where he worked in North Carolina, he met Fred. Nancy, his wife, is so cute and has us in stitches constantly. Their little girl, Judy, is seventeen months old and such a darling. Fred and Elva are enjoying them so much and are nuts about Judy.

It felt so good to sit at a pretty table in peace and quiet, eating slowly and without interruptions. They insist that I don't lift a finger, just have a good rest. After dinner we looked at pictures and read parts of your letters.

I have the bedroom with the ivy wallpaper just like ours. When I woke up this morning, there was a gorgeous red sunrise. I went back to sleep and didn't get up until nearly nine. What luxury! Our breakfast was delicious, orange juice, bacon, eggs, toasted English muffins, and jam. It pays to rent to people who can shop at a commissary!

I'm not getting much done on this letter, but I am having such a good time. Nancy's father is a Baptist minister and head of an orphanage. Also she is from Georgia. It's interesting that we have those three things in common. Apparently she is from one of those old Southern families with scads of servants and houses with tall white columns. . . .

Friday, May 26, 1944

Dear Daddy,

I have the measles and I am sick in bed. Mother is typing this because I mustn't use my eyes. I have measles all over my feet, and Dr. Beede says I will have more tomorrow. He came to see me last night. I wish I didn't have to have the measles and be sick in bed because it's terrible.

I have two Lt. bars just like you, that Captain gave me. I also have a rifle, and Mother bought a clock from the Lembecks so I know when to get up in the morning. I like the helmet and the leggings you sent me.

I understand about the horse and will try hard to get more bonds. I have five now and am starting on my sixth. I also have thirty books of stamps.

I have fun at school especially when we play kickball. Also I got 100 on all my spelling papers. Down at the bleachers there is going to be a track meet. Everyone who is in it can get ice cream.

Next week I am going to be in a show to raise money for the Red Cross. Mark Evans and I are going to sing, "Home On The Range."

The boat hasn't come yet but I know it is going to be good.

Love, Donny.

May 26, 1944

Honey:

Right after I wrote you yesterday, Rae phoned to say Donny has the measles. The call scared me to death. I knew she wouldn't phone unless it was something drastic. It was because she had to leave for S.F. this morning at eight and couldn't very well expect anyone else to take on the responsibility of caring for Donny and exposing their own children.

I decided to enjoy myself until I had to leave, and I did. We went to the village. I never realized what a metropolis Lafayette is compared to Larkspur! No dime store or hardly anything else. But it is a cute little place.

When we got back, we lunched outside, then sewed, pulled weeds, and played with Judy. When Fred got home, he was terribly disappointed to have me leave. We had a grand Southern style dinner cooked by Nancy.

Going home it was still light. I had never seen Marin City before. It looks like a huge cliff dwelling and is as incompatible with the topography of Marin County as Louis XVI furniture would be in our Colonial house! Well, I suppose it is unreasonable to expect a city thrown together with any available materials and as quickly as possible to house hundreds of families brought here to work in the shipyards, to be a gem of architectural beauty! The bus was jammed and tore along, getting to Market St., right outside your office, in less than half an hour. I stepped right on a streetcar from there, and straight from the streetcar to the Claremont Key System train. Talk about perfect connections!

I had a strange experience on the train. There were four couples together who had been prominent in our class at Cal. I couldn't remember any of their names. The thing that was strange was, instead of feeling lonesome and miserable because I was without you, I felt rather smug and proud because the husbands all looked kind of soft, middle-aged, and uninteresting. I felt proud that you are doing what you are doing.

When I got home Dr. Beede had just left. Donny was pretty unhappy but felt better when I got there. It is awful to think how many children he has exposed. Chuckie will get it and get it hard as he does everything.

Bert came in while I was scrubbing the kitchen floor tonight and said, "Oh, you poor kid! Let me do that." I told him not to be silly, I was fine. But it was surprising how good it felt just to have the sympathy. I was grateful. He gave the lawn a good watering and swatted a zillion flies in the kitchen.

When Rae was in S.F., she arranged with the manufacturer of children's coats for Livingston's to make coats for our girls. They are 100% REAL wool and would sell at Livingston's for $19.75. We are getting the two for $25, and in ONLY TWO WEEKS! That is miraculous. Goodnight Darling. . . .

May 28, 1944

My Darling Honey:

Since the girls from your office were coming this morning, Bert cut the lawn, and it looks beautiful. When they arrived I was still making formula for Frances, so Mr. Edwards played with Chuckie, and the girls insisted on doing the dishes. What a way to treat guests!

When our girls got home from Sunday School, we all started laying out the food. The day had turned cold, dark, and windy. It was disappointing to have our buffet indoors. They look forward to an outdoor day whenever they come. The table looked like pre-war days with five salads, three cakes, sliced meats and cheeses, pickles, olives, crackers, radishes, onions, cokes, milk, and my huge bowl of chili beans.

Afterwards they climbed to the top of the high hill behind the Browns, quite a climb for city folks. Before they got to the top, the sun came out, the wind subsided, and they said it was just marvelous.

It was killing Donny to miss all this, but he was a brick. Miss Gold was so good to him, spending lots of time with him and taking him goodies to tempt his appetite. We sat outside, read parts of your letters, and looked at the pictures. They enjoyed the children and were in ecstacy over Frances. Chuckie had a wonderful time showing off his beloved chickens, which the girls thought were marvelous. What a different life people live in San Francisco. Coming to the country is a whole new world for them.

Just as the girls were leaving Jim Phelan phoned and then came out. The kids remembered Jim from the days at the beach and enjoyed him so much. After they were in bed, we took a walk. Golly, I enjoyed it. It was fun to be walking up our road with a Lt. j.g. in blues. The last time I saw you, that's what you wore. I always visualize you that way and get a thrill out of that stripe and a half whenever I see it. When we got to the end of the road, we ran all the way back. It was so much fun.

When we got back, we stopped by the rumpus room and visited a while with the Lembecks. Then we all came in to our place. Bert had us all in stitches, including Rae, on the subject of "How Wonderful Harry Is!" It felt so good to laugh. Bert is very good at making us do that.

After they left, we looked at the pictures you sent and discussed things. He is waiting at Treasure Island to be sent out as Communications Officer on a merchant ship. Evelyn and the girls will stay in Washington, since they have no assurance of being able to be with him anywhere. He is excited about your new duty and has a very high opinion of your ability. . . .

May 29, 1944

My Sweet Precious:

It's a shame that your typewriter is acting up again. It seems to happen so frequently, but I suppose it has to be expected with a typewriter you bought second hand for $5 in 1925! After the war when they start making them, we'll try to get a new one. I'm sure there will be a long waiting list.

All day I've been thinking about your day with my office staff. I'm sure they all had a good time, and hope you did too. I'll bet they were surprised at how much you have accomplished.

I started another Navy correspondence course today. That should keep me plenty busy in my spare time.

It was a thrill to learn how beautifully everything went when you met Bob. How on earth could he hear you, clear across that busy intersection? I knew you would like him and feel perfectly comfortable with him. It was a shame he couldn't spend the weekend.

Tomorrow at home it's Memorial Day. I wonder if it will be observed in spite of everything that's going on. Will there be parades, speeches, and picnics just as there used to be? It all seems so far away and long ago.

Also tomorrow I will be paid again. I'll send a small check for birthday gifts from me for Chuck, Judy, and Rae. . . .

May 29, 1944

Honey Dearest:

Rae and Marky went to Oakland to take Susan to the eye doctor and Frances for a measles shot. This will either prevent her getting it or give her a lighter case. Betty wants to take her boys and Chuckie over to St. Mary's tomorrow and get the shots for them. When she phoned St Mary's about it, they told her we would have to bring our own serum, as they don't have it, and it is very hard to get. I phoned Mr. Winkler, and he phoned all the supply houses unsuccessfully. We phoned the drugstore in Martinez, also the ones in Concord, Pittsburg, and Danville. Finally we were able to get some in Orinda. It is only good for one exposure, so I hope it does the job.

When I got home from Orinda, I found that Rae and Marky had left our box of groceries on the front porch. Chuckie had eaten all the chocolate chips, and the dogs had eaten an entire three pound box of Pablum. Chuckie was fussy, so I sat on the steps with him on my lap. He began to heave. There I was with my lap being inundated. It was dripping through my dress and down my legs. Poor little kid. He got white as a sheet and lay inert. I managed to stagger into the bathroom in a crouching position with him in my arms and skin off his clothes and mine. I washed him off, threw on a robe, and gave him Milk of Bismuth to settle his stomach. Although he seemed asleep, he kept clutching my hand and wouldn't let go. It was really scary. But he seems to be ok now.

Jack has a new post hole digger which is a vast improvement on the old kind. After dinner Bert and I amazed ourselves by getting all the posts for the grape arbor in and starting the framework. Jack's digger is a marvel. It works like a corkscrew.

Bert brought more good sturdy lumber and replaced the flimsy railing around the top of the playhouse. Whatever would we do without him? I told him how much you appreciate all he is doing. He said to tell you that they are so glad to have a chance to show how much they appreciate being able to live here and that he hopes to know you some day.

The poison oak spray is something new by Du Pont. Dan learned about it at work and managed to get some. Jack mixed up a huge quantity, Bob Underhill supplied the spray rig, and they are doing everyone's place. I think we get the best of the deal. I, the helpless female, am having it all done for me. No one else has a two hundred foot stretch growing all the way down the bank.

Tomorrow Uncle George plans to be here early to start moving Rae's things. Today I filled the gas tank and had the car checked for them. . . .

May 31, 1944

Dearest Honey:

Uncle George arrived yesterday at the crack of dawn. By the time he left with the first load the morning was half gone. In the meantime, Dan laid out the pipes for my vegetable garden. I helped him put them in, and in a few hours, the watering system was working. What a thrill!

Betty took her boys and Chuckie to St. Mary's for the measles shots. By 5:30 the reaction to the shots was already making them miserable. Chuckie refused to eat his dinner sitting down!

Donny was able to have the freedom of the house today. He dressed Chuck in his military gear, and they had a wonderful time together. Chuckie's attachment for Donny grows stronger each day. Today he pinched his fingers in a door, and when I was comforting him he kept sobbing for "Nonny, Nonny."

I found one of our hens dead this morning. Jack says it was a "blow-out" caused by heavy egg laying. Poor thing.

Rae, Stevie, and Frances left with uncle George when he came back for the last load. It will seem quite different without them here but I think I am going to enjoy it, even though I know we'll miss those wonderful meals Rae has been making for us. It's lucky for Chuck he still has Mike and Lance. . . .

Part Six

"THIS IS WORTH FIGHTING FOR"

I see a peaceful old valley

With a river that winds through its floor,

And a voice within me keeps repeating,

"This is worth fighting for."

I see a little log cabin

With the corn patch that grows by it's door.

And the voice within me keeps repeating,

"This is worth fighting for."

Didn't I build that cabin?

Didn't I plant that corn?

Didn't my folks before me

Fight for this country before I was born?

I gather my loved ones around me

And I gaze at the face I adore,

While a voice within me keeps repeating,

"THIS IS WORTH FIGHTING FOR."

Edward DeLande and Sam H. Stept
From the Musical "Cabin In The Sky."
Starring Ethel Waters, 1941

Part Six

June 1, 1944

Honey Dearest:

Chuckie has the measles, but thanks to the shot, he's not very sick. He woke up hot and shaky during the night and has a temp, sore eyes, and no appetite. He can't be terribly ill because he is furious at having to stay indoors. I hope Stevie and Frances haven't caught it.

Donny brought Duane home after school. Duane must be "in the money" as he gave Donny fifty cents for comic books and treated him to a milk shake and an ice cream cone. How can people give their children so much money? I was shocked. Donny begged me to let them sleep in the playhouse but I felt Duane would enjoy sleeping in a comfortable bed, and he did. After dinner Bert supervised boxing and wrestling matches. They were evenly matched, and Donny did well. Duane won the "championship" and gave it (a nickel) to Donny saying, "I have plenty of nickels at home, you take it." Donny says he is the only boy at school who plays with Duane. The others taunt him and call him "Okie!"

The kids were a joy today. They sailed into their chores without a word from me and soon were out collecting bottles. They came home hot and tired with the most unbelievable load of bottles and jars—somewhere between 150–160.

After dinner I laid down for "just a minute." The kids said to stay there until they called. They washed, wiped, put away the dishes, and swept the kitchen floor, and while the girls got ready for bed, Donny scrubbed it. Was I amazed? It was wonderful!

The folks got a letter from John saying his squadron returned from their eleventh mission. Also one of the Chung Mei boys was on the ship that cracked up on the Farallons. . . .

Your lonesome, loving Honey

June 7, 1944

Hi Babe! Hey Babe!

There was a lot to talk about at mess tonight. We had just heard the good news about the landings in France and of the fall of Rome the day before. That plus our own Pacific war provided plenty of conversation and speculation. We don't often talk about the war, but all these events happening so nearly simultaneously have us pretty excited.

I ran into Jack Mainzer today, and we talked for quite a while. He told me about a number of mutual friends who are out here. If I had only known, I could have seen many of them in the various places I have been. When I got the free haircut and ice cream on Washington's birthday, he was on that ship. His best friend, whom I also knew, was killed in an Army plane crash in Santa Ana while his wife was watching. Eight months later she had a baby girl. She had secured a job there so they could be together before he went overseas.

Today I met a couple of war correspondents. One, who was from Berkeley, seemed to be much older than I because his hair was completely white. Then I learned he graduated from Cal nine years after we did and is only twenty six. Both of them had some extremely interesting tales to tell.

After I left Jack, I found the officers' club, which is made of old wood and screening but is rather interesting. As I stood at the doorway to see if I knew anyone, I noticed a young Navy flier near me. When we spoke, he said he was going home soon. It turned out he's from Lafayette and is the Whitakers' son. We had never met because he's been in the Navy ever since we moved to Lafayette. I took a liking to him immediately. He plans to phone you when he gets home. Meeting him just made my day.

The Chaplain here is very well liked. First he holds a general service and later a Catholic mass. I don't understand how he can do that, but he does.

I am so happy you had the opportunity to spend two days at the Banduccis'. It sounds as though you enjoyed yourself in spite of the untimely ending. How could the bus driver go so fast? Have the war regulations been relaxed?

I think it's wonderful the way Bert enjoys being Daddy to two families. It sounds as though Chuckie is crazy about him. In fact it seems all of you are. I was so thrilled to receive the pictures. My Poochie looks so sweet. Chuckie looks like an armful for her. Donny looks so proud on his bike, even if it is that old thing which causes him so much trouble. That dimpled smile of Judy's is something to behold.

The reason I am in different places at different times is that an Admiral's staff goes with him, whether he is ashore or afloat. There is a lot more to explain, but that is the best I can do. . . .Goodnight my love.

June 7, 1944

Honey:

I asked Dr. Hartman today about sending Donny to camp for the month of August. He says it's all right, so long as he can plan in advance. He liked what I told him about the Sturtevants' ranch camp and is going to see if they have room for his son who is about Donny's age.

When we left there, we went to Bob's Cyclery to see if Donny's bike was ready. He hunted all over for his shabby little old wreck. When he couldn't find it, he was worried. Then they showed him this handsome shiny large one. He was popping with delight.

Next we went to take Mama and Midge the shell necklaces you sent. They were tickled to death. In John's latest letters he sounds more cheerful. They now have a shower right outside their tents instead of having to walk fifteen miles to the village. What I'm wondering is where does one go to get a shower in a small Italian village?

I wish you could have seen Judy this morning, entertaining all the little ones in the neighborhood. She put on both the grass skirts you sent the girls, bound a folded kerchief around her "bosom", parted her hair in the middle, stuck sweet peas all around it, and danced. She made up a very pretty and appropriate dance. For a five-year-old, sometimes she amazes me.

Yes, I too think Judy's letters are the cutest because she is so fluent. No, I don't have to prompt her. She wiggles and wriggles, looking around the room and thinking, and all those things come popping out.

It sometimes annoys me, the way everyone thinks I enjoy gardening. I often have to force myself outside because I know it has to be done, and it won't wait like indoor things will. I enjoy seeing the results of my labor, but it's hot, painful, and dirty, not to mention also cold, wet, and discouraging sometimes. I would much prefer to be sewing or making the house shine.

I love to sit here and talk to you on my typewriter, but Goodnight Honey.

June 8, 1944

My Wonderful Darling:

I received two especially marvelous letters from you today, and I loved the cartoon of the lady saying, "I'm tired of being wonderful. I need HELP."

I am so pleased to learn the Dads' Club is going to sponsor a Boy Scout troop. Will they have Cub Scouts? I am anxious to see Donny's playhouse. It sounds super with all the things he and Bert have done to it. I am glad to hear you are doing something about the watering system. Did you have much trouble getting pipe? I was flabbergasted at the price of the serum for the measles shots, but so glad you were able to get it.

Isn't this the week the high school pool opens to the public? I'm wondering if any of you have gone yet. I hope there isn't a polio epidemic again this summer. Remember how it was when we were first married, and no one dared go anywhere? At least we saved enough money that way out of our $1 a week "recreation fund," so that when fall came we could buy season tickets to the Cal football games.

I wanted to send you a copy of our daily paper but found we aren't allowed to. I know you will be ecstatic to learn that Li'l Abner is about to get a job at the "skonk" works and has told Available Jones that he will be available whenever Available is available! Now aren't you a lucky lady to have a husband off fighting a war and sending you such thrilling news?

Yes, I am quite a seasoned air traveler by now, and I like it. I am hoping that after the war, the Prudential Home Office can be persuaded to allow the managers to fly to the conferences. Think how much time could be saved that way, taking only a few hours rather than four days each way by train.

June 8, 1944

My dear precious Judy:

I loved receiving your letter. Every day Mother tells me in her letters about the things you do, but it is so much more fun to hear it from you.

Do you miss Rae and Stevie and Frances? How did Susan like the things you took her when she got home from the hospital?

I love you very much and miss you a lot too. Just think, you will probably be in the first grade when I see you. I'll bet you will like that. You are getting to be such a big girl. I love you so much. Please write again soon. . . .

June 11, 1944

Dearest Honey:

Yesterday was a big day for Donny. I let him go to Lafayette on his bike to get a couple of things for me which I needed. Was he THRILLED!

It is so exciting that you met Austin Whitaker. Yes, Donny always rides when he is at David's. Tomorrow he is going to ride the pony while David rides Donny's bike. One more week before the pool opens, and so far no polio.

Yesterday Judy helped me can cherries, and we got sixteen quarts done. Then a strong wind came up, so I decided to dig post holes for the grape arbor and get the posts in before the grape vines, which are already six feet high, blow over and break.

Today after Sunday School, I let Donny go to Happy Valley to visit Ernest and told him to start home at 4:30. At 3:45 he came tearing in red as a beet and soaked with perspiration. Someone had looked at the clock wrong and told him it was 5:10. He was all in, so I gave him some orange juice and told him to flop on the lawn for a while.

This morning I received a telegram from Leta asking me to find out if Sally and Bud's house is for sale or for rent. I dashed over there right away. Bud is leaving for Seattle tomorrow. Sally and the boys will stay with her aunt until he finds a place for them. They sold their house for $12,000. They figured out it cost them $7,750 counting all improvements. The buyers have offered $1000 for their Bendix.

I have solved the panty problem for the girls by getting them Jockey shorts like Donny's. They are sturdy, comfortable, and THEY STAY UP! They love them!

I wish I had a letter to answer. I wish I had a husband to cuddle with.

Sunday, June 11, 1944

My Own Sweet Poochy:

I love your letters and enjoy hearing from you so very much. Please tell me all about what you are doing, now that it is vacation.

When Mother writes about what a big help you are, it makes me so happy. She also told me about how you and Judy have been collecting bottles for the Junior Commandos, to help Donny. You certainly have a lot of them, don't you? I miss you so much and love you so very much.

June 13, 1944

My Honey:

Today I made two sunsuits for each of the girls. They are all as cute as can be. Believe it or not, they were made from men's striped Madras shorts given me by Mrs. Rogers. They were a gift to her husband. Like you, he won't wear anything but plain white.

Bert is on the phone about an available house. I am dying to know the outcome. I can't blame them for wanting to live in more than one room, but I'll die if they leave. He says nineteen officers are on the waiting list. It's the first to be listed at St. Mary's in three months. It has one bedroom with a sun porch, no washing machine, and no refrigerator, just an ice box. They want $75 a month for it. Did you ever hear of such highway robbery?

What a relief! Bert just hung up. He decided against it. It wasn't the price. He just felt they would rather be here with us.

NEXT DAY. I left Chuck with the Lembecks while we went to Berkeley and the dentist. When we returned and I picked him up, Bert handed me the $36 rent. Then, when I went into our kitchen, I discovered that Betty had washed and dried the awful mess of dishes I had left undone. I dashed back to the rumpus room and said in wild tones, "There's something wrong! I don't know what it is, but something is terribly wrong!" They looked very worried and wanted to know what was wrong. I told them, "First you take care of my child, then you do my dishes and then on top of all that, you pay me for it."

There was another article in the paper tonight about what I am assuming is your unit. I am getting very puzzled and somewhat suspicious. The fellows who came home said, since you are on the Admiral's staff, you are well protected by all the other ships around yours,[1] and there is absolutely nothing to worry about. You tell me you are safe. But how come I read all this in the papers? How come you have all these weird hours and sudden changes of

---

[1] The aircraft carriers are surrounded by the battle ships, then by the cruisers, and finally by the destroyers of the entire fleet.

duty and have to leave in the middle of writing a letter?[1] I am trying very hard not to worry because it is the only way to keep going, but what's going on?

Tonight we had hot boysenberry cobbler for dessert, loaded with whipped cream. It was SO good, and I ate far too much. Right now Bert and Betty are having seconds. It is getting so we practically always collaborate on our dessert. She makes a perfectly delicious apricot upside down cake. Our berries are absolutely overpowering. You can't even imagine what they are like. There are thousands of them. I'll have to start making jam if I can get hold of enough sugar. We can't eat them fast enough.

Did I tell you Bert graduated from high school at age fifteen? He stayed out and worked for three years and then graduated from UCLA in '29. With only one year at San Diego State Betty feels her lack of college education very keenly. She was "Miss San Diego State" and was having too good a time. She felt she shouldn't be wasting her mother's money if she wasn't willing to buckle down, so she quit. Her father died of lung cancer when she was eight.

Besides the three birthday presents you wanted me to get for Chuck, Rae, and Judy, I will also use that $25 you sent to get birthday gifts for Mama and Ken and a graduation gift for Midge.

Bad news! The Schneiders sold the cow. No more wonderful thick cream for us. Also it will add at least $4.50 a month to the cost of our milk, and getting it at the store in Lafayette will be so inconvenient....

Sunday, June 18, 1944

Honey Dear:

I keep forgetting to tell you how glad I am that you insisted on building such an enormous sandbox. At times yesterday there were eleven playing in it with plenty of room for all ages.

Today when we got home from Sunday School, the kids decided to celebrate Father's Day. Beverly and Judy picked bunches of flowers for Bert, Jack, and Dan. They gave Bert a card on which Donny had written, "To Captain Lembeck who is such a nice Daddy to us." Bert was so touched. After that they picked flowers for the other men in the neighborhood— Gary, Tom, Jack Imrie, Bob Underhill, and even Mr. Cole, Mr. Rodgers, and Mr. Hink. Donny went on his bike up the road to deliver the last three, with Gretchen and Blackie flying along beside him. They love it when he rides his bike.

---

[1] Staff officers rotate being on duty and the rotation is changed from time to time. When the ship is at "general quarters" due to attack or anticipated attack, everyone is on duty at his battle station.

This afternoon Chuck and Mike climbed into the barbecue. When we discovered them they were a solid mass of ashes and were the funniest sight! Chuck's face, hair, ears, and eyebrows were white with ashes, in fact everything except his eyeballs, and they were beginning to sting.

The Woods came unexpectedly about four and brought ME a box of CANDY for FATHER'S DAY! The kids all had a great time with Herb. He got down on the floor and tussled with them. They didn't stay long because they had to get back to take care of their little granddaughter. I hope caring for her helps ease the pain of their son's death in the Jap prison camp. . . .

JUNE 20TH. Yesterday Lila Burke came over, bringing the boys to play with Donny. They all had a wonderful time cooking eggs, toast, and potatoes outdoors and riding their bikes. She told me they tried to file an application with Childrens Home Society for a baby girl, and C.H.S. wouldn't even take it, since they already have children of their own. How heartbreaking that must be to know that you are never going to have a daughter.

Today I left the children at Live Oak Park to play while I got a permanent. When I got back I couldn't get over how filthy they had gotten in that dusty place. I scrubbed them up as well as I could. Then we took Donny to his dentist. When he was finished, which took about two minutes, he checked the girls' teeth and cleaned them. I am glad we decided on Dr. Hartman. It's handy to have someone who does plain ordinary dentistry as well as orthodontia. They were quite interested in the whole process and seemed to enjoy it. He says Judy won't have to have her teeth straightened after all. Beverly's are fine, too.

On the way home we stopped at the folks to discuss the plans for next Sunday. Midge has a beautiful formal for the Senior Ball. She is going steady with someone who is only five feet nine inches, and you know how tall she is. I think she is more interested in him than anyone she has ever gone with.

At last I have seen pictures in the paper of your admiral[1] and know he isn't just a figment of the imagination. He certainly looks rugged, not at all as I had visualized him—tall, distinguished looking, and "admiralish". The news in the paper today was thrilling. It is strange to think of you in the midst of all those sea battles, land bombings, and landings, while I go on peacefully growing vegetables and nailing lathes.

After dinner Chuckie played with Beverly and Judy and had a glorious time. It is such a delight to see how much fun he has with each one of the older children, more and more each day, I long to have you see him. He is so unique.

The high school pool opened, and the children are going tomorrow. At twenty cents apiece each day, it will play havoc with my budget. . . .

---

[1]Vice Admiral Mitscher

June 18,1944

My Sweet:

Guess what I saw today. Something I had never seen before—the end of the rainbow! In fact, I saw both ends, but there wasn't a pot of gold at either end. It was a large one, and the colors were so rich and deep. We were all fascinated with it. It formed an almost complete circle with both ends terminating not more than a hundred yards from where I was standing. What a spectacular sight! I wish I knew what caused it to be that way.

I finally had the pleasure of buying some Palmolive soap. It is amazing how much small things mean over here. But I also have some bad news. After all you went through getting a new head for my Schick razor, I discovered the rubber on the cord had completely melted from the heat.

I'm beginning to get used to the irregular hours and snatching sleep when I can. For example, after working since midnight, I had breakfast at 4 a.m., then slept from 5 a.m. until 10. I was on duty again until mid-afternoon, got an hour's sleep, and went back to work again. As soon as I finish this, I will hit the sack because I have the duty again at 3 a.m. and so ad infinitum.

I finally was able to attend the church service. I guess the Catholic Chaplain doesn't know too much about conducting a general service. All he talked about was what sinners we all are and about repenting. However, the opening prayer was good and made tears come to my eyes when he spoke about our wives, children, parents, and sweethearts. I'll go again the next chance I have and see if it's any better.

I enjoyed George's letter which you enclosed with yours of June 2nd. I couldn't figure out exactly where he is stationed. I was surprised to realize I no longer mind his signing his letters to you "love and kisses." I guess it's about time. What a long friendship you two have had. Say "Hello" to him from me next time you write.

The letter from your cousin in England was very interesting. She never has much to say about the air raids, does she? I'm sure Bristol must be getting the blitzes as badly as London. She always sounds so matter of fact—"a few noisy nights." Their food shortages are really drastic, aren't they? One egg a month per person struck me as the worst.

Tonight I am going to try sleeping out on the forecastle[1] because of the heat in my room. I simply must get rid of this heat rash and can't do it when I perspire all night. Your breathlessly and hopelessly in love, Honey.

Dear Daddy,

No, I didn't get the measles. Yes, I miss Rae and Stevie and Frances. Yes, Susan liked the things we took her. She wanted to hold my hand while I was there and she wanted to sit on her mothers lap.

It is a lot of fun playing with Philip. We swing and he falls off, and when I stand up he keeps making me fall off.

---

[1]The forecastle is an open area at the bow on the hanger deck just below the flight deck where the planes take off. There is always some breeze from the movement of the ship.

I love the grass skirt you sent. Thank you Daddy. I'll write to you every night if I tell my mother if I can stay up to write a letter and if you write me a letter tonight I'll write you one every night for you. I hope you come home very soon. We are collecting bottles in a big box to get the war over and they are all Donny's. Dear Daddy, I hope you come home soon. Love, Judy.

June 25, 1944

Oh Honey!

I just got back from Midge's big day—her graduation from Cal. Bert had the duty today, so Betty was happy to take over for me here.

At the luncheon in Faculty Glade, we sat with Midge's friends and their families. The crowd was enormous, but I saw no one from the class of '30.

The graduation, which was small and informal, was held in the Greek Theater instead of the stadium. The audience was so small it fitted into the lower part of the Greek Theater. Can you imagine?

There were only three LL.Bs., a whole slew of Navy dentists, but only four M.Ds., all in uniform. Cal graduated only two teachers! There were only three men from Letters and Science and a dozen from Engineering.

Four LL.Ds. were conferred. They were to Alfred Noyes, the English poet, an astronomer, a priest, and a member of the class of 1894 who has done outstanding work in agriculture.

As always, President Sproul's speech was outstanding. He is so endearing and continues to be so well loved and respected.

We went to the Claremont Hotel for dinner. It was a new experience for my family. What that poor waitress went through before she got our order! The cheapest dinner on the menu was $2. Although that included all the other courses, Mama thought she couldn't have anything but the entree for that price. When the waitress asked whether she wanted soup, salad, or fruit cocktail, she said very firmly and primly, "No cocktail." I could tell she thought the cocktail was, heaven forbid, a COCKTAIL!

Mama ordered baked ham and sweet potatoes. When it came, she mentioned to the waitress, she thought there were to be sweet potatoes. The waitress pointed to a small lump on her plate and said, "There they are." It was so funny. We all just doubled up. It reminded me of that old cartoon during WW I where the waiter says, "How did you find your meat, sir?" The man answers, "I just lifted up my knife, and there it was." The food was delicious, but we forgot to bring butter for the corn on the cob and fresh asparagus. No restaurants serve it. The orchestra was terrific but it killed me to think Daddy had to spend $10 plus the tip on our five dinners, and I didn't even get to dance. What a waste.

When we woke up this morning, it was such a gorgeous morning, we all went around singing "When Morning Gilds the Skies," at the tops of our voices. The girls were in their sunsuits, and we planned to go to the pool. Just before noon the sky turned black, and a terrific gale came up, along with a torrential rain. We had the most violent hailstorm we have ever had. All of us watched it from the patio. The children could hardly contain themselves. I let them play outdoors in the rain that followed, to compensate for not going to the pool.

Now they are "camping" in the attic. When I said "yes," they could hardly believe it. I think it's a terrific idea. It leaves the downstairs looking so neat! They are now building a "town" to live in. They hung all their wet clothes on the line and made shacks out of boxes and tents out of old quilts.

Are you the "Task Force 58"[1] referred to in the paper tonight? You aren't in the 5th Fleet, are you? I'm enclosing the article. During WWI you couldn't go by what the papers said at all. Does this seem to be accurate? I thought it was kind of cute where he says you caught the Japs with their planes down[2].

Beverly got in bed with me during the night because her tummy ached. She was so uncomfortable, she wiggled and fussed all night. When Dr. Beede came, he said it is a mild intestinal infection and to keep her in bed. During nap time I accidentally fell asleep too, then became aware of a strange noise. Judy was playing in the bathroom instead of sleeping. She was standing on her head kicking the wall and had also painted the door with my nail polish!

When I went to the depot in Walnut Creek to get the rock wool insulation I had ordered, no one was there. Finally a doddering old soul arrived. Feebly he searched the office for over fifteen minutes before he found the papers and offered to help me.

The freight room was almost entirely filled with my order. It was blazing hot. I handed the stuff to him as he fitted it into the car. I had four huge cartons on the roof and eighteen sacks inside the car and trunk. It took an hour-and-a-half. I was scared stiff to drive home, but I managed to arrive safely. When I got here, I discovered that when he roped the stuff on to the roof, he also roped me in! Finally Betty and Donny managed to untie all the knots and open the door. I was black with grime and soaked with perspiration.

After dinner I went over to see how Marky is feeling. When I got back, Betty and Donny were finishing OUR dishes. I shooed Betty out, and the next thing I knew, she and Bert were unloading the insulation.

The insulation I brought home was only part of it. Tomorrow I have to get the rest, and I don't know how I can face it. There are ten bags and sixteen boxes measuring approximately eighteen inches square by about four feet long.

---

[1]Admiral Mitscher was Commander of the entire Navy and Marine Air Force carriers for both Task Force 58 and 38. The two Task Forces (consisting of the fifth fleet and the third fleet) alternated operations with Admiral Spruance in command of the fifth Fleet and Admiral Halsey in command of the third fleet. The same aircraft carriers were used for both fleets. The Lexington was the flag ship for Admiral Mitscher for both task forces.

[2]The "First Battle of The Philippine Sea." Three hundred enemy planes were downed. Finally the enemy fleet was located and a total of 216 planes were sent after it. Three carriers and two oilers were sunk. Twenty of our planes were lost in combat. One hundred planes survived. The rest went down as a result of empty gas tanks or from landing accidents. However all but 16 pilots and 22 crewmen were rescued.

I promised Mama today's picking of berries, so that too, has to be done before we can leave for the dentist. Also tomorrow evening there is to be a meeting of all parents interested in having their boys in Cub Scouts. I'm delighted they are to get started, but I'll be glad when tomorrow is over.

Oh, my Darling! I can't bear it. Marge Hoffer just phoned. Little Lou Anne Dingus died tonight. That little doll. It isn't right. Why do things like that have to happen? What poor Walt and Anne must be going through. She had chicken pox, measles, and then brain fever. They took her to a hospital in S.F. today. At five they were told she was better and were sent home. At 7:15 the call came that she was gone. I didn't even know she was sick. It's a blessing that they have little seven-week-old Larry. I wish you were here so I could cry in your arms. Everyone wants to go over and do something for them, but Dr. Feiler says it isn't safe. There are still germs around. Lou Anne was the sixth Lafayette child to die from this same brain fever, which is a complication from measles. It is called encephalitis. How do people live through things like this? Oh Honey, please hurry home. We are wasting precious time. . . .

June 28, 1944

Honey:

When Betty and I arrived at the freight depot this morning, the agent opened the freight room so we could carry the insulation to the platform. As soon as we had it piled outside, we went to see if he would help us load it. He moved a couple of boxes around while Betty and I tried to load her car. That was all he ever did. We finally got the trunks, the insides, and roofs of both cars filled. By the time we unloaded at home, it had taken the entire morning. We were filthy and dripping with perspiration. Needless to say, we were boiling mad at that man.

When we got back, Bert said an insurance man phoned to ask how old I am, how old the house is, what it's made out of, whether I am white, Oriental, Hebrew, or colored, how far we are from a fire hydrant, how far from a fire department, and whether I leave the house locked! Bert said he told the man he doesn't think I ever even leave the house!

First thing this morning Betty and I started insulating. We soon learned the process is absolute torture. It was hot everywhere, so you can imagine what it was like under the roof. We decided to get into swimsuits. That was our big mistake. We hadn't realized how lethal insulation can be until we had most of our skin exposed. It's made of pulverized glass. All those millions of tiny pieces of "glass" got into our skin. Between that and the perspiration we were in misery, but we kept at it until we had done the area over the rumpus room.

We couldn't take any more, so we quit to take baths. I don't know when we'll have the courage to tackle the rest of it. I've been going around singing,

"The Navy's made a man out of me, a man out of me, a man out of me." The worst part is that the baths didn't take out those little prickly things. We are still extremely uncomfortable.

Donny came home from the pool so excited today. A "BIG boy, a SIXTH GRADER," bet him seventy-two cents he couldn't swim under water. He succeeded in doing it half the length of the pool. He was so proud of himself and felt so wealthy coming home with all that money. He had also jumped in and retrieved a purse for a high school girl who dropped it as she ran past. He told me he felt so good because he made himself do two things he was afraid to do.

The girls had been looking forward to swimming, but during nap time, Judy swiped some chewing gum, and also spilled nail polish on the floor. I grounded her and offered Beverly the alternative of having Betty Jean come down to play in the lawn sprinkler.

Bert and Betty just returned from their regular Friday "date." She found some pink rickrack for me, and at prewar prices! She also found clothespins, and in desperation, bought them, although they were six times what we paid last time—twenty-nine cents for one package! At last she found some elastic. It isn't as good quality as prewar and is also six times as expensive. She let me buy three yards from her...

I received stacks of letters from you today. When the mail lady arrived, she honked her horn repeatedly and yelled to me.

I had to tear myself away from your letters to take the kids to the pool because I had promised them. Donny came home so impressed with Judy because she is so wonderful in the water. He was quite proud to say she is his sister. . . .

July 2, 1944

Hello, my Lovely Lady:

I spend most of my free time trying to figure out what kind of duty to request. I look at one angle and then another. My primary consideration is how to work it so I can get out as soon as possible after the war or get shore duty in the Bay Area. However, I am hearing more and more frequently that the WAVES are taking over so many of the duties on shore, so men aren't needed there.

Tonight I waited on the forecastle for the sunset. It was spectacular. I wish I could describe it adequately. There was every kind of cloud imaginable in the sky, with patches of deep blue in between. Every cloud seemed to have a different shade of red, depending on its position in relation to the setting sun. For a while the entire sky reflected a deep maroon on the ocean.

The biggest news around here is that Li'l Abner finally became fumigated and is no longer the inside man at the "skonk" factory. You can see that our life here is just one big exciting event after another. Perhaps you have noticed that I haven't seen any movies for a long time. When we see them, it means that we are where they can be shown—in port. Goodnight my darling!

July 4, 1944

Dearest Honey:

We are getting panicky about the mosquito and fly situation. The current trend of thought is that they are carriers of polio. When I woke up this morning my left eye was swollen shut and puffed in two directions. I was the most grotesque thing you could possibly imagine. Everyone doubled up when they saw me, and so did I when I looked in the mirror. Oh those mosquitoes!

Yesterday was a strange day. We needed milk, and I drove everywhere but could find nothing open. Finally I saw a man inside the creamery. He came to the door and told us they were closed and that they didn't have a drop of ice cream left. I told him what we needed was milk for six children and bread. He let us in and sold us eight quarts of milk and the bread. What a nice man.

After the ferocious heat of yesterday, this morning we had black clouds and a bitter wind. We started the day with many renditions of "Happy Birthday," and Chuckie was so tickled. He kept dancing around singing "Bu Day Bu Day" and yelling for "CAKE." The children "helped" make the cake and ice cream. In spite of that, it was, without a doubt, the best cake I have ever made.

Chuckie kept wanting to get down from his high chair between bites to play ring-a-round-a-rosie. He thinks that is the greatest! There were no presents. We hadn't found anything worth buying except the bond. His gifts from the other members of the family hadn't arrived. Fortunately, the Lembecks were back in time to make him deliriously happy with four gaily wrapped packages. . . .

July 7, 1944

Dearest Honey:

I always enjoy the enclosures in your letters, particularly Aunt Nettie's. I can never decide whether she is living in a dream world or is trying to write letters "as they should be written to a man overseas." Do you understand what I mean? Everything is being seen through rose colored glasses.

Tonight I paid bills. I have already paid Dr. Hartman $141.50. Is it any wonder I'm always broke? I talked to Yvonne today. She too is having a terrible time making their Navy allotment stretch.

When I gave the children their allowances tonight, Donny had a shock. This past week he has had Bev do his jobs. She does them well and enjoys it. As a result, Donny got fifty cents instead of $1 and Beverly got seventy-five cents instead of twenty-five. He has decided to do his own work from now on.

Your letters from the girls at the office are always so sweet, especially Miss Carlson's. It thrills me to pieces the way they all adore you. However,

Alkire's letter really griped me. Poor thing, suffering from all the terrible deprivations caused by the war and saying that you must be getting to be a really good golfer by now. What does he think you do—use the deck for a fairway and the Pacific Ocean for water hazards?

We are getting a $10 reduction in the water bill this year because of our victory garden. We have sold fifty dozen eggs. We should have been farmers!

Today I tried to straighten out your closet. It contains Harry's clothes, Rae's clothes, Donny's best clothes, the sick-a-bed toy box, gift wrappings, fall clothes to be fixed for the girls, old clothes to be given away, a lamp shade, four hula skirts, all your letters, and the movie equipment.

I'm trying to get Chuckie's baby book up to date. I must weigh and measure him tomorrow. Oh dear, there are so many things that need do be done. He hasn't had his tetanus shot. He and Donny must go to the eye specialist. Judy must go to Oak Knoll about her tonsils, and I must go to the dentist. Also it's time to start working on clothes for them to start school in September. . . .

July 9, 1944

My Dearest Young Man:

I just received your letter written in April. It was one you typed, and I think you did it very nicely. I have lots to write to you, but will do it in a few days as I have very little time tonight.

In this letter you told me about your gun. Captain Lembeck surely does a lot of nice things for you. I am glad he is there to do things with you and to help you with your playhouse. I love you and miss you so very much. . . .

July 10, 1944

My Wonderful Honey:

No matter how late it is or how tired I am, I need thinking time, not just about you and the children, but also about other things, principally about "after the war." It's the indefinite future stretching endlessly ahead that gets me down. Thinking about plans for the future helps.

The newspaper clipping you sent was accurate. You surmised correctly. Wouldn't it be nice if I could ever come right out and answer your questions? It's hard to think of ways to answer without breaking any rules.

I guess everyone at home got excited about D-day as you did, but we know how long drawn out those things can be and how many lives can be lost. I wish so-called civilized people would get some sense into their heads and stop this mess. Once the Germans and the Japs have seen their situation is hopeless, they should give up and stop the slaughter. The Germans appear to have realized it's hopeless but are too stubborn to give up. The Allies seem determined not to end the war until they reach Berlin.

If Charlie gets orders to come where I am, please be sure to send his Navy number and the name of his ship. I would have a very good chance of locating him. Have you heard from Leta lately? I wonder how they are doing. She must have her hands full with five as young as theirs are.

I got such a kick out of your letter describing Midge's graduation day, especially the part about ordering the dinner. I can't get over the unusual distribution of the graduates. Why do you suppose there were so many girls in agriculture and so many more dentists than doctors? To have only two graduating in education is disgraceful!

Oh Honey, It must have been so awful when you got the phone call about little Lou Ann Dingus. You have so many things to go through without me. . . .

July 13, 1944

Honey:

We have been without butane for nearly two days. We can't cook, wash dishes or clothes, or have showers or baths. I spent a lot of time phoning. Finally they delivered it, but we can't get a flame.

Donny went to work at the Browns' yesterday, and the girls took a hike up into the hills with Bernice and Philip. In the afternoon they all went swimming. Oh what a blessing that pool is. It was an opportunity for them to have showers, too.

Today on our way to the dentist we picked up an Ensign from St. Mary's who was hitchhiking to Berkeley to meet his wife. By an odd coincidence she is a play ground director at John Muir School two blocks from the folks. Later we stopped for a young woman with a frantic look who was trying to get to a hospital in Oakland where she is a volunteer.

After the dentist, we headed for the Matthews'. While we were there, Chuckie, who was exploring the place, locked himself in the bathroom. We couldn't make him understand how to unlock the door. He was screaming hysterically, first for me, then for Donny. Don Matthews climbed up a ladder, took the screen off and finally got in. We were all wrecks.

You should have seen the piles of clothes she had for Donny. Her boys are growing so fast and barely wear their things before outgrowing them. There were eight pairs of school pants with ZIPPERS!

I was sitting on the patio last night with Bert and Betty and kept saying "I must go and do the dishes." Betty kept telling me to relax. I said I had to sort and fold the clothes and learned that Betty had already done that! Then I said that I really did have to write to you. Bert started giving me a silly line of chatter that made no sense but was very funny. He said he would write my letter for me so I could go to bed right now. I gave up, gave in, and had a wonderful sleep. . . .

12 July 1944

Dear Fibush:

Betty and I were sitting in the patio last nite and finally prevailed upon Dot to slow up long enough to join us. We chatted until 2145 when Dot became "eager", had many things to be done. We analyzed her situation and took care of everything except her letter to you. I volunteered to write you and gave Dot a vocal sample of my correspondence. She agreed to hit the sack, so this is the reason for this missive.

Yesterday was quite a hectic day for your gal. She took the gang into town, made some calls, and left Bev with Dot's folks for a few days. The highlight of the day, however, was when Chuck locked himself in the head and then yelled like hell to get out, thinking he had been trapped and locked in by someone. This episode threw Dot clear off her schedule (you know how she loves to schedule her day), as it required almost two hours to spring him. Incidentally, that Chuckie is a great little character.

I can further report that your family is in good condition. They are all swell, and don't ever worry that they are forgetting you. They refer constantly to their Daddy.

Now as to St. Mary's U.S. Naval Pre-Flight School, we get lots of boys, from the farm and city but the uniform doesn't make the man, they all look alike, especially on a basketball court where they throw the ball across the court and most of them can't so you give them a dollar if they can make a basket and nobody makes a basket so you have to give them all a dollar as everything emphasizes individual effort for which they are being trained in teamwork as the man on your wing may be from the city and couldn't find a hammer and all the sweat shirts belong to Washington and the Admiral wears a towel over his arm and what the hell's the difference everybody catches a cold anyway. I've been here fourteen months and there's nothing wrong with me. Lots of the fellows around here are a little squirrely and stir crazy, but I'm all right.

Weather—stinking—however today looks like it might qualify as a fair day. This, I believe covers "My Day".

We, Betty and I, want you to know that you're not the only one who realizes what a great gal you have in that Dot, we know she's a Honey. Don't ever have any concern about the home fires, everything is Copasetti.

Lots of luck, Fibush, and hope you can soon be stateside.

Best regards,
BERT LEMBECK

July 15, 1944

My Honey:

I woke up on the wrong side of the bed this morning and stayed that way all day. The first thing I thought was, "I'm sick and tired of checking on everyone's, neck and ears, food, sleep, eyes, dispositions, and behavior. I'm sick and tired of being responsible for everything. But that's ridiculous because, when they all get to the point where I don't have to do any of that, they will be grown." That appalling thought snapped me out of it.

Bert went to the commissary at Mare Island with some other officers today. When he arrived with his arms full of groceries, he walked in our front door, which surprised me. I kidded him about showing off. He admitted he let them think he owned the whole place and told them it was "just a little place we have in the country to make it nice for the kids in the summer time." He even told them all the kids playing on the front lawn were his! Isn't he the limit?

You have asked me to describe how I look and what I am wearing, and I feel funny doing it. It seems so vain, but here goes. You would just love me tonight. I am wearing my new pinafore with my red shoes and a red ribbon in my hair, I feel quite glamorous. When the children saw me, they raved.

I was really down today. Then as I stepped out the back door, I saw Dan and Bernice greeting each other after a week's separation. That really got me! When Betty came in, I told her how I felt. She told me I should have a good cry, take a relaxing bath, put on something pretty, and take it easy. I did all those things, and it really did help.

Leta phoned from Oakland to say they had just seen their kids off for camp and would be out after dinner. I persuaded them to come right away. It was so much fun. We had a grand day and hated to see them leave.

Charlie is waiting for transportation to his ship, the Sagittarius, which is somewhere out where you are. He will be commanding a net tender. He looks so old with his white hair. Bert said he would have guessed him at least fifty-five rather than thirty-three. Leta and the children will be back in their home while Charlie is at sea. How wonderful to have them around again.

Charlie isn't very happy about going out to sea again but says he has had his year of shore duty, and now it's someone else's turn. The fellow who is relieving him has been out for two-and-a-half years. I hope you and Charlie do run into each other. It would mean so much to both of you. Goodnight, Darling.

July 18, 1944

My Sweet Honey:

I expect you heard about the terrible tragedy in Port Chicago. Myrna, Mabel, and I were at the movies. Suddenly we heard a loud explosion which shook the building. We thought it was in the building or right outside. Everyone started screaming and rushing out. We thought we had better remain where we were until we knew what was happening. Someone came in and told a young girl right behind us that an ammunition ship at Port

Chicago had blown up, and all the Lafayette store windows were broken. She screamed, "Oh my brother, my brother. He's up there tonight!" and rushed out.

Gradually some people came back. When the movie was over, we discovered a huge crowd had gathered, and cars were heading for Port Chicago. When we got home, we found our skylight smashed. Cupboard doors were open, and plates were knocked down, but no windows were broken. I suppose that's because the panes are so small. Betty said when she dashed in to check on the children, she found Chuckie had bumped the head of his bed and was crying. His forehead was bruised. All who heard or felt it thought it was right at their door. Betty thought one of our butane tanks had exploded.

I'm sorry you don't have the snapshots yet, but that is only half the story. I don't have them either. Everyone gets more and more behind. The shoe man I told you about who was getting repairs done so fast, had just gotten out of the army and was an expert. Now he is so well-known that he is swamped and can no longer give quick service.

Last night Bert went over everything with me, and I do mean everything. He does this almost every night. Do I need milk from the store? Is there anything he can get me from Ship's Service? Tonight he said he'll talk to the doctor at St. Mary's about giving Chuck tetanus shots, our other children their blood counts, and Donny a basal metabolism test. He certainly takes good care of us.

The folks were here for dinner today. It was rather hectic getting a company dinner so early in the day, but the folks always eat Sunday dinner at one, so I felt we must. They arrived shortly after we got home from Sunday School. Our dinner turned out beautifully. The fried rabbit was a big success, Judy made gingerbread, and Beverly fixed apple sauce and squash. The folks thought that was pretty wonderful for little girls of seven and almost six.

How do you expect to get the shore duty you want if you don't ask for it specifically? Bert says if you want Alameda, you should say so.

Yesterday I received a letter from a Mr. Elwood, who is manager of N.B.C. in San Francisco. His son Mickey is to travel with Donny on the train to the ranch. He has gotten Donny's ticket on the Daylight for August 1st and will meet us at the Oakland Mole at 8 a.m.

I'm so glad you can have that happy feeling about being in love with me, in spite of what you are going through. I know exactly what you mean. Sometimes I have days like that too, when it seems the separation doesn't really matter because we love each other so much. Having just said that, I'll have to admit that right now is not one of those times. . . .

July 20, 1944

Dearest Honey:

Marky said she heard some mention of your Admiral Mitscher on the radio, so I figured you must be out to sea again. That is sooner than I expected and, in my mind, it means another mess-up in the mail.

Today the girls went with Betty when she shopped for all of us. They can only sell two pounds of meat at a time, so the girls went along to stand in line with the ration points and give our meat order separately.

Jack cut bean poles for me this evening. When I started putting them in, Bert took over. He is making a helpless female out of me, and I love it.

We were eating lunch on the patio when Bert came home. The children asked him and Betty to join us. Bert said he couldn't eat with us because he was mad at me (I had told him that in my dream last night he was mad at me for digging up all the onions without letting him help). When we asked him if he was too mad to eat ice cream, he replied that he practically never gets that mad. He sat there with Chuck, Mike, and Lance all on his lap as he ate. After that he and the kids played mumbletypeg[1], and marbles until they left for the pool.

After dinner Donny and Judy went into a huddle. Soon he had her working like a beaver with him to clean up around his play house. It tickles me to death when they get together like that. As you know, they get along like oil and water. I am beginning to catch on that a lot of the things for which we punish Donny are caused because she started it or egged him on. I must take sides with "poor little Judy" less often and watch to see that Donny isn't always the one in the wrong. Goodnight my Honey....

July 22, 1944

Hello, my Loveliness:

Yesterday I read about the ammunition ships exploding at Port Chicago. It said the blast was felt for twenty-five miles and that the windows in Pittsburg were all blown out. Did you feel it? I hope it didn't do any damage to our place. It must have been terrible for all those fellows on the ship.

I had hoped to attend the service this morning, but I didn't get off duty in time. When I got off duty tonight I played bridge for a couple of hours. One of the fellows I played with has had a rather interesting career. He was in the first flying squadron at Guadalcanal and has been decorated four times. Now he has been "retired" to a sort of semi-safe job. However he dislocated his shoulder last week while doing his work.

I finally feel rested and caught up on my sleep for the first time in many weeks. Perhaps it is because of the funny dream I had. I got on a plane with other officers to take a long flight. There were a lot of other people on the plane, and among them were several women officers. Each of them asked one of us to

---

[1]A children's game played with a pocket knife.

sit down beside her. The one next to me said "Now, you hold my hand and imagine it is your wife's hand. Then you tell me all about your family." You can imagine what a good time I had pretending I was holding your hand and talking endlessly about you and the children.

That picture of our admiral you saw in Time Magazine is an excellent likeness, but he is not at all rugged. He is very small, thin, and so wrinkled from constant exposure to the elements, that he looks at least fifteen years older than he is. He has plenty on the ball.

You have asked why it is that we can sometimes receive mail but not send it. Of course our main business is to win the war, and mail is secondary. It is only through unusual circumstances that we are able to receive it from time to time. As for not being able to send it, there is no way I can explain that to you at present. If you have not seen Time Magazine for July 3rd, please try to get hold of a copy. It is very accurate in describing what has been going on.

I read an article in the May Readers Digest about a new insect spray that sounds quite wonderful. It has a long name, but I think they call it DDT. Have you heard about it? It might be the solution for your hordes of flies and mosquitoes. Why don't you see what you can find out?

This past week I have been more lonesome than ever in spite of the fact that our activities have been EXTREMELY INTERESTING[1]. As a result, I have become very optimistic about the war in Europe and feel that it might be finished by early fall. Today's news was encouraging as far as the Russians are concerned, too. If only they would let us use their fields in Siberia, I think we could finish up in the Pacific in about six to eight months.

It's wonderful but terrible to love you so much. . . . Goodnight Dearest.

July 24, 1944

Dear Daddy:

Five more days and it will be my birthday. The presents are all wrapped up and I can't see them. I'll be six years old and I will be an old lady.

I play with Nancy and Lois and Betty Jean's gone to Lake Tahoe. I could swim almost and I could duck my head under water and kick my legs up holding on to the edge and I could go into the deep part and I could jump in. I'm a good girl and I love you and I miss you and I hope you come home and stay home, and the war's over pretty soon. Goodbye Daddy.

Judy.

July 26, 1944

Hello my Bunny:

I always think of you as my darling little Easter Bunny because I love you so much. Do you like that name? I have been thinking about you an extra lot

---

[1]Retaking Guam and also Saipan and Tinian.

lately because it will be your birthday soon. I'll bet you are excited. Be sure to tell me all about it.

Mother says you play in the attic on rainy and dreary days. That is a good place to play, isn't it? Do you have a lot of fun up there?

I miss you very much and wish I could be there with you, especially on your birthday. I love you SO MUCH! XOXOXOXOXOXO . . . .

July 29, 1944

Honey:

The girls were awake bright and early this morning, and the fun began. Judy found slippers from you and several other packages beside her bed when she woke up. They no sooner climbed into my bed than Donny came downstairs to give her a coloring book and crayons. After they cleaned up their room and went outside to play, I called them back and told them they had better come finish the job. They were highly indignant until they discovered a Storybook Doll from you on each of their beds.

By the time everyone arrived, there were fourteen, twelve of them under six. Things got pretty lively. After they had eaten and then played games for a while, I piled them into the car and took them home. I have already learned it is simpler to do that than to wait for mothers to arrive.

While I was gone Betty cleaned up the lawn and patio areas as well as the kitchen. Anyone reading this letter would think Betty was my maid!

Bert was quite impressed when he read the article in Life Magazine about Task Force 58. I wish I knew for sure whether that rear view of someone on the staff is you. It would be fun to show the article to one and all, point to that and say, "That's my husband's fanny!"

Yesterday I tried to get Donny some fishing tackle for camp. Mr. Gibson at the hardware store was surprised I didn't know it has been frozen for ages. He tried without success to fix my flashlight. Mr. Winkler from the drugstore next door came in for some change. Knowing I couldn't possibly find a new one to buy, he was absolutely determined to fix it and finally did. What a dear.

I woke up at 3:15 and couldn't go back to sleep, because I just KNEW we were going to miss the train. I just KNEW Mr. Elwood wouldn't be there with Donny's ticket. How was I ever going to find the Oakland Mole? How was I ever going to find the right train? It's lucky we got there in plenty of time because he was in car sixty three! With Chuckie in my arms, I felt as though I could have walked home to Lafayette before we got to it!

I left the car at Howard Auto, and when we got back to pick it up, the bill was every bit as bad as I expected. Here it is: tune and burn motor, $7.50; overhaul and clear out carburetor, $6.90; install distributor exchange, .90; then $10 for the distributor, five cents for a gasket, and two bits tax—$26.11! Only a year ago I spent $25 on that darn car.

Don't ever think it isn't necessary for me to can as much as I do. With every can costing one person's ration points for a week, we need at least five hundred quarts of fruits and vegetables to keep this family healthy.

Well, my Darling, I am off to bed. Would you care to join me?

August 7, 1944

Hello, my Honey:

It's a whole year since we have been together. Just thinking about it gives me a sick feeling in the pit of my stomach. I went to the blood bank again this morning. It was a breeze this time.

Last night, after we all did the dishes together, we piled into my bed, and Bev read "Little Black Sambo" to Chuckie. As she read, Judy rubbed my back. Have I told you how marvelous she is at that? She is better than most adults. She has not only the force, but also the knack to get to all the right places. She also makes beds beautifully and never makes a fuss over shots and medicine. She is very tender-hearted, especially over animals. Don't you think she would make a good nurse? Or perhaps an even better veterinarian?

The girls went to Bucky Hall's birthday party today. I had put curlers in Judy's hair last night. When she saw how soft and fluffy it looked, she kept looking in the mirror and saying in amazement, "I don't look like Judy, do I?"

Betty and I took our boys to St. Mary's for tetanus shots. The doctor told us that he has four children of his own and has just recently returned from duty in the Pacific. He says that soon there will be one shot which will take care of all the childhood diseases. He also told us that in New York, babies one-day-old are being vaccinated!

This evening Frank Brown brought Aunt Bertha over from San Francisco. We are so lucky that he works there and could do this. We were so tickled to see her. She is amazing. It's hard to believe she is eighty seven. She was such a help in the garden and also helped hem blankets for Red Cross. She is such a dear and so much fun.

At ten we listened to the Richfield reporter. He said that you are about 650 miles from Japan. Is that correct? It bothers me to have you so close to Japan. I'm afraid they might have some hidden strengths we don't suspect and come out and surprise you.

Today Anne Dingus came to wash for the last time. She is amazing the way she has taken Lou Anne's death. She is very willing to talk about it. She said she and Walt often wonder how they stand it, but she has to keep going for him and the baby and he for her. It's terrible that he has to go overseas right now. When he leaves, Anne and the baby will go home to Kansas. The doctor at Children's Hospital thinks there should be an investigation. He wants to find out why six out of 150 cases of measles in Lafayette resulted in encephalitis, when in the general population it happens only once in 10,000 cases.

Tonight after dinner, I flopped on my bed for a minute. The girls then put on aprons, barred me from the rest of the house, cleaned up everything, and had a good time doing it. I must be doing something right!

It's a shame Donny isn't here. He could make some real money. Bernice picked pears for Gary and made $3.50 today just in her spare time. Poor Les Underhill. Bob is away, and his father has a cracked rib, so Les has to do all the picking. Pears are $80 a ton this year, up $20 from last year. In spite of the poor crop, we may make a little profit.

Gretchen and Laddy get along just fine, but Gretchen never goes over to the Schneiders'. She is a loyal family dog. We are her family, and she stays with Blackie and the children exclusively.

Your lonely, longing, languishing Honey.

August 7, 1944

"Dearest Sweetheart Darling":

I am so glad you sent me the magazine story by that name. When I finished reading it, I was all choked up because it made me feel as though I was reading a letter from you. In fact, it sounded EXACTLY like you.

After I came off duty this morning I slept restlessly, then was awakened two hours later to attend to some business. I used the "Admiral's Barge." It is pretty fancy, you know. I'll tell you all about it when I see you.

Two of your recent letters had that lovely powdery fragrance that I enjoy so much. Why don't you do it oftener? Isn't it amazing that they retain the fragrance over all the miles and time that elapse?

Yes, I am just a cog in the machinery, as is EVERYONE, including His Nibs. I'll have to explain that when I see you.

It's a shame you couldn't get any fishing tackle. I'll have to take Donny fishing for trout when I get home.

The reason I am optimistic about the war is that I am sure the Germans will quit before they are annihilated by the Russians. The Japs are a different story, but I have a feeling that, when we finally have a landing operation there, they will quit too, unless bombing does it before then. Due to topography, their supplies and manufacturing centers can't be diversified as to location, like the Germans, so it should be easier to destroy them by bombings.

It must be tough on John to be right in the middle of a war, with his increasing feelings of Pacifism. If he saw someone assaulting his wife, would he just stand there and try to reason with him? That is one of the many things that would have happened if we hadn't gone to war.

What you heard from the Richfield Reporter was true, except that we were A LOT CLOSER to the enemy's base than he said.

I just received oodles of mail including one piece sent to Port Hueneme a year ago! When I think of a year ago today, my heart stands still—our last time together.

I could go on writing to you forever, but I simply must get some sleep. That sounds like the boy who phoned his girl and said "I love you. I would go through fire and water for you. I'll be over tomorrow, if it doesn't rain."

August 12, 1944

My Precious Honey:

Bert just got home, and great is the rejoicing by one and all. We are all going to have dinner together to celebrate his birthday. Yesterday Jack gave us a chicken which had been attacked by a weasel. It was in such bad shape that he had to kill it, and since Marky is away, he gave it to us. This was our first experience with picking, plucking, cleaning, and cutting up a chicken. When we finished it was midnight, and we were exhausted.

Due to the gas shortage, our garbage hasn't been collected for over three weeks. With all the fruit peelings and the cleaning of the chicken, it is just awful. When we step out the back door we are met by hordes of flies and bees. The odor is horrendous.

The insulation is doing a wonderful job of keeping the house cooler. There is still enough left to do the rest of the attic when I can. Do you realize I figured out all by myself how much we would need? For someone who claims she can't do arithmetic, that's not bad.

I sent the girls on an adventure this morning. They took Chuck and Mike with them, across the bridge and up to the Ingrams' to pay for the rabbit we bought when the folks came for dinner. I also sent some chard and lettuce, since they don't have a garden. When they came home they were all absolutely filthy and very happy, after stopping to play in the Underhills' orchard and in the truck that was sitting there.

You asked what is so unique about Chuck. I don't know exactly how to explain it, but everyone thinks he is. I guess it's because he is such a clown and so very happy. Everything is exciting to him, his curiosity is limitless, and he is so loving.

You also asked about the campus. The student body president is a girl. She got practically all the votes. The sororities are still going strong, but their main activities are for the war effort. I haven't heard of a fraternity in ages. Many of the fraternity houses are now boarding houses for war workers.

A lonesome goodnight from your Honey

August 13, 1944

Hello My Honey:

That chicken Jack gave us was superb. No one would ever have suspected it was a tough old hen. When Betty brought out Bert's birthday cake, you should have seen Chuckie, Mike, and Lance trying to blow the candles out. It sounded as though they were all blowing "raspberries".

We can probably expect little Miss Lembeck along about next May. Betty has been trying very hard to persuade Bert that they really need a third child, and he has agreed. What a change in her since a few months ago, when she was so terrified she might be pregnant again. She says now she wouldn't mind if it's another boy or even twins.

Bert dreamed last night that a fellow in a pin stripe suit, with a straw hat pushed way back on his head, and smoking a big black cigar, came into his office at St. Mary's and handed him your business card. You started trying to sell him insurance. He asked if you had seen me yet. You said you hadn't and went right on trying to sell him insurance. He kept worrying about me, asking you if you weren't going home right away, but you just kept up your sales pitch. You were trying to convert his government insurance to Prudential! I can't wait for Bert to see what you are really like.

Beverly's duties consist mainly of taking care of Chuck. It is handy to be able to call on her whenever I need her. The girls get twenty-five cents a week. Since Beverly is making extra money doing some of Donny's jobs while he is gone, she is going to buy stamps and a Storybook Doll. I think you have gathered that Judy is quite helpful in a number of ways. So aside from keeping their rooms neat, I just call on both of them when I need them.

There is no end to the good things that happen when Bert is around. He was able to get my Mixmaster fixed at St. Mary's. I haven't been able to use it for so long. I couldn't find a shop that had time to repair a "nonessential".

August 15, 1944

Dearest Mine:

The heat gets worse and worse. As a result, so does my heat rash. Just as I had taken my cot outside and was getting settled for a cool night's sleep in the forecastle, someone came to tell me we are no longer allowed to do that. The Flag Lt. said he would try to find a cooler room for me, and just now he phoned to say he has a bunk for tonight he thinks will be much cooler.

I was interrupted by the arrival of the mail. It included a letter from Donny. He said, "Dear Daddy, How are you? Mother wanted me to write you a good letter, so I hope this is a good letter. I can't write much because I have a job to do. We all have jobs here at camp. Love Donny. S.W.A.K." I think his handwriting has improved a lot, but I must say that he is far from loquacious.

The U.S.O. show we have been hoping to see finally came, and it is quite a thrill to see a woman (other than a native) after so long. There are five of them, and right now they are all in the wardroom with officers crowding around them. They are very hard looking, except for one who isn't really pretty, just kind of cute. The show was nothing wonderful, but you can't possibly imagine what it was like to see a woman and have her smile at you, even though the smiles were collective. At the end of the program, they asked everyone who was celebrating a birthday to come up. There were five enlisted men and one officer, also the cute girl. They held hands, and we all sang "Happy Birthday."

We have a small newspaper here called "The Sunrise Press" which I will send you. I think you'll enjoy it. As far as world news is concerned, it prints only what you would get at home. Due to the nature of my work, I get all the news a day before it's printed, so I only read the funnies.

I saw Life Magazine for June 26th, and it contained a very interesting article about the island where we were at first. I think you would enjoy reading it if you can get a copy. . . . I have to quit now, darn it.

August 16, 1944

Honey Dearest:

It has been a rather trying day. I woke up feeling perfectly awful and had quite a bit to get done before the Chung Mei boys arrived. Daddy told me he would send all the gardening tools they would need, but they forgot them. I had to scurry around to all the neighbors borrowing everything. Also he had said they would bring bag lunches, but at the last minute before lunch time, I discovered they hadn't. So I sent Beverly to the garden to pick squash while I made a large platter of sandwiches. Then I poured a half gallon of milk. In absolutely no time at all there wasn't a crumb left, so I put on another big bowl of squash, made chocolate shakes and a few more sandwiches. Everything was devoured with enthusiasm. After that they explored the whole place before they started working again.

After chopping all the weeds, they cleaned out the chicken house and chicken yard, dug a compost pit and filled it with everything they had just chopped, dug out, or scraped up. It is going to be wonderful to have a compost heap again. In no time it was 4:30 and time for them to quit. They piled all our old newspapers and magazines into the truck, then did likewise with the Schneiders', Condits', Underhills' and Wooley's, all of whom were delighted to have them taken care of. The boys were tickled to death with their haul and especially with the pears and peaches I let them take home.

Chuck was in all his glory playing in their truck all day. You should hear him trying to make all the car noises that he hears the bigger boys making.

August 19, 1944

Hi there, My sweet Poochy:

I love you and miss you so very much. From Mother's letters it sounds as though you are having a nice vacation. What a lot of birthday parties you have gone to. It must be a lot of fun.

Mother told me how you helped her make the dinner when Grandpa, Grandma, and Midge came. I am so proud of you.

It must be fun for you and Judy to have the playhouse all to yourselves while Donny is away. I think of you so many times every day. X 0 X 0 X 0 X 0

Your Daddy.

August 20, 1944

My Honey:

After the kids were tucked away this evening, I joined Bert and Betty in the patio. It was an exquisite starlit night. The newly mown lawn looked super. Beverly does a good job of mowing and enjoys it. Bert was in top form and had us in stitches. He seemed to think I got off some pretty good cracks, too. The delightful thing about Bert is that all his humor is absolutely clean, not even one innuendo which is rather unusual these days.

Today Mama and Midge came to pick pears. It was obvious they hadn't just come for pears because Mama made a point of leaving Midge alone with me much of the time. Midge must be really getting serious. She was asking, "How do you KNOW when it is really love?" That's the question of the ages, isn't it?

This morning Betty Jean and Johnny were here. The three girls took charge of the four little boys. They had a wonderful time playing with the pear lugs that are waiting in the orchard to be filled. They built houses and forts, and also used them as cars and boats, piling the little ones into them and pulling them around. Then they used them as tables when they had their picnic lunch.

I love you and miss you and would love to kiss you. Hey! I'm a poet!. . .

August 23, 1944

Dearest Mine:

This morning I was assigned a new room. It's much cooler, and I have only one roommate. I think I am going to enjoy him very much.

When I moved from the old room, I talked the owner of the typewriter I have been using into selling it to me. He charged me $10. It's ten years newer than the Remington you have.

My new roommate, Mac, had three near misses before he left the states, which goes to show you I'm safer out here than I would be at home. First when he was flying in a training plane, the motor caught fire at 6,000 feet. He and the pilot had to bail out. He hadn't the slightest idea how to operate a parachute or how to pull the cord but managed to land safely without a scratch. The pilot broke his leg.

The next was when he was walking down the airfield beside parked planes. A fifty caliber gun inside a plane went off and killed the man beside him.

The third time was when he was watching gunnery practice. Suddenly he felt something hit his side pants pocket. He looked down and saw his pants had been torn from the waist to and through the pocket. At his feet he found a piece of shrapnel which had done the dirty work. He certainly leads a charmed life.

NEXT DAY. I like my new roommate. His conversation is very interesting, BUT he came in last night and talked nonstop for over an hour when I was trying to write to you, and he is doing it again right now. I think I'll take a nap and assume he'll stop talking while I'm asleep.

You should know by now that noise never bothers me when I sleep. I can sleep with a power saw going right next to my bunk and the loudspeaker over my head. Here, I have a winch operating about fifteen feet from my bunk, and I don't even notice it. There is nothing noisier than a winch.

I am a sight! My heat rash is so bad I am really repulsive-looking, especially where it has become infected. I have a lump the size of a walnut on my neck. The Doctor says it is a sweat gland swollen from overwork.

NEXT DAY. Doc Peabody dropped in to look at me again. As a result, he felt I should go into sick bay before these infections get any worse, so that's where I am. I hated to do it because we are terribly busy now. I don't like leaving the others with so much extra to do, but he felt it was imperative.

A DAY LATER. My roommate here in sick bay has been in the Navy a long time and attained the rank of warrant officer shortly before the war started. At that time he was stationed on an island[1] which was captured and occupied when Pearl was attacked. He's been hiding all this time and was rescued by us a few days ago. He is here to recuperate from his deprivation. He has some very interesting tales to tell.

The war in Europe is looking hopeful. In the last war the Germans weren't nearly so badly beaten as they are right now, when they decided to sign the Armistice. . . .

The Doctor just came in and thinks my heat rash is so much better that I can resume my regular duties tomorrow. I'll be so glad to get back to work.

August 26, 1944

Honey:

Yesterday noon Mr.Sturtevant phoned to say he was putting Donny on the train which was due in Martinez at 6:05. This was a surprise. He said Donny decided to leave early to be home for his first Cub Scout Pack meeting.

When the girls and I got to the depot, we learned they no longer have time to check on whether or not the trains are on schedule. You just wait till they come. It was terribly hot and absolutely unbearable in the waiting room. We walked up and down the platform while train after train came in loaded with soldiers heading for their port of embarkation.

By seven-thirty, I was frantic. I kept thinking of Donny already on the train for over seven hours and with no dinner. Finally I overheard one man in the depot say to another that they had better let such and such a train go ahead because Number 51 wouldn't be here until 9:48. I found a little cigar shop where they had Eskimo Pies which pacified our hunger pangs for a while.

Finally at 10:40 a train-load of Japanese prisoners of war came in. I was surprised. I didn't realize we capture them. Just then we detected legs on the

---

[1]Guam.

other side of the P.O.W. train, rushed around the end of it and found that the Daylight had arrived with Donny. After all my worries about him, he had spent a marvelous day. He had made friends with any number of soldiers and other passengers who had supplied him with candy, popcorn, and all sorts of junk all day long. He had the time of his life while we were all worrying and waiting.

His time at the ranch was marvelous too, especially on the camping trip at Lake Tenaya. He can now dive in and swim clear across their swimming hole.

I found out today that Judy will only be going to school a half day. The second grade will be doing that too. The Pleasant Hill school will be having half days through third grade and in Vallejo it will be half days for everyone. Imagine what it will be like with a whole town full of teenagers free for half the day. With so many fathers in the service and mothers working in the shipyards, they are anticipating problems.

Did I remember to tell you I actually got some Palmolive soap the other day? That's the first we have had since long before you left. Goodnight Honey.

August 27, 1944

Dearest Honey:

Today was the annual Horse Show Parade, and it would have to be the hottest day we have had this year. We had a good view because we all got into the Halls' truck which was parked in a fine location. With all of ours and theirs that made ten children.

It's a shame we haven't been able to get Beverly a horse. She has wanted one so desperately for so long and would dearly love to ride in the parade. I know it would do her ego a world of good. Right now it certainly needs a boost. I haven't figured out why. Perhaps she thinks you left because of something she did. Of course you have always meant everything to her. Remember how she was when she was tiny? You were the absolute center of her existence. Perhaps she wonders why you went to war when none of the other daddies on our road have.

The Woods came today, which I thought was very brave of them, considering the temperature. They said they almost turned back when they came through the tunnel and felt the blast of heat on this side. I guess they must figure their contribution to the war effort is to check on us every once in a while. They shouldn't feel that way. Losing a son is the ultimate contribution.

Yesterday we went to San Francisco with Bernice and Philip, who had appointments not far from ours. I'd hoped that by getting to Dr. Burns' office early, we wouldn't have to wait too long. When we arrived, there was barely standing room. Our appointment was for nine, but I counted seventeen people ahead of us and only six chairs.

After forty-five minutes, Chuckie got restless and started crying bitterly. I'm sure the other impatient patients thought I must have pinched him to start him off, because the nurse ushered us in immediately while everyone glared. Dr.Burns said Donny's eyes are making excellent progress. Much to my delight, he took a look at Chuckie's eyes and said there is nothing to worry about. So much for all the people who feared he was going to be cross eyed.

As soon as we met Bernice and Philip, we headed for Fleishacker Zoo. First we had our picnic lunch and then enjoyed the animals, especially the monkeys. Afterwards the kids had a wonderful time on the swings and slides.

Next we went to Golden Gate Park where they enjoyed the rides. Maybe you don't think it's expensive these days buying rides for four children at a nickel a ride! The prices have doubled since we were there last, and the parents no longer can ride free on the merry-go-round with a child too small to go alone. I spent $1.85. We got them away from there by promising them donkey rides. Chuckie, who had just loved everything all day, liked that best of all. His lazy dreamy donkey had to be poked along—perfect for a two-year-old.

I have so much fun planning the way it will be when you come home on leave. Starting the day with a leisurely breakfast on the patio with large dishes of fresh strawberries (if it's December, I don't know about the strawberries and the patio). We could then have a wonderful time working together on all the projects around here that I long to complete. Honey, you can skip the fur coat, the diamonds, the new car, and even the spinet piano. What I want most of all is to get the grounds looking perfectly beautiful. When it comes to the evenings and the nights—well I'll leave that to you. After all, I shouldn't do ALL the planning! . . .

August 30, 1944

Hello Honey:

Before taking Donny to the dentist today, we went to Live Oak Park. Chuckie made a beeline for the slide, and oh, how he loved it. He would come down lickety-split and land face first in that filthy sawdust pile, get his mouth and eyes full of it, and laugh so hard. One time he came down too hard and fast, turned head over heels half way down and whacked his head hard on the side. He cried wildly for a minute, and then suddenly laughed through his tears, "Ha ha I go boom," and was right back on the slide.

Apparently you were shocked when I mentioned Midge wearing jeans when they came out Sunday. That shows how long you have been gone. Remember how amazed you were that the coeds at U. of Arizona were wearing them on campus when you took your indoctrination there? Now all girls wear them.

Yes, we finally did get our canning sugar. The ration board has a hard time keeping up. It takes ages to receive the actual coupons after we get the "request granted." I thought the coupons for the girls' shoes would never come. In the meantime I had to borrow some. People are very good about giving us their shoe coupons, since adults don't outgrow their shoes and sometimes don't use all their tickets. Judy often wears out a pair in six weeks. Little kids like Chuckie can easily outgrow theirs in that length of time too.

I must have forgotten to tell you, when I phoned Oak Knoll Hospital to see about having Judy's tonsils out, they said they weren't taking out tonsils in August. It's the worst time for polio. Actually there are very few times of the year when it is safe.

September 3, 1944

Dearest:

The time was finally appropriate. I spoke to my IMIC (immediate superior in command) about putting in my request—thirty days' leave and stateside duty in the 12th Naval District. He is a rather peculiar fellow, and others have not had much luck with him, but I was lucky. He said it would be ok to put it through. Thus it will get the Admiral's endorsement. That assures me of leave but not necessarily the duty I want. I'll be getting the papers off tomorrow.

Why do I say he's peculiar? He has had sea duty for the past four years with only ten days' leave. He can't see why a Navy man would want anything but sea duty. If they do, according to him, they shouldn't be in the Navy!

What a dream I had last night! I was in a crowd of people all in uniform. A WAVE came up to me and asked if I was on the staff. When I told her my duties, she said I was to get leave now and would be flying home. She asked if I had my tag. I thought she meant my dog tag, but she said I had to have a cardboard tag on a string around my neck. This would entitle me to go on leave tomorrow and to fly. When she said she would get one for me, we fought our way through the crowds but got nowhere. Then I woke up. Now even if I believed in dreams, how would I decide whether to be encouraged or discouraged by that one?

Isn't it marvelous the way the war in Europe has been moving so rapidly? The scuttlebut continues to fly thick and fast. From the way things are going, I wouldn't be surprised if they could wind it up by the time you receive this letter. Then we could really dig in and put the finishing touches on those blankety blank Japs! . . .

Dear Daddy

I am telling this to Mother. Um, I love you and I wish you would come home very very very very very soon. And I went on a train at the Merry-go-round and on real donkeys and I played in the slide, a ring around a rosy slide. And I went on the double swing with two seats with Pat and Beverly and myself. And mother gave me a black velvet hair ribbon with a little comb and I put it on myself and I did it all by myself.

Now Daddy, I been at school and I make pictures with the color crayons and I make pictures nice. I make grass and hills and sky and sun and flowers. My teacher is a nice teacher and she teaches us to do words and points to the words and points to the numbers. My room has pictures on the wall made by the children coloring, and pictures not made by the children and we count to ten and then recess came and I'm a first grader. And I came home on the bus and I went to the school on Joe's bus with two people in it. Everybody else went to school in the morning.

Captain makes ice cream and Betty makes cupcakes and Captain buys some gum and some food and milk. Betty has her hair pretty, rolled up off the back of her neck with blue ribbons in it and we got thousands and thousands and thousands of bottles, a whole attic full.

Love, Judy

September 3, 1944

Dearest Honey:

Yesterday I made a BIG mistake! I forgot the whole world would be shopping for Labor Day weekend. First I went to the meat market, and at 9:30 a.m. they were out of everything and closing for the day. That's when I learned that practically everyone would be closed Sunday, Monday, and Tuesday and some shops on Wednesday as well. I went from one store to another trying to find food we would need for the next few days. Thank goodness for our garden and our fruit.

The children came home all excited over their accomplishments at the pool this afternoon. Bert got Beverly to jump in and submerge her whole head, which she never would do before. Both Donny and Judy can now jump in and swim across the deep end. The Lembecks enjoyed the pool very much, and I had a lovely time taking care of Mike, Lance, and Chuckie, uninterrupted by "the big kids."

Big news! John wired last night that he is back in the U.S. Isn't that marvelous? It's also inexplicable. When you think of all the husbands and fathers who have been in Europe for a couple of years or more without getting home on leave, it doesn't make sense. . . .Goodnight Honey

FIRST DAY OF SCHOOL. The school bus situation is awful. Since the first day was a short day, we expected our children home by 12:30. Donny arrived at one, but the girls did not. Donny said when his bus left, so many children were still there that he assumed they must be running another one. I phoned the school, but there was no answer. Just then Jean Hall drove up. She had her three plus our girls and Betty Jean, Nancy, and Lois. Beverly and Nancy insisted that Mr. Ellis said there would be another bus. Nobody knows yet just what happened.

Judy was crying because "Nancy socked me because I was fighting Bucky Hall, and it wasn't any of her business, and he won anyhow because he bit me on the arm." She hates school, "because I knocked someone down, and the teacher wanted me to say I'm sorry, but I couldn't and I just cried and cried, so she sat me on a chair."

When I asked her what her teacher was like, she said she didn't know. When I asked if she was pretty, she said, "OH YES! And I think she talks English. Anyhow she doesn't talk like us, but she talks nice. I think maybe she comes from some other country."

They had been given notes that the government is not paying for the milk this year. It will cost a nickel a day instead of a penny, so that means $1.00 a week instead of the twenty cents I had expected to pay.

Betty and I sewed all afternoon. I made Chuck a bathrobe out of the non-worn-out-parts of three old blue bath towels. It's as cute as can be on him. The war shortages are certainly teaching us that the old adage, "Necessity is the mother of invention," is true.

Today I spent nearly four hours swatting flies and cleaning up after them. By the time I finished it was noon and I had to meet the bus, since it was Judy's first day to come home alone. The bus didn't come until one-thirty. There was a line-up of mothers and their kindergartners waiting all that time for the bus to the afternoon session. Donny, Sonny, and some others walked home dripping with perspiration. The rest arrived eventually after much confusion and many tears. Something must be done.

Beverly is thrilled to death with school this year. She has Mrs. Burkhead, that little doll who is married to a sailor. She is the type who, by her smile and greeting, makes everyone feel like the one person in the world she is most delighted to see. . . . Goodnight Honey.

September 8, 1944

Honey Dearest:

Today we stopped by the Barrows' to invite David to Donny's party. I was amazed at the changes since the last time I was there. They now have a huge lawn with stepping stones leading to the porch and a very tall flag pole with a large flag waving. The house is painted white, and inside it is cozy and charming. Mr. Barrows was there. He is a big handsome man—very distinguished looking like his father. They were delighted at the invitation.

When Bert got home all six children went after him, practically tearing him limb from limb. This evening they all had a great time together with the hose sprinkler. Chuckie was in swimming trunks and your helmet, Mike and Lance in nothing at all. Donny, Beverly, Judy, Susan, Philip, and of course Bert, all tore around on the lawn having a perfectly glorious time.

Yesterday Millie and I talked about the school situation. Something must be done about the overcrowding! Last year the school board was criticized for spending $8,000 for two new rooms. It would now require $11,000 for two more, and the county school board would have a fit. Consequently our school board decided against more building. I think something must be done NOW. We have classes in the basement of the town hall, the basement of a church, and in the auditorium, which is divided into four classrooms. Those basements flood almost every winter. I don't know how anyone can be expected to teach or to learn, with approximately one hundred twenty children and four teachers working in the auditorium. Can you imagine the din?

DONNY'S BIRTHDAY. Monday morning I bought the last-minute things for Donny's party, plus fourteen quarts of milk. Then I picked up my cleaning lady. I actually have a cleaning lady. Can you believe it? Her name is Mrs. Wilbur, and she has two sons in the Air Corps. She cleaned everything thoroughly, and the place looked beautiful when she finished. She charges $1.25 an hour, so the day cost me $10, but I think I can handle it.

After school the horde descended. From then on the air rang with shouts of, "Put him in front of the firing squad! Halt who goes there? Charge!" and other warlike phrases. The boys were very impressed with the playhouse (fort), the gun, and all the things for which Bert is responsible.

I asked the boys to gather wood and cut sticks for roasting the wieners. Only one made the mistake of cutting a poison oak stick, and luckily I caught it in time. After the hot dogs had disappeared, I brought out the ice cream and cake, and in nothing flat four quarts of ice cream and the whole cake had also vanished. Most of the boys had three helpings.

When the folks arrived, the boys besieged John with questions—how many Germans had he killed, etc!

While I took the boys home, John went to the Imries' to pick up Beverly and Judy. Then he put all the paraphernalia Donny had received; two new tubes, a rear-view mirror, reflector, and basket, on Donny's bike. Donny said it was the most wonderful birthday ever. He got EVERYTHING he had ever hoped for.

Yesterday morning I drove the children to school and visited each of their rooms. Beverly's teacher is adorable, so sweet and patient. During recess I asked how Bev was doing. She said she reads and spells very well, but is easily distracted. She thinks your being away is very upsetting for her, as she talks about it constantly.

I spent the next hour in Judy's room. As soon as they went out for recess, I said "Well, how is my little roughneck doing? Has she knocked anyone down lately?" She said in a tone of great relief, "Oh, then you know how she is!" Apparently she dreaded telling me. Well, the gist of our talk was that she thinks Judy is the prettiest, cutest, most adorable, and most interesting child in her class. She loves to watch her on the swings or bars because she is so agile and graceful, but she isn't sure she'll survive the year with Judy in her class! They have been at swords' points several times already. When I told her Judy's history, she was very understanding. However, I hope she doesn't go to the other extreme and let her get away with unacceptable behavior.

When I got to Donny's room, Mrs. Christian was delighted to see me.

She was happy to hear that Donny is crazy about school this year and about her, but says she has quite a bit of trouble with him and Charles. I was not especially thrilled about having Donny classed with that troublemaker. She is simply grand, so natural and loving. She calls them "darling," stands with an arm around them, gives them a pat on the head or a swat on the behind, according to what they deserve at any given moment. She called Allan Stanley a nosy neighbor and Jerry Hoffer a wiggle worm, and it just tickled them to death. She's definitely a teacher of the old school, a very good teacher who really likes kids. As Donny says, "She is just like a grandmother", which she is.

Late news flash. Catharine just phoned. They are getting a baby girl at last—born August 4th. They are desperate for baby things, since there is nothing in the stores. I'm sure I can gather some in the neighborhood, and of course our family bassinet is available. Goodnight my precious Honey.

September 16, 1944

My Precious Dear:

I've been in sick bay ever since I last wrote. They gave me all sorts of tests and numerous pills, brown ones, white ones, black and white ones. I am in what is called the "quiet room." It's the most comfortable room in sick bay, but far from quiet. A noisy machine beside my bed which is supposed to cool the room rattles constantly. It is called an "air conditioner". The carpentry shop overhead has power saws going continually. Doc wants me to stay one more day.

I just learned that George Brown's duty is about the most hazardous anyone can get. For goodness sake, don't mention that to ANYONE.

The news from Europe was good this morning—confirmation that we had crossed the German border, and also the capitulation of Bulgaria. If Harry is involved in any of those places, he should be coming home before long.

I too, hope we don't have too much company while I am home. Perhaps we could arrange to devote just one evening to ALL the relatives and have the rest of the time for ourselves. I think the first thing we must do is install a sprinkler system. The watering is still much too time consuming for you. I'm pretty sure I could install it myself. Oh Honey, just thinking about being there gives me tingles up my spine. Goodnight my very lovely Lady. . . .

September 20, 1944

Darling Honey:

We all felt rotten when we woke up yesterday morning, so I kept everyone in bed. I started on the matching jumpers for the girls and myself, but by the time they were cut out and the major seams sewed up I was feeling really awful. Betty gave me a huge glass of freshly-squeezed orange juice and sent me to bed.

222 DARK CLOUDS AND SILVER LININGS

I just heard a ruckus in the patio and got out of bed to see what was wrong. Mike and Chuckie were having a knock-down-drag-out over the tricycle. Neither would give in. Betty started to stop them, but they were so well matched, I thought we should let them fight it out. Lance was very distressed. He picked a long blade of grass and was hitting them both with it and saying, "'top it! 'top it!" He was a riot. We finally broke it up and told them they must take turns. Then I caught the dickens from Betty for getting out of bed!

NEXT DAY. I picked up Mrs. Wilbur the first thing this morning, and she concentrated on just the living room, dining room, and kitchen today. When she finished they looked beautiful. It has been so long since I could do anything more than give things a lick and a promise.

A news flash just came about what happened yesterday. As soon as the flash finished, the phone rang and, just as I thought, it was my Dad. He had heard it too. It is sheer coincidence that I happened to have the radio on when they flashed that news. Now I fully realize how perfectly awful it must be to write your seemingly (to you) DULL "my day" letters, when things like that are going on all around you.[1]

I feel right in the pink today, but the kids are just well enough to drive me crazy. I've done nothing all day except give them aspirin, juice, sulfa, meals, and HECK!....I wish I didn't have to say goodnight to you, my Honey.

September 24, 1944

Dearest Honey:

On Friday Donny had a rough session at the dentist. Fortunately, getting his upper bands on isn't as painful as the lower ones were.

Afterwards we looked for a tricycle seat for Chuckie without success, but next door to Berkeley Cyclery was a meat market with a sign "HORSE MEAT TODAY." I bought two pounds at twenty one cents a pound, and NO ration points! We have never tried it before but I have heard it is delicious.

On the way home we picked up a sailor who was heading for his home in Reno. He had just come from twenty-nine months in the Pacific, which he said was just about two years too long. As far as I'm concerned, the thirteen months since you left us at Port Hueneme is thirteen months too long!

At dinner Bev sat and moaned because her feet hurt. Immediately, Judy's did too! When they mentioned wanting tap shoes, I told them I would fix some as soon as they cleaned up their plates. The effect was miraculous. In no time at all their plates were empty, and the dishes were done. I pushed thumb tacks into the soles of their shoes, and they went outside to dance and dance. How badly their feet must have been hurting!

---

[1]Another successful air strike by the carriers preceding a landing to retake a strategic island.

Before we left for Sunday School this morning, I prepared my casserole for the Springhill Road picnic. I baked it when we got back and took it sizzling from the oven up to the Slavens'.

Their place looks perfectly lovely. I think they have planted every square inch of their six acres. After we all enjoyed the fabulous spread, there was basketball, volley ball, badminton, and horseshoes, as well as three-legged races, potato races, and sack races. The children had a wonderful time. It was fun watching Chuckie trying so hard to enter into EVERYTHING! At dusk a big bonfire was lighted, and it looked beautiful. Finally I had the children say their thank-yous, and reluctantly we left.

I still had to iron the girls' dresses for tomorrow, sew the insignia on Donny's Cub shirt, clean their shoes, bathe them, curl their hair, and pack their lunches. If "man works from sun to sun", I wish I were a man!

Tons of love from your down-in-the-dumps, fed-up with it all, Honey

September 25, 1944

My own sweet Poochie:

Thank you very much for the extra nice long letter you sent me. I keep reading it over and over. I think it's the best letter you ever wrote me.

I can't tell you when I'll be coming home, but I'll get there just as quickly as I can as I am very lonesome for you. When you write again, be sure to tell me all the things you want us to do together when I'm on leave.

Mother says you are a big help to her, and I am so proud of you. I finally received the picture of you and Judy in the grass skirts I sent you, and you both look so pretty in them. I look at your picture for a long time every day.

Thank you for the hugs and kisses you sent me. Here are some for you. X O X O X O X O X O X O X O X O I love you so very much. . . . .

September 29, 1944

Sweetheart Mine:

After I wrote you yesterday I saw the Flag Secretary. He said my requests for leave and change of duty were sent air mail, endorsed, "Forwarded with recommendation for favorable consideration." My leave should start whenever they find a replacement for me, which shouldn't take over two months.

While I was on the forecastle today a good strong breeze came up. In fact it was such a cool breeze that I suddenly realized I was all goose pimples, and it wasn't from thinking about you!

I am so relieved that Bev is happy with school and her teacher. Sometimes the most awful wave of lonesomeness for her sweeps over me.

Since mail arrived in great volume, I am celebrating my birthday today. It makes me furious that the schools are so neglected. They should come before

everything else. I wish I were there to do something about it.[1] I think if the school board was approached in the right way, something could be done. Our taxes should be taking care of all that, and now is the time to meet the problem if it is ever going to be met. . . .

October 1, 1944

Darling Honey:

I wonder what you have been doing to celebrate your thirty-fifth birthday today. I hope it has been something big and exciting involving lots of Jap planes and ships. Betty made a perfectly marvelous banana cake with whipped cream, which we called your birthday cake.

When Betty shopped for me today, I forgot to give her our ration books, Who but Betty could have talked the butcher into letting her have the meat anyway—fifty three points worth! She told him I would bring them in this afternoon. When I did, he looked so pleased and also astonished.

Marky came over to see if our phone was out of order as well as theirs. It was. When she went to the Condits' to report it, she found theirs was ok, because they have just been changed to a different line. Even though they are no longer on our line, we still have nine families on ours.

After we went to Dr. Hartman today, we went all over Berkeley trying to find brown shoe polish and finally managed to get some. Since we had been dying to see "Going My Way" with Bing Crosby, we had planned to have a picnic in the park and go straight to the Orinda Theater. It got so late we had to eat in the car while driving there. It gave the kids the giggles to see me signal for turns with a sandwich in my hand. We just made it to the show on time, and we all absolutely loved it. We laughed and cried and had a wonderful time.

I don't see why you have to be so secretive about George Brown's amphibian duty.[2] Everyone knows it is like having your death warrant signed. When Walt Dingus got his orders, Ann said, "They say you get a promotion every time you make a landing. But no one has ever gotten further than Lt. Commander."

I have been feeling sunk because I have a hunch you won't be coming home as soon as we had hoped. Every day I hear about someone whose leave has been canceled. I can see why. From the news I read now, it seems the only thing to do is for all branches of the service to keep pounding away and not take a chance on losing the advantage we have at present. . . . Goodnight my Love.

---

[1] Eventually he did "do something about it." After doing all he could on boards and committees for the next twenty years, he retired at age fifty five to spend the next twenty four years with no pay, working full time for the betterment of children, youth, and families.

[2] In landing operations, the personnel who are trained to be the first to go ashore from small landing craft, and meet the remaining enemy after heavy bombing by the fleet and aircraft.

October 2, 1944

My Honey:

I had been looking forward to a day in Oakland unencumbered by anyone so I could get a lot done. I left Chuckie with Betty, and on the way in I picked up a lady heading for a doctor appointment. She had been waiting over an hour for a bus to stop. They all sailed right by her loaded with servicemen.

I dropped her off, parked on 6th, and headed for Snides, because I was desperately in need of shoes. I hadn't found any since the spring of '41. Oh what luck! I found two pairs of Foot Delights from Werner's that usually sell for $14. They were $3 a pair. I LOVE them!

Next I walked to 21st, where I finally found some seat covers for the car. They are like the ones we could have gotten for $3.95 when I first thought we needed them. They are now $12.20. I had to get them because the stuffing is coming out, and the drivers seat is down to the springs.

After dinner Bert came in to tell me that Betty hadn't wanted to upset me, but when I left this morning, she went looking for Chuck and found him in the Schneiders' chicken pen with Gretchen. Gretchen had killed twelve of their pedigreed chickens for which they had paid an astronomical price. It must have been a gruesome sight.

When Bert went over there Jack had all their name tags and pedigrees on the table trying to figure out what to do. He was nice about it. So was Marky, but it has been a tremendous investment in both time and money. They were guaranteed to lay at least 350 eggs a year. Just figuring the eggs alone that they will lose before they can get others to replace them would amount to well over 3600 eggs, to say nothing of the cost of the chickens and their feed.

As long as Bert has been there, I haven't gone as yet. I just couldn't face it tonight. I'll go over in the morning. But when I think about it, I don't know how I can go or what I can say. It's really my fault for not having checked on Chuckie before I left, and Betty considers it her fault. Chuckie must have discovered he is finally tall enough to reach the latch on the gate. He loves those chickens. He must have been overjoyed to find that he could get right in with them and wanted his pal Gretchen to share his joy!

NEXT DAY. The very first thing this morning I went to see Marky. You know what a terrible pregnancy she has been having. This is all she needs. When I got there, she was trying to salvage for the freezer what she could of those twelve mangled bodies, and she looked miserable. She was sweet about it, but I don't think any of us can really comprehend what this means to them. It will take some figuring to tell just how much they are worth. Even split with the Lembecks, it's bound to take over half my Navy allotment.

This has proved to be quite a day between that, the trip to Oakland, picking up Mrs. Wilbur, taking her home, picking up fourteen Brownies, running out of gas, waiting for a push, and being pushed by all fourteen little girls.

Helen finally came for the bottles. It was wonderful to get those 2200 bottles out of the garage. I was so amused at what she said. "I'm half an hour late—well—uh—actually I'm usually half an hour late." She didn't even realize that it was eighteen days since she promised to get them.

When Donny got home from school, he said something so embarrassing happened at school that he just couldn't tell me, but he finally did. Mrs. Christian asked him why he wasn't doing his arithmetic, and he said he wanted to get a zero. She made him come up to the front and gave him three little spanks. He was so terribly embarrassed. Afterwards, when he was getting a drink of water, she came by, put her arm around him, and told him that he should always come to her for help instead of being a smart aleck. Now he just adores her. . . .

October 3, 1944

Lovely Precious Mine:

We had a change of plans, and, as a result, we will be unable to get mail for at least the next week. "C'est la guerre." However, every cloud has a silver lining. We will be able to send mail out for the next few days.

The last time I received mail, you sent that picture of the little girl saying, "I'd like to make an appointment to see my Daddy." It gave me a lump in my throat. She seemed to be just about Poochie's age.

I learned today that Charlie will arrive here the day after we leave. Isn't that a shame? I was so sure we would make connections that I arranged for twenty-four hours off so we could spend plenty of time together.

I think you might as well give up all hope of my ever finding out by experience what being seasick is like. After our experiences of the past few days, I KNOW it will never happen[1]!

The past forty-eight hours have been extremely interesting, but not in the same way they have ever been before. Are you thoroughly confused? If the enemy were to get hold of this letter, let's hope they would be equally confused. . . .

October 5, 1944

Hello my Darling Honey:

I have been having fun pretending that since I haven't heard from you for so long, you'll phone and ask me to pick you up at Treasure Island. By the way, when you do come, be sure to make it a Friday or Saturday so the children won't have to go to school the next day. I'm sure the Navy will be happy to arrange things that way for you!

---

[1] A typhoon struck the Task Force creating waves of 60 to 80 feet. Each wave completely covered the destroyers and swept over the flight deck of the Lexington, damaging the catwalk in the forecastle of the hanger deck.

Bert was successful in putting the strip of synthetic rubber around the wheel of Chuckie's trike. He also contrived a seat, which made Chuckie supremely happy. His feet don't reach the pedals, but he sits on it endlessly, saying, "Cap'n fix it. Cap'n fix it."

Bert's other accomplishments of the day: he brought home a sturdy tarp from St. Mary's and "carpeted" and "roofed" the playhouse with it, nailing it way over the edges so it can't possibly leak. Then he fixed Judy's toy piano, Bev's doll bed, and Chuck's wheelbarrow. After that they all went to meet Betty's mother who came in on the Daylight.

Donny has been feeling very lonesome for you lately. I am glad to see that. I was worried because he never expresses anything about your absence. Last night he said, "Getting letters from Daddy doesn't make me unlonesome for him. It makes me want to cry." Then he talked about you a long time, and I read him parts of your letters to me. Of course I always read them the parts pertaining to them but not always a great deal of the rest of it.

Yes, I think our chickens will have paid for themselves at the end of a year. Of course prices fluctuate, and so does their laying, but I figure we will probably have sold about 180 dozen eggs. If I figure an average price of fifty cents a dozen, that would do it. Right now eggs are seventy cents. It makes me feel guilty to charge that much, but people are delighted to get them.

This morning Judy had an extremely bad case of the slows, couldn't get dressed, and couldn't eat breakfast. Beverly, bless her kind little heart, waited for her. They missed the bus. However, I learned later that the driver for McNeill's Dairy picked them up and took them all the way to school. People are so thoughtful, aren't they?

When I checked on Chuck, who was playing outside, I discovered he and Gretchen were already at the gate of the Schneiders' chicken pen! I made a dash, and Marky did too. She beat me there and sent them packing in short order. She was practically hysterical, and I don't blame her. We had locked them in the backyard, but they dug their way out under the fence where the soil in the flower bed is soft and loose.

I am mad at you for standing me up tonight. How dare you not phone me from Treasure Island the way I planned for you to do? . . . Goodnight, Honey

Monday, October 9, 1944

Dearest Honey:

Since today is Betty's birthday, I made her a cake. We were all joining them for a "party" after dinner. Judy ate absolutely not one bite of dinner and got just too smarty for words. I gave her every possible chance to make the grade, but she was simply outrageous. I had to send her to bed.

First, I let her take her gift to Betty, which made her happy momentarily, and she went skipping out our door bubbling over. She crossed the patio and, as I heard from them later, burst through their door sobbing and saying, "You're going to hate me. You're going to hate me," then a long sobbing tale of woe. Bert said it was so dramatic and so pitiful. I'm glad they told me about it. It is so hard to know when she is acting and when she is sincerely heartbroken.

Betty's mother brought Betty some real silk stockings! Imagine! She got them in Tijuana. It's close to three years since we have seen any.

I talked to Yvonne Brown today. She and Buster are going down to San Diego to join George before he ships out. She is so scared and shaky over his duty. She knows how dangerous it is and says that almost every day someone in the outfit gets killed or injured just in training.

You've heard of people who have a hard time "keeping up with the Joneses." Well that is not my problem. Mine is "keeping up with the Brownses." Lois stopped by after school today, and while she was here managed to tell me the following items of interest: Judy and Beverly don't think I am nearly as good a mommy as hers is. She and Nancy have three times as many dresses as Beverly and Judy (poor B and J have only eleven apiece). She says they get to stay up and listen to the radio until nine every night, go to a movie every Friday night, take dancing lessons, and get fifty cents apiece to eat lunch uptown whenever they want to, plus every time they go anywhere they get to have ice cream cones or sundaes. How would you like to have that kind of competition?....

NEXT DAY. Helen Brown brought Beverly home from Brownies. I laughingly told her what Lois had said yesterday. She told me her girls have four decent dresses apiece, practically never get to see a movie, are allowed to stay up until eight on Friday nights to listen to Bob Hope, provided they have had their baths and are ready for bed.

At dinner Donny was feeling terribly sorry for himself and talked again of leaving home. I think he would like to find a home where he didn't have to take baths, eat regular meals, do homework, chores, or go to bed....

October 13, 1944

Dear Young Man:

There are so many things I wish I could tell you because I think you would find them very interesting. When I get home won't we have fun? You can ask me all the questions you want, and I can answer them.

I am very anxious to hear more about Cub Scouts. I want to know about Den meetings and Pack meetings, what you have to do to earn your promotions, and all about your friends.

I must get back to work now. I love you very much and can't wait to be home and be with you....

Part Seven

OCTOBER 27, 1944 – NOVEMBER 21, 1944
AUGUST 10, 1945 – NOVEMBER 11, 1945

"WHEN JOHNNIE COMES MARCHING
HOME."

"When Johnnie comes marching home again
Hurrah! Hurrah!
We'll give him a hearty welcome then.
Hurrah! Hurrah!
Oh the men will sing, the boys will shout,
The ladies they will all turn out.
And we'll all feel gay when Johnnie comes
   marching home.
Yes, we'll all feel gay when Johnnie comes
   marching home."

Patrick Sarsfield Gilmore
Famous old song from Civil War days

(OCTOBER 27, 1944)

PRESS WIRELESS DISPATCH

UNDATED PACIFIC WAR:

AFTER SMASHING TASK FORCE ATTACK ON MANILA BAY, CAPITE NAVAL BASE, AND TWO ENEMY AIRFIELDS NEAR MANILA, DONE THURSDAY NIGHT IN AN ENGLISH LANGUAGE BROADCAST HEARD BY FEDERAL COMMUNICATIONS COMMISSION STATED THAT MARTIAL LAW DECLARED IN THE PHILIPPINES TO BECOME EFFECTIVE NINE AM PHILIPPINES TIME FRIDAY. PROCLAMATION ISSUED BY JOSEPH LAUREL PUPPET PRESIDENT. TOKYO RADIO ALSO ANNOUNCED ATTACK ON MANILA AREA CLAIMING THE SEPARATE ATTACKS WERE MADE BY CARRIER BASED PLANES. BROADCAST HEARD BY SAN FRANCISCO, CLAIMING QUOTE DAMAGE ON OUR SIDE REPORTED AS BEING NEGLIGIBLE UNQUOTE. ASSERTED THAT THIRTY UNITED STATES PLANES SHOT DOWN, AND SIX OTHERS DAMAGED. AMERICAN BROADCAST STATES AMERICAN AIRCRAFT BOMBED MANILA BAY ON THURSDAY. THEY DESTROYED AT LEAST TWENTY FIVE JAPAN-ESE AIRCRAFT. THEY SANK ELEVEN SHIPS, AND THEY DESTROYED TWENTY-SIX OTHER JAPANESE VESSELS. ADMIRAL CHESTER NIMITZ ANNOUNCED THIS GREAT ATTACK EARLY FRIDAY AT PEARL HARBOR. HE STATED THE ACTION AS BEING EXTREMELY SUCCESSFUL, THAT NO AMERICAN SURFACE CRAFT HAD BEEN DAMAGED. AMERICAN AIRCRAFT LOSSES ARE FIFTEEN PLANES. A TOTAL OF ONE-HUNDRED-TEN AIRCRAFT OF THE JAPANESE WERE SHOT DOWN IN COMBAT OVER THE MANILA BAY AREA, AND ANOTHER NINETY FIVE JAPANESE PLANES WERE DESTROYED ON GROUND. THE AMERICAN CARRIER BASED FLIERS PROBABLY WIPED OUT A FLOATING DRY DOCK AT CAPITE NAVAL BASE AND THE AMERICANS HIT HARD AT JAPANESE SHIPPING IN MANILA, AND SUBIC BAY, AND THEY CAUSED EXTENSIVE DAMAGE TO JAPANESE INSTALLATIONS AT CLARK AND NICHOLS FIELDS. THE ENTIRE OPERATIONS WAS MADE BY PLANES. U.S. THIRD FLEET UNDER WILLIAM F. HALSEY

Tuesday, October 31st. 1944

Hello my Darling Honey:

Yesterday was quite a day. I accomplished a lot outside, and it was a grand feeling. First I reseeded the lawn and covered it with a layer of peat moss and fertilizer, then cultivated and fertilized the flower beds in back. After transplanting two lilac bushes and two rose bushes into that bed, I put in eight clumps of iris, tied up the chrysanthemums, and planted larkspur, sweet peas, and bachelor buttons. If everything works out, the area around the lawn should look beautiful in a few months.

Last night because of the rain, we went straight to the auditorium for the Halloween party, rather than meeting at the gas station and parading to the school. Donny went as a pirate. Beverly looked lovely in the hula skirt you sent her with a pretty flowered scarf for a "bra" and nothing but her pride to keep her warm. Judy was in pantalettes and hoop skirt and, when she was asked what she was supposed to represent, our kids all chorused, "an old fashioned." There were some darling little clowns and ghosts who didn't look any bigger than Chuck. I had longed to take him but decided to be sensible.

When the party was over, the rain was coming down in torrents. Donny dashed ahead, and I wrapped my coat around the girls. When we got to the car, Donny was cuddling a darling little grey kitten, so tiny and so wet. She was immediately accepted by the rest of our cats when we got home, and is now sleeping with her head on the shoulder of one of them.

It was still pouring hard this morning. Since it is impossible to buy rain gear, I cut up an old shower curtain and made scarves to tie over the girls' heads. The children are so tired this morning. I fail to understand why the party was last night. I thought the object was to keep the kids occupied on Halloween night itself, not the night before. Goodnight, my Honey.

November 1, 1944

Dearest Precious:

Grand surprise today—mail! Since we swore always to be frank and tell each other everything, I think I must tell you that your letters didn't make me feel wonderful as they usually do. I was so depressed after I read them, thinking of you with all the work, worry, and responsibility you have to bear by yourself. I am so thankful that I had already received the later ones and knew all of you were all right. Now PLEASE don't start holding anything back because of what I just said. Remember our agreement.

I am getting cynical enough to wonder if the upcoming election will have any influence on when the war ends. I still think it will be over in Europe in a few more months but not until some time in 1945 in the Pacific. I hope I am not being too optimistic.

We have been listening to the broadcast of the World Series. Americans are funny people. Who else would go to the trouble of giving a play by play report over our P.A. system? It is relayed here by several stations. It seems impossible to me that we can hear what is going on in St.Louis only a few seconds after it happens. I often wonder how long it will take us to hear when peace is declared in Europe.

It is now Halloween at home, and I keep thinking about our children, wondering how they are dressed for the parade and the party at school, and wishing I could be there to enjoy it with you.

Honey, don't compare the way our place looks with the others you see. There probably isn't another place in Lafayette where the Daddy had to leave before the landscaping was in, and the Mommy had from four to six children to take care of without help, plus vegetables and fruits to raise, harvest, and can. Please remember you are only one person, and there are only twenty-four hours in the day. Don't try to be all things to all people all the time.

Remember that night and day, waking or sleeping, busy or bored, hot or hotter, I love you to pieces my Darling.

November 2, 1944

Honey Darling:

Today Mrs. Wilbur cleaned the whole house while I cleaned what we can now call our guest room and bath, getting it ready for the Banduccis. It's really nice to have that spare room again, and it's getting good use.

When I got back from taking Mrs. Wilbur home and picking up the children from Brownies and Cubs, Fred and Elva were already here. Donny took them on a tour of the neighborhood, playing the genial host and being a real life saver while I fixed dinner.

We had what I suppose was a really delicious meal, including steak, which took most of our ration points for the week. Donny was a perfect gentleman at the table, but our adorable Chuckie has NEVER been such a BRAT! The girls waved their forks, messed around with their food, chewed with their mouths open, and continually left the table to go to the bathroom. If the Banduccis ever had doubts about whether or not they wanted children, I'm sure they decided the answer was a resounding "NO." In fact they didn't even pretend they weren't shocked by the children's behavior. Elva said she's sure it's because you are gone, and they will be fine when you get back.

This morning it had stopped raining and was beautiful. Chuckie was now his irresistible self and they were enchanted with him. Frank Brown had driven them here from S.F. and took Fred back this a.m. As soon as the kids were off to school, Elva and I went for a walk. Then we had a nice lazy day enjoying the three little boys plus Philip and Susan. Verna Slaven was driving over to San Francisco in the late afternoon and took Elva to meet Fred.

Goodnight Honey

November 10, 1944

Dear Charlie:

I'm home at last, and will be stateside for my next assignment. What a wonderful feeling. Here's how it happened. Not long before I left the ship, Commodore Arleigh Burke gave me his home phone number in Bethesda and said he would be on leave there while I am on my thirty-day leave. He suggested I check around and decide where I would like to have my duty, then phone him, and he would arrange it at BuPers[1]. Upon arrival at Com12[2], I talked with the commander in charge of communications. Yesterday I phoned Commodore Burke, who is now a Rear Admiral, and told him I would like to be stationed at St. Mary's Pre-flight. I just received a call from him. He told me my orders were already written, and I will be at Com12 in San Francisco as the Administrative Officer for Communications for the entire 12th Naval District. Just think, I'll be thirty-five minutes from home and just one block from my Prudential office!

Charlie, I was terribly disappointed that we never got together. Whenever I thought your ship would arrive, we would leave too soon. While we were in the second battle of the Philippine Sea, after MacArthur went ashore and took over the command, we went to Ulithi. When we arrived there, my relief came aboard, but there was no transportation.

A few hours later we received our long awaited mail. I took mine to the forecastle to read in peace. I had hardly started when word was passed on the speaker, "Members of the Admiral's staff who are eligible for leave report to the quarterdeck in fifteen minutes!" Of course I made it, even though I had to leave some of my things aboard, including my typewriter.

The reason for the urgency was just as we expected. MacArthur was too anxious to become a hero, and his message that all was secure was definitely premature. The Lexington had to return to battle immediately. What a very considerate person Admiral Mitscher is. He had his Exec arrange for the three of us who were eligible for leave to be taken aboard the mail seaplane.

That was quite an experience. It was a PBM flying to Saipan, and we sat on the sacks of mail. After we had been flying a while, the plane changed it's course, and the crew started manning the guns. They informed us that they had a bogey on the screen and were taking out after it! They must have been frustrated fighter pilots who had lost their minds. Imagine how we felt about the prospect of being shot down in the ocean while on our way home! Fortunately, they gave up the chase before too long.

My orders were for priority air travel. Consequently, I left Saipan on the first Army plane leaving for Hawaii. The plane I took from Hawaii was a DC4 headed for Hamilton Field. I was delighted that I would be landing only forty miles from home. However, to add to my anxiety en route, two of the four

---

[1] Bureau of Naval Personnel. Keeps records of all personnel and issues assignment orders.
[2] Commanding Officer, Twelfth Naval District.

props went dead. Nevertheless we arrived safely at Hamilton about midnight. There was no transportation to be had, not even any taxi service at that time of night.

I think you remember our friends, the Banduccis, who live in Larkspur. I phoned them. A lady, whose voice I didn't recognize, answered the phone. When I asked, "Is this the Banducci residence?" Her reply was, "No, but they are here at a party. Would you like to talk with Fred?" They happened to be on the same party line and had heard the double ring. Fred immediately came to get me and loaned me his car to drive home. It was 2 a.m. when I opened our unlocked front door on November 5th, went to our bedroom, and awakened Dot with, "Happy Birthday!"

I'm sure you heard that a dive bomber landed on the Lexington. It hit my battle station less than twelve hours after I left. I understand that all but one person in that area became a casualty. How can one not be a fatalist?

We expect to see Leta and the children some time next week before my leave ends. I hope it won't be too long before you will be home, too. What a great day that will be. As always, warmest regards,

November 12, 1944

Dear Leta:

I'll be so glad when you are able to get a phone. I have been dying to tell you the wonderful news and FINALLY have found a chance to write. I know that Charlie is still way off in the Pacific somewhere, but I'm sure you will be happy for us. Don is home! He arrived at 2 a.m. on my birthday.

It was so dramatic, and so exciting. I had taken the children to a movie that night, Friday the 4th. When we got home and they were all tucked in bed I started reading the paper. I read a very small item that said the Lexington had been hit. Well, I didn't panic. Naive me! I believed it when all the fellows who visited us while on leave solemnly and most emphatically told me there was nothing to worry about. They said that on the Admiral's ship you are well protected by the other ships around it, so there's no danger of it being hit. Consequently, remembering the well known admonition, "Don't believe everything you read in the papers," I dismissed it from my mind and went to bed.

A couple of hours later, deep in sleep, I realized someone was coming through the door calling exuberantly, "Happy Birthday, Honey! Happy Birthday!" I was dazed and bewildered. Was I dreaming? Was this a romantic movie? Could this be really happening? No, that was impossible! But it was true!

One by one we awakened the children. Chuckie wasn't at all sure he knew this strange man who was creating such a commotion. He stood there hanging on to Don's pants leg, looking up at him uncertainly. The others were suddenly wide awake and practically tearing him limb from limb.

His coming was so sudden and unexpected. He had been hoping against hope and pulling all possible strings but had no idea when his request for leave might be granted. I had been fantasizing for weeks about his arrival, but with no real basis for hope.

They had been in battle for days and had retreated to an atoll for more supplies. Suddenly the loudspeaker announced that those on the Admiral's staff who were eligible for leave were to be on the quarterdeck in fifteen minutes. Somehow he made it. He collected his shirts from the laundry and his shoes from the repair shop. I assume you know how huge the Lexington is. It must have been like running all over "downtown" Lafayette. In fact I wouldn't be surprised if the Lexington is considerably larger than that. The crew alone is over 2000, and that is more than the population of Lafayette.

You know from experience how wonderful it is having him home. In some ways it's strange, too. I have had to become so independent since he left, I find myself making decisions that have always been his to make. The children have gotten so used to me as "the boss" that they turn to me for every little thing. It gets pretty ridiculous when Don is driving the car and Donny asks ME instead of Don why he is going in a certain direction!

We are anxious to get together with you. Our nine kids always have such a fine time together. We have been inundated with family, wanting to see their "Donny," which is what the aunts and cousins still call this Navy Lt. home from the wars! PHONE SOON so we can arrange something. Much love to ALL of you.

NOVEMBER 21, 1944

MRS HARRY CAPLAN:

REGRET TO INFORM YOU YOUR HUSBAND

SERIOUSLY WOUNDED IN ACTION IN FRANCE.

DIARY

November 21st. What a ghastly day. A messenger came to our door with a telegram for Rae from the War Department. We both shook as Don opened it. "How am I ever going to break this to Baby?" he groaned, and left for Burlingame.

November 22nd. Don got back about 2 a.m., a complete wreck. He said it was the hardest thing he ever had to do. He would have stayed overnight but she wanted to be alone. The trouble is, "seriously wounded" is so vague. It conjures up all sorts of horrible thoughts. Will Harry ever be a whole person again? Poor Rae! How is she ever going to live through this?

THANKSGIVING DAY! WHAT a Thanksgiving day! What that DARNED War Department has put all of us through. Rae just phoned. She has a cable from Harry saying, "Feeling fine. Don't worry."

December 31st. Had fine day with Rae in Burlingame. She finally has letters from Harry. It turns out he "merely" had the very tip end of his finger shot off and hopefully will be home soon. Don's leave is over. He starts work at Com12 tomorrow.

January 6, 1945. Charlie's back. We had a grand reunion. Showed our combined home movies for the last two years. The kids had a great time.

January 16th. Hallelujah! Harry is home! He and Rae want some time to themselves so Stevie and Frances arrived this morning. They are so darling!

January 19th. It is such fun having Stevie and Frances back again, but I am SO tired. The kids are so darling, I wish we could keep them forever.

January 21st. Stevie and Frances are gone. I feel as though I am on a vacation, with only four kids. But I miss them so much already. Bert got his orders—Camp Pendleton. They are ecstatic. They'll be back in their own home at Mission Beach again. What a break. I can't bear to have them leave.

February 28th. To the Claremont with Bert and Betty. Joined a j.g. and his VERY beautiful wife. Bert says he is one of the Kings,[1] of Texas. All that money doesn't help to find a place to live. They and their little three-year-old girl are living in a refurbished storeroom behind a hat shop on Main St. in Walnut Creek. "Nurse Peggy[2] was there too, with a party of eight. Everyone was buzzing! Poor thing! I couldn't get over her teeth. Many gone and the remaining ones black! It was a marvelous evening but our last fling with Bert and Betty.

March 12th. Bert and Betty left at 5 a.m. Worked like mad getting the rumpus room ready for our next tenants, who come tomorrow. They have a darling little two-year-old named Karen. He was on the Lexington with Don but they didn't know that until now.

April 2nd. Chris and Irene are a gift from Heaven! Instead of paying us rent she helps me with the housework and he helps Don outdoors. They are great workers and very congenial. Karen is adorable. We share baby sitting.

April 14th. We have Frances for a few days. What fun.

May 8th. V.E. Day!!!![3] Listened to the radio much of the day as we gardened. THRILLING! But chilling. The casualties are horrible.

June 17th. Rae and Harry and the kids for the weekend. Fun time. Lots accomplished outdoors too. Don finished putting in the sprinkler system and he and Harry started the front fence. All this company gets wearing. Almost every day someone from the Navy comes for lunch, dinner, or overnight. I hope they don't all decide to move to California after the war is over.

---

[1] One of the wealthiest families in Texas with huge land holdings.
[2] Became famous in the news, then in a book and a movie as one of the nurses captured on Bataan and held as prisoners for the duration.
[3] Victory in Europe.

July 1st. Frances will be here for a week while Rae and Harry take Stevie camping. Fourteen for lunch, eleven for dinner. The food shortages are getting worse and most of our guests are Navy, and don't have ration stamps to help out. Don feels horrible and can't find out what's wrong. Back to Oak Knoll Hospital. He's been in and out of there for the past four weeks with no solution. One Doctor said something about "war nerves," whatever that is. He loves his work at Com12 though it is very demanding. Sometimes he is there for eighteen hours at a stretch. He feels that he is very useful there and very effective, so it's not that.

July 23rd. Canned 75 quarts of apricots!!!!!!!!!!!!. Will it ever end?

August 10th. WHAT A DAY! THE JAPS HAVE OFFERED TO SURRENDER! It's hard to do anything but listen to the radio. I guess the bombing of Hiroshima must have done the trick. The suspense is terrible!

August 11th. No news yet. It's hard to think of anything else.

August 12th. Still no news. Special prayer service at church.

August 13th. Still no news. Canned thirty-nine quarts of peaches. Don says they are going through the motions at the Com12 office, but all they can think of is the news we are all waiting for.

August 14th. The news finally came at 4 P.M! It's really over! It's really over! We took Donny, Beverly, and Judy to S.F. to see all the excitement. WHAT AN EVENING! It was fun and exciting, but we certainly took our lives in our hands!

August 15th. Don started the red tape unwinding towards getting his discharge from the Navy.

August 22, 1945

Dear Leta, and Charlie too, I hope!

Isn't it wonderful? Isn't it marvelous? I hope that by some miracle Charlie is home by now. Don has already found out that the red tape doesn't unwind as quickly as he had hoped and has been told he can not be a civilian for another eleven months. He is fit to be tied. He is so anxious to be running his Prudential office. It would be nice to have an adequate income again, but, of course, as long as he is here, that's all that really matters to me.

He has thoroughly enjoyed his work for the 12th Naval District. Ever since he started there he has felt that he was contributing far more to the war effort than in his other assignments. He has discovered and put into practice any number of ways for the Navy to reduce large numbers of military and civilian personnel as well as to save large sums of money. You know how big he is on efficiency. He also enjoys the people with whom he works. But oh how he wants to get back to his beloved office.

I must tell you about V.J.[1] night. Don was at Oak Knoll Hospital having some tests when he got the news. He phoned to tell me and also to have me

---

[1]Victory in Japan

get the children dressed for San Francisco. We felt this was something Donny, Bev, and Judy should have the opportunity to experience and remember.

We drove the car to Berkeley, parked it at the Claremont, and took the Key System Train from there. That ride was a circus! Somehow, a man on the train had been able to get hold of balloons. You know how long it is since we have seen any. He gave one to each of our children. The engineer was wonderful. He let each one of our kids take turns blowing the whistle repeatedly all the way to the City. What a thrill for them!

When we got off at the foot of Market St. everything was a teaming, seething mass of people. All sorts of antics were going on, and as soon as Don saw this, he pulled the decorative strap of his officer's cap down under his chin so no one could snatch it. A lot of them had started "celebrating" the moment they heard the news and were already "three sheets to the wind". Cars were being rocked, girls were being grabbed and kissed, willy nilly.

As I watched one girl fighting off a very enthusiastic sailor, I said into Don's left ear, "Look, Honey. Look at that poor girl. That sailor is trying to kiss her, and she doesn't even know him." At the same moment Donny was saying into Don's right ear, "Look Daddy! See that poor sailor. He is so happy because the war is over that he wants to kiss that girl, and she won't let him. Isn't that mean?" It just "shows to go you," it's all in the point of view.

In the beautiful new coat with the fox trim that Don had just bought me, my high heels, gloves, hat, and veil I felt very much the sedate married lady of thirty-six. However, Donny kept glancing up at me with a worried look on his face, and when I asked him what was wrong, he said, "Mommy, I'd feel better if you were just a LITTLE bit older." I thought that was the nicest compliment I had heard in a long time. In a way it reminded me of the time the truant officer stopped you as you walked along eating an ice cream cone after having just dropped your four boys off at school! Remember?

It was difficult to make our way up Market Street through the crowds. Confetti and serpentine were everywhere, and sirens were screaming with joy. A snowy avalanche of paper descended from office windows. Statues were being climbed. Streetcar trolleys were being pulled from the wires overhead.

When we finally reached the second floor of the Federal Building where Don's Navy office is, we watched from a safer vantage point as things got wilder. Light fixtures were being torn out and thrown from the top stories of the surrounding buildings on Market Street. At that point we decided it was time to head for home.

You must be getting so tired of the waiting. I hope it will soon be over for you too. . . . Oceans of love for all of you from all of us.

DIARY

November 1st. 1945. Don is out of the Navy! Somehow he pulled it off and got out eight months earlier than the date originally anticipated.

"Home is the sailor, home from the sea,

And the hunter home from the hill."

from "Requiem"
Robert Louis Stevenson

Addenda

"THE FROSTING ON THE CAKE"

You can have your pies and cookies,
And other things you bake,
'Cause there's nothing half so lickin' good
As the frosting on the cake.

Author Unknown

November 1, 1946

Dear Leta and Charlie,

How maddening it must be for you not to have a phone after all this time. Maddening for me too, bursting with the WONDERFUL news I am DYING to tell you. You would think that fourteen months after the war ended we could have telephones, bedding and baby clothes wouldn't you? Now how did I happen to mention baby clothes? Well, by now you have guessed, I'm sure.

You know how desperately we have been wanting another baby. Well, it has finally happened! Day before yesterday, John Davis, the new head of our Probation Department since Mrs. Edgar was killed in that horrible auto accident, phoned. He said, "The baby Mrs. Edgar told you about is here. Judge Bray and I have been talking it over and he has decided he wants you folks to have it. . . . We arranged for me to be there the next day at 2 p.m. Just as we were about to hang up, I remembered to ask whether it was a boy or a girl. "It's a boy," he replied. As you know, I had been longing for another girl, or better yet, twin girls, but suddenly a baby boy was the answer to my dreams!

I immediately phoned Capwells. For starters I asked for three dozen diapers. "Oh my dear," she replied, "I'm So sorry. We finally received a shipment this morning of one hundred dozen, but they are all gone." I asked about wrappers, gowns, shirts, bottles, and a sterilizer, to no avail.

It was time to rally the neighborhood. The good news spread like wildfire and soon the doorbell was ringing constantly. People were bringing what they could spare: two shirts, one wrapping blanket, a tiny sweater, three diapers. Someone I had never even met came out from Berkeley with bottles and a sterilizer. They were in the midst of building their home up the road and a mutual friend had passed the word to them.

The next day, when I arrived, they were bathing the baby. I held him for a moment. What a thrill! Now Don didn't know anything about all this! He was on his way home from a Prudential Conference in Seattle. The train was late. The other wives were there too and I was DYING to tell them the news, but it didn't seem fair for them to know before Don. We waited and waited. Every little while we would be told that the train had been delayed but would arrive soon. When it finally came after several more hours we learned that rock slides over the tracks had caused the delays. My poor Honey looked So tired when he got off. I greeted him with, "How would you like to go see our new baby boy?" Suddenly, he no longer looked the least bit tired!

It was so late by now that they told us to go have something to eat and come back in an hour. While eating, we spent the time making a final decision on his name, Stuart Brett. We call him Brett, but we know that what he really is for us is "the frosting on the cake."

When we finally got home, the kids were impatiently waiting to see him before they went trick or treating. When each of them had held him, they were off. That's when I remembered I had been too excited to think of buying anything for "trick or treat"! All evening long, when I answered the doorbell, I would say, "Well, we have a REALLY SPECIAL treat for you tonight," and lead them to the bassinet. Every single one of them was thrilled over him and no one objected to the fact that there were no sweets.

He is fifteen days old, weighed less than six pounds at birth, but is now six pounds three ounces and is SO adorable! It's wonderful having him so young. This is our first experience with the 2 a.m. feeding! If you recall, the others were two months old or more.

We hope to see you and your tribe soon.

Much love.

May 10, 1982

EPILOGUE

The day itself couldn't be more beautiful: the same sort of flawless day in May that it had been just fifty years ago. A gentle breeze riffles the leaves of the birch, elm, and Japanese maple trees shading the area where the picnic tables are set up, in and around the lacy white gazebo, lush with cascading wisteria.

Throughout the house and grounds is the happy hubbub of old friends and loved ones, greeting each other with delight. Leta and Charlie, and others from our days at Cal, former Prudential cohorts, our nearest and dearest neighbors from Springhill Road and their children, now here with their own little ones.

As a taxi from the airport pulls up, the dear and familiar bald head of "Baby Brother" John, emerges. Appropriately our three balding sons rush to greet their favorite Uncle: "Donny," still crazy about cars and horses, "Little Chuckie," now a successful building contractor, and Brett, our "frosting on the cake," an investigator with the Sheriff's Department.

Baby Sister "Midge," can't be with us. She and her husband, Tal, are in the Orient, and this very day are exploring the village where I spent my early childhood. However their four children are well represented. As Bev flies here and there seeing that all goes smoothly with the catering, her daughter Stacy presides over the guest book, aided by her fiance, Mike. We are eager to chat with Bev's son, Pete, whom we haven't seen since his graduation from U.C. Davis, with Melanee, Chuck's stepdaughter, recently back from college in Minnesota, and with Tami, Chuck's daughter-in-law, and her two little girls, Tawnie and Mindi, our great-granddaughters. After a delicious lunch has been consumed, we gather for the cutting of the gorgeous four tiered Golden Wedding cake, baked and decorated by Cheryl the wife of "Stevie," who is now the owner of a thriving furnishings business. Cindy, Judy's daughter is surprised to find that she is sharing honors with the "bride and groom." Since just twenty-five years ago today her birth had made us grandparents for the first time, Steve proposes a toast to her, and everyone sings, "Happy Birthday."

Now another surprise! The State Legislature, both the Senate and the Assembly, have gotten together a "Joint Resolution," beautifully framed, and ready to hang. It honors us for the twenty years Don has spent at the Capitol, since his early retirement from Prudential, as a full time volunteer advocate for children and youth, as well as our other volunteer activities elsewhere.

Throughout the day, a collection of old scrap books dating back to 1921 containing pictures, dance cards, theater programs, restaurant menus and other memorabilia, are a source of constant amazement, particularly to the young. The prices fascinate. "How about this complete prime rib dinner for fifty cents!" someone exclaims. "Oh, that included a marvelous floor show and a ten piece dance band," we inform them. "It was at a gambling dive way out of town during prohibition, where the real action was going on in the back rooms."

Far too soon, it is time to say goodbye to our guests. As we drive home, taking Rae's four teenage grandsons with us, the sons of Steve and Cheryl and Frances and Roy, it is interesting to listen to their comments. The consensus is that the party was "not too shabby," in fact "it was cool."

At home Bev has prepared a post-party spread for the immediate family, twenty four in all. When that grand finale is over, our celebration has lasted eleven hours. What a Golden day! So much love put into it by so many people.

DOROTHY S. FIBUSH

Born in Montezuma, Georgia in 1908.

Canton, China 1913–1917. A fascinating time to be there. Enormous changes were taking place and my parents made me aware of them at an early age.

Back to the U.S. in 1917, after my mother died of smallpox. The ship had to be blacked out at night. With portholes closed to avoid attack by German U Boats—a slow, stuffy, and unpleasant trip.

Illinois until 1919 and then Berkeley, California. My father had been appointed superintendent of Chinese Baptist Missions on the Pacific Coast. By night he often risked his life in raids on brothels in San Francisco to rescue little Chinese girls as young as eleven, from white slavery. (Scary for me, the Chinese Tongs, or gangs, were very strong at that time.)

U.C Berkeley, Class of '30, followed by two years at the Oakland Tribune while waiting for my husband-to-be to finish law school at Boalt Hall.

Marriage in 1932. Adopted five children between 1934–1946.

Contra Costa County 1940—Built our "dream house" on Springhill Road in Lafayette—a little dirt road which wound through a mile and a half of orchards and passed a half dozen homes. Now enjoying life at Rossmoor, but too busy to get involved in the many activities here other than swimming and walking.

World War Two. The housing situation was desperate, so since our home was expandable, we could always make room for a few more. Part V, "Two's Company But Twelve Is Definitely A Crowd!" refers to a period when a young army wife with two babies under two, a Marine Captain with his wife and two boys, age one and two, shared it with the five of us while my husband was serving in the Pacific during 1943 and 1944, also in 1945 while he was stationed in San Francisco upon his return.

Volunteer Work. Starting in the early fifties and continuing at present; Mental Health, preschools, Friends Outside, clothing room and food room at our church, working with teenage boys and girls at Juvenile Hall. From 1973–1984 helping my husband with his full time, unpaid work at the state legislature in behalf of children and families. He retired in 1964 expressly for that purpose and continued full time (60–70 hours a week, ten months out of the year) until 1984, but is still introducing and guiding some bills through the legislature each year. He is also a literacy volunteer, working individually with students from six different countries, four days each week.

THE PRESENT. The most exciting part of life is being very actively involved with our ten grandchildren and ten great-grandchildren, and enjoying each other.